Praise for
Unions Matter

Unions Matter is a timely counterpoint to a divisive political narrative aimed at weakening the labour movement in Canada. Whether the purpose of unions is to protect human rights or to reduce income inequality, this book is testament to why unions matter. It's a great resource showcasing stellar research. *Unions Matter* is a vital contribution to Canadian democracy, in which unions play a key role.
— Trish Hennessy, Canadian Centre for Policy Alternatives

Unions Matter! The Harper government has launched an all-out assault on working people and their collective rights. This powerful book reminds us that unions have fought for every basic right we enjoy as Canadians and of the debt we all owe them. It made me angry and more determined than ever to stop the travesty of this agenda.
— Maude Barlow, National Chairperson of the Council of Canadians

Why are one in three workers in Canada union members? And what does the labour movement do for the rest of us and for Canadian society in general? *Unions Matter* is an informative handbook for anyone interested in finding out why unions matter to our quality of life and our future. Buy one copy, buy many, and spread the word.
— Elaine Bernard, Executive Director, Labor & Worklife Program, Harvard Law School

Unions Matter

Advancing Democracy, Economic Equality, and Social Justice

edited by
Matthew Behrens
for the
Canadian Foundation for Labour Rights

Between the Lines
Toronto

Unions Matter: Advancing Democracy, Economic Equality, and Social Justice

The Canadian Foundation for Labour Rights (CFLR) is a national voice devoted to promoting labour rights as an important means to strengthening democracy, equality and economic justice here in Canada and internationally. CFLR was established and is sponsored by the National Union of Public and General Employees and the United Food and Commercial Workers – Canada.

First published in 2014 by: Between the Lines
401 Richmond St. W., Studio 277
Toronto, Ontario   M5V 3A8
1-800-718-7201
www.btlbooks.com

Cover design by Jennifer Tiberio
Front cover photo © Erlo Brown / Shutterstock.com
Page preparation and text design by Steve Izma
Printed in Canada

Second printing August 2016

Library and Archives Canada Cataloguing in Publication

Unions matter : advancing democracy, economic equality, and social justice / edited by Matthew Behrens for the Canadian Foundation for Labour Rights.

Includes bibliographical references.

Issued in print and electronic formats.

ISBN 978-1-77113-132-2 (pbk.).
ISBN 978-1-77113-133-9 (epub).
ISBN 978-1-77113-134-6 (pdf).

1. Labor unions — Social aspects — Canada. 2. Employee rights — Canada. 3. Labor movement — Canada. 4. Social justice — Canada. 5. Equality — Canada. 6. Democracy — Canada. I. Behrens, Matthew L., editor of compilation
HD6524.U57 2014   331.880971   C2013-907914-9
C2013-907915-7

Between the Lines gratefully acknowledges assistance for its publishing activities from the Canada Council for the Arts, the Ontario Arts Council, the Government of Ontario through the Ontario Book Publishers Tax Credit program and through the Ontario Book Initiative, and the Government of Canada through the Canada Book Fund.

Contents

Introduction / 1
James Clancy

Part 1 Reducing Income Inequality through Labour Rights

One   Why Unions Matter / 13
            Garry Sran with James Clancy, Derek Fudge, and Michael Lynk

Two   Income Inequality in Canada / 43
            Armine Yalnizyan

Three   Increasing Inequality / 67
            Lars Osberg

Four   Labour Law and Labour Rights / 79
            Michael Lynk

Part 2 Promoting Democracy, Economic Equality, and Social Rights

Five   Unions and Democratic Governance / 93
            Nathalie Des Rosiers

Six   Advancing Human Rights for All Canadians / 101
            Paul Champ

Seven   A Changing Union Tide Hurts Vulnerable Workers / 115
            Naveen Mehta

Part 3 Constitutional Protection of Labour Rights

Eight   Who Owns *Charter* Values? / 125
            Fay Faraday and Eric Tucker

Nine   Freedom of Association / 139
            Paul J.J. Cavalluzzo and Adrienne Telford

Ten   Constitutional Protection for the Right to Strike / 149
            Steven Barrett and Benjamin Oliphant

Eleven   Working towards Equality / 163
            Fay Faraday

Twelve   The Power of Collective Bargaining / 171
            John Hendy

Notes / 179

Contributors / 203

Introduction

Unions Promote Fairness

James Clancy

MORE THAN TWO YEARS after the Occupy Wall Street movement rocketed the concept of the 1 per cent and the 99 per cent into mainstream North American consciousness, business and government leaders, right-wing think tanks, and conservative pundits have been working overtime to shift the focus away from the rapid growth in income inequality. Indeed, those who make up the 1 per cent rely on the hope that the 99 per cent will not draw the connection between their own difficult economic circumstances and the huge concentration of wealth and power that continues to reside in the hands of the very few.

To the dismay of the 1 per cent, however, those connections are not only being drawn, but also acted upon. The Spanish *indignados* movement, the uproar of Chilean students, and the mass demonstrations that have rocked France, Greece, Portugal, Brazil, and a score of other nations in recent years have occurred because people are resisting the globalized inequality that reared its head in the trillions transferred by governments to near-bankrupt banks and other corporations whose policies brought on the 2008 recession. In an all-too-familiar pattern, subsequent reports emerged of million-dollar bonuses for disgraced brokers while the unemployed faced foreclosure and single mothers with three part-time minimum-wage jobs struggled to get by.

At home, Canadians face the highest levels of income inequality since 1928. As Bruce Campbell of the Canadian Centre for Policy Alternatives points out, "The 61 Canadian billionaires have a combined wealth of $162 billion, twice as much as the bottom 17 million Canadians."[1] In 2011, the average CEO received compensation worth 235 times more than the annual pay of the average Canadian worker. The fact that the CEO of Canadian Pacific took home $49.2 million in 2012[2] is not generally flaunted in the manner of a Donald Trump, but for the convenience store clerk nursing a massive student debt or the working family too busy juggling low-wage, part-time jobs to spend time with each other, the idea that Canada is an increasingly unequal society is all too real. Indeed, in May 2013, the Pew Research Center found that 76 per cent of Canadians felt income inequality had grown since the 2008 recession, while nearly half of respondents believe inequality is a significant problem, and 22 per cent said reducing inequality should be the government's top priority.[3]

The standard canards about working harder to get ahead simply do not apply in an economy so lopsided in favour of the few. Indeed, the awful truth is that the more Canadians work, the less they get. Canada's real economic output today is twice as big as it was in 1981, but growing the economy doesn't count for much if the increases just mean bigger slices for the top 1 per cent and crumbs for everyone else. Most Canadians have gained nothing from decades of economic growth: the poor are getting poorer, the middle class is shrinking, and the top 1 per cent continues getting a lot richer. The income gap has been skyrocketing, and Canada has become a radically less equal society.

Despite this very clear picture, efforts continue to convince Canadians that things are not as bad as they seem. As participants headed to the starting point of Canada's annual Labour Day parades on September 3, 2013, perhaps some of them caught the headlines screaming out from *National Post* newspaper boxes: "The myth of income inequality" and "It's the 1% who are flatlining, while the 99% surge."[4]

As with previous Labour Day events, 2013 was a time to focus on such issues, and who better to do so than the leaders of the Canadian labour movement, whose research, reports, public statements, and solidarity actions have for decades played a major role in publicizing and resisting income inequality? That leadership role, however, means unions are squarely in the crosshairs of corporate targeting. The business-friendly *National Post*'s Labour Day message was clear enough, warning to "Beware of bogus union wage claims," with an editorial called "The union disadvantage" and a Fraser Institute piece touting the benefits of so-called right-to-work laws thrown in for good measure. It is clear that one way of diverting attention from the income divide is to demonize those who talk about it the most: unions.[5]

"Unions were good at one time, but haven't they outlived their usefulness," wondered Canada's other national newspaper, in an editorial by *The Globe and Mail*'s predecessor, *The Daily Globe*, on May 8, 1886. This sentiment, which could have been ripped from any number of today's business publications, is a stark reminder that as long as

---

unions have existed, those who have profited from economic inequality have questioned organized labour's relevance, effectiveness, and social role.

The heart of what unions do and why they pose such a threat to the dictates of the 1 per cent can be boiled down to the fact that they promote fairness in the workplace and in the economy, they strengthen democracy, and they participate in broader social movements for social justice. In other words, they have the very qualities lacking in the 1 per cent.

Unions Promote Workplace Fairness

Through unions, working people have a voice at work and an avenue to equality and fair treatment. In addition to job security and economic security for unionized workers and their families, unions provide an important check against discrimination by employers and the almost total power of management in the workplace. The popular bumper sticker reminding drivers that "unions brought you weekends" could be expanded to include decent wages, vacation and overtime pay, leave for care of newborns and sick family members, medical, disability, and life insurance, minimum wage, pay equity, protection against employment discrimination, employment insurance, occupational health and safety, and workers' compensation. Needless to say, such workplace gains have translated into general social improvements that benefit non-unionized workers as well, raising the bar for everyone.

Less well recognized perhaps is the important role that unions play in ensuring that these employment protections are not just "paper promises" at the workplace.[6] Unions have been crucial in this aspect by providing all workers relevant information about their rights at work and the necessary procedures to ensure those rights are adhered to. Unions have also mounted major campaigns across the country aimed at ensuring workplace rights are not only respected, but also protected and enhanced.

Unions Promote Economic Fairness

The struggle for economic fairness does not end in the workplace. If all unions did was to represent workers in their workplaces then it would be fair to say that they are simply a business, providing a service that workers purchase by paying union dues. But unions have a wider vision. They are interested in raising the economic floor for everyone who works for a living. Indeed, unions raise the wages and benefits of non-unionized workers in related industries, in part because non-unionized employers seek to dampen the appeal of unionization.[7] Studies have consistently proven that in geographic regions or industries with high unionization rates, non-union workers benefit because it gives them higher bargaining power for their own job as well. This dynamic is sometimes called the "union threat effect," the degree to which non-union workers get paid more because their employers are trying to forestall unionization.[8]

Unions also play a role in sustaining significant economic benefits for business. Unions not only make workplaces safer and more productive, but they also raise professional standards and work with management to keep companies in business. The cyclical spinoff effect is also clear, given that union members have more purchasing power through good jobs and fair wages, allowing them to support local businesses (and thus create more local jobs) and bolster the local tax base, which in turn supports public works and community services that add to everyone's quality of life.

There is no question that when unions are stronger, the economy as a whole does better. Even the conservative-leaning World Bank has noted the positive role unions have on national economies. Based on more than a thousand studies of the effects of unions on the performance of national economies, the World Bank found that "high rates of unionization lead to greater income equality, lower unemployment and inflation, higher productivity and speedier adjustments to economic shocks."[9]

Unions Promote Democracy

Unions also make democracy work better by being relentlessly democratic. At every local meeting, job action, and convention, and throughout the collective bargaining process, unions are one of the most democratic institutions in our society, providing workers with a training ground to learn and participate in all facets of the democratic process, from advocacy to electoral politics. Recent research has found that union membership in Canada is associated with a roughly 10–12 per cent increase in the propensity to vote, while voter participation data in Canada has confirmed that union density acts as a complement to voter turnout.[10] As unionization rates have declined for the past three decades, there has been a downward trend in voter turnout.

This trend is also reflected in voter-turnout research conducted by the Organisation for Economic Co-operation and Development and the Institute for Democracy and Electoral Assistance, both of which confirm that countries with higher unionization rates have higher voter turnout.[11] Looking at average voter-turnout data between 2000 and 2010, they found that the top ten unionized countries have a 77.9 per cent voter turnout, compared to 61.8 per cent in the bottom ten countries.

Unions Promote Political Fairness

Most union members recognize that anything they win at the bargaining table can be taken away by regulation, legislation, or political decision making. It's for that reason that unions and their members organize politically – through campaigns, coalitions, and social movements – and as a result help build more civic engagement. Unions often help working people make the connection between public policy and the overall well-being of their families, their communities, and their daily work life.

Ultimately, unions provide a democratic counterweight to the growing power of corporations and the super-wealthy to determine public policy. The importance of this counterweight cannot be underestimated, as increasing corporate power in recent years has resulted in massive inequality and social exclusion. Unions consistently push back by helping build greater social inclusiveness and supporting initiatives that improve the lives of all people, including poverty reduction strategies, the fight for gender equality, combating racism, advancing human rights, and advocating for healthy communities.

Unions Promote Social Justice Fairness

Unions make an important contribution to social cohesion by helping build greater social inclusiveness within societies. Unions have supported initiatives that improve the lives of all people. From organizing education events to holding mass rallies, unions have mobilized the broader society in order to educate and to resist the erosion of human rights associated with greater inequality.

The critical role that unions play in advancing social rights is reinforced by a major 2008 International Labour Organization (ILO) study that found that higher rates of union density had a positive impact on the range of social rights afforded to citizens: "The countries in which union density rates are higher are also the ones in which the welfare state is more developed, taxation levels higher and more progressive, collective bargaining more centralized and labour law both closer to international labour standards and better implemented."[12]

Unions Promote Global Fairness

Unions play an important role advancing democracy, economic equality, and social justice within the international community, and have played a critical role in the transition from dictatorship and corruption to democracy and the rule of law in many countries. Whether it was opposing the military dictatorships in Latin America in the 1970s, supporting Solidarność and the pro-democracy movement in Poland in the 1980s, leading the boycott campaign against South African Apartheid, or supporting struggles for democracy and social justice in Colombia and more recently in the Arab countries, unions have been a major force in bringing about democratic change around the globe.

Unions have also worked with the poor and disenfranchised around the world, campaigning against child labour, working in partnership with humanitarian organizations on the AIDS crisis in Africa, lobbying the Canadian government and the G8 on maternal health, or by providing international disaster relief to countries that have been stricken by war, famine, or earthquakes.

Future Pathways: Unions and the Struggle for Fairness

Ultimately, there are far too many examples that could be included here to point out why unions matter to achieving a greater degree of fairness, social justice, and healthy economic growth not just for their own members, but for society in general. Suffice it to say, however, that this collection of essays serves as a reminder of the good work that continues to be done as well as of the challenges that lie ahead. In March 2013, the Canadian Foundation for Labour Rights hosted an international conference that brought together experts on human rights, economic justice, and the role of unions in achieving a more equitable society. The foundation is a national voice devoted to promoting labour rights as an important means to strengthening democracy, equality, and economic justice in Canada and internationally, and provides a forum for its members to promote and publish their independent research, policy papers, and articles. While fostering greater public awareness and understanding of labour rights as a critical component of human rights, the foundation also acts to build effective political momentum and public support for progressive labour law reform (and against regressive labour laws), promote fundamental labour standards in Canada that enhance union organizing, and support legal challenges to strategically move labour rights ahead.

Given this background, it made logical sense for the foundation to bring together some of the leading players on these issues – including conference co-sponsors United Food and Commercial Workers (UFCW) Canada, the National Union of Public and General Employees (NUPGE), and the Canadian Teachers' Federation (CTF) – for what became known as the International Conference on Labour Rights and Their Impact on Democracy, Economic Equality and Social Justice.

Those attending the conference were struck both by the passion and intellectual rigor of the conference presenters, and by their wealth of knowledge on a significant range of issues. Some 160 conference attendees were inspired by what they heard, and we felt that a logical next step was inviting some of our guests – as well as other leading figures in the struggle to remind people that labour rights are human rights – to put together a book encompassing the themes that comprise their daily work. Thus, *Unions Matter* was born, and we are proud to have brought together the thoughtful voices of individuals who took time out of their jam-packed schedules to put their thoughts to paper and share their valuable insights on some of the most compelling issues facing not just the labour movement and those struggling for a more equitable world, but also all those who work to put food on the table and keep a roof over their heads.

Unions Matter is divided into three parts, the first of which focuses on labour rights and the critical role they play in reducing income inequality. As a starting point, Garry Sran, Derek Fudge, and Michael Lynk join me in providing a review of Canadian and international research that affirms the critical role that labour rights and unions play in reducing income inequality, promoting the social well-being of all citizens, and advancing democracy within nations. Armine Yalnizyan builds on this foundation with a review of the history and trends of income inequality in Canada, examining how a growing gap between the rich and the rest of us continues to drive today's political and economic processes, including volatile stock markets, troubled housing markets, and a newly escalated attack on labour that paints unions as yesterday's answer to yesterday's problems.

Lars Osberg contributes an analysis of the connection between union density and income inequality based on economic theory and available international empirical evidence. It addresses the dilemma facing Canada's union movement by pointing out that a focus limited to workplace bargaining issues does not, on its own, directly confront the core inequality issues facing Canada. This part is rounded out by Michael Lynk's explanation of the connection between eroding levels of unionization in Canada and the country's stagnant labour laws. He also presents empirical social science suggesting that labour laws matter, not only for unionization levels, but also as important tools to enhance economic egalitarianism.

Part II discusses the role of unions in promoting democracy, economic equality, and social rights. Nathalie Des Rosiers gives an overview of how unions have contributed to the intellectual framework of modern democracies in developing concepts of solidarity and group rights. In particular, she writes about how collective bargaining and the right to strike – the key elements of freedom of association – support modern democratic ideals. Paul Champ presents a historical overview of unions' lead role in advancing human rights in Canada, not only in the workplace through bargaining and litigation, but also by using their organizational strength to promote legal reform through education, lobbying, and social action to secure protections for all Canadians. Naveen Mehta of the UFCW argues – with a particular focus on vulnerable temporary migrant workers – that when unions thrive and commit to broader social unionism, the union tide raises all boats: standards of living, democratic participation, and increased social and economic justice.

The final part focuses on constitutional protection of labour rights as they relate to Canada's *Charter of Rights and Freedoms* and international labour standards. Fay Faraday and Eric Tucker examine the potential for labour and progressive social movements to use the values expressed in the *Charter* to mobilize direct political action and to advocate for reform against the backdrop of austerity. They focus on historical examples of radical organizing that have leveraged constitutional values, as well as recent Canadian social movements. In a separate chapter, Faraday explores the disconnect between the right to equality being praised as reflecting the dreams, hopes, and aspirations of Canadian society, and its elusiveness in practice. This chapter also reflects on how labour and progressive movements can measure success in advancing equality in law.

The ongoing push and pull over the meaning of the *Charter*'s freedom of association guarantee for the labour movement is explored in great detail by Paul J.J. Cavalluzzo and Adrienne Telford, while Steven Barrett and Benjamin Oliphant dig deep into the three main doctrinal approaches adopted by Canadian courts to determine the scope of freedom of association, suggesting that under each approach, there is strong support for the conclusion that the right to strike is constitutionally protected.

Finally, an international perspective on the role of neoliberalism is provided by Britain's John Hendy, who reminds us that a series of international labour law instruments remain in place to protect basic rights to strike and to collective bargaining, all of which can be employed to protect against the tide of neoliberalism.

Taken together, these voices represent the democratic strength of inquiry, research, and discussion that animate so much of the labour movement and the social movements supported by unions. The business press will no doubt continue trying to convince us that unions are unnecessary and irrelevant. Those who benefit from the work of organized labour know better. *Unions Matter* is one more tool in the pushback against inequality and towards a more just and hopeful future.

Part 1

Reducing Income Inequality through Labour Rights

One

Why Unions Matter

Unions, Income Inequality, and Regressive Labour Laws

Garry Sran with James Clancy, Derek Fudge, and Michael Lynk

FOR OVER THIRTY YEARS, income inequality has been rising in Canada and throughout the world. The elusive promise of increased living standards through globalization and free trade has clearly not materialized for everyone. Indeed, while most of the gains have gone to the very rich, increasing public concerns about inequality gave rise to the North American Occupy movement. Like related movements globally, Occupy has focused on the significant roles played by large corporations and the global financial system in perpetuating the growing social and economic inequalities that plague most industrialized countries.

Inequality affects everyone: unequal societies generally produce greater levels of social dysfunction, higher rates of crime and incarceration, lower educational scores, and decreased life expectancy.[1] And while economic inequality has traditionally been viewed as a social justice question, growing evidence suggests the rich-poor gap also hurts economic growth.

While generally a healthier country than its southern neighbour, Canada ranked twelfth out of seventeen peer countries on income inequality and received a C grade in the Conference Board of Canada's

January 2013 Society Report Card.[2] The report states that high rates of poverty and a large income gap between the rich and everyone else put stress on a society and the economy. Rising poverty rates and greater income inequality can also mean a weakening in labour force attachment and declining social cohesion.

The rise in income inequality is not an inevitable phenomenon. History shows that the problems of inequality can be tackled when there is political will. From the late 1940s to the early 1980s – often referred to as the Great Compression,[3] a period of economic growth and rising living standards – income inequality was reduced through government policies such as a progressive tax system; adequate levels of public spending on education, health, and infrastructure; and protective labour and employment standards. During the Great Compression, unions played an important role in fighting for greater income equality. Higher levels of unionization made it easier for the labour movement to bargain fair wages and benefits for their members, with the subsequent spillover effect on the wages of non-union workers, whose demands were more readily met in part because non-unionized employers sought to dampen the appeal of unionization.[4]

"The important contribution of post-war Canadian labour law has been to assist in advancing the growing egalitarian character of our country while fulfilling our commitment to promoting social rights," writes University of Western Ontario law professor Michael Lynk. "This was most clearly visible in the years between 1945 and the mid-1980s. As labour laws do their job, the distribution of income, wealth and social opportunities becomes more equitable, and our society becomes more cohesive. Allow labour laws to fall into disrepair, or actively deconstruct them and the virtuous circles that promote egalitarianism become smaller, our economic life becomes more disfigured, and our sense of mutual reinforcement wanes."[5]

Since the 1980s, a series of governmental actions – promoted by powerful corporate interests – has eroded labour rights and undermined the income redistribution effects of unions. Empirical evidence exploring the results of these regressive policies suggests that labour laws matter, not only for union members, but also as an important tool to reduce income inequality: in countries where unionization rates decline, inequality tends to rise.

Indeed, as Lynk writes, the dramatic drop in union density and the erosion of Canada's labour laws have had profound implications for Canadian society. "Labour and employment rights and the laws that buttress them are not the accumulation of privileges by a vigorous lobby of special interests, but the expression of core constitutional and human rights that benefit, directly and indirectly, the majority of citizens living in a modern democratic society."[6] In a 2002 paper based on more than a thousand studies of the effects of unions on the performance of national economies, the conservative-leaning World Bank found that "high rates of unionization lead to greater income equality, lower unemployment and inflation, higher productivity and speedier adjustments to economic shocks."[7]

Even the International Monetary Fund, once a leader in promoting neoliberal policies to advance economic growth, has now changed its tune, declaring that income inequality must be tackled given its strong correlation with weaker economic growth.[8] Moreover, a growing body of international literature across the political spectrum has established that unions play a critical role in reducing income inequality.[9] A major 2008 International Labour Organization (ILO) study found that the countries in which income inequality was lower tended to be those in which a greater proportion of workers were members of unions. "Highly unionized countries and countries where collective bargaining is more coordinated tend to have low income-inequality, and greater compliance with [international labour law standards] tends to be associated with lower inequality," the report concluded.[10]

Over the past thirty years in Canada, regressive labour laws have significantly contributed to declining unionization rates, with one consequence being the steady rise of income inequality. Research shows that from the 1950s through the early 1980s, Canada experienced high income growth, shared proportionally across all income groups. During the same period, union density in Canada rose from 28.4 per cent in 1951 to a high point of 41.8 per cent in 1984. Much of this rise in union density coincided with a major expansion of labour law, establishing a comprehensive framework of collective bargaining rights for most Canadian workers.[11] Conversely, a May 2012 study by five University of British Columbia economists attributed 15 per cent of Canada's growth in income inequality during the 1980s and 1990s to declining unionization.[12]

Social scientists have consistently demonstrated this correlation, with Jacob Hacker and Paul Pierson writing, "On the one hand, [unions] push policy makers to address issues of mounting inequality. On the other, they recognize, highlight and effectively resist policy changes that further inequality."[13] Clearly, federal and provincial governments need to recognize that one surefire path to reducing income inequality is the strengthening of labour rights.

Paul Krugman, the 2008 Nobel Prize winner in economics, explains the difference between average and median income. If there are ten people in a bar earning between $34,000 and $36,000, the average and median income in that room is around $35,000. But if Microsoft founder Bill Gates walked in and his annual $1 billion income were included in the calculation, the average income in the bar would suddenly soar to $91 million, even though the ten people already there would be no richer than they were before. Inequality rises because the median income would remain around $35,000, and only one person would be better off.[14]

Current Economic Climate: A Cause for Concern

There's no doubt that the big reason for the income differences [is] not so much the poor getting left further behind, it's the rich running away from the rest of us with the bonus culture.

— Richard Wilkinson[15]

While the Harper government boasts about Canada weathering the 2008 recession and heading into an economic recovery, the majority of Canadians have not bounced back. Canadian purchasing power is falling and the average wage has not kept up with inflation. Canadian economist Armine Yalnizyan calls this the "wageless recovery," noting that from the lowest point in the recent recession in 2009 to 2011, real average hourly wages have declined by 0.6 per cent, falling from $23.11 to $22.99.[16] At first glance, this decline may seem insignificant, but a closer examination of wage distribution reveals that Canadians on the bottom half of the income scale have experienced significant losses. As figure 1 illustrates, the purchasing power of Canadians across all income groups has fallen. But those in low-income percentiles experience the biggest declines in real wages.

In Canada, working people have been squeezed by stagnant earnings, the rising costs of everyday goods, and worsening household debt. While figure 2 shows a growing gap between the average and median yearly earnings from 1976 to 2010 – average yearly earnings results have increased by 7.7 per cent during the period – average earnings are typically pulled up by the gains of the rich. When considering median incomes, which declined by 5.5 per cent, one can see that the lion's share of income gains was enjoyed only by the rich minority at the top of the income chart.

To offset income losses, many Canadians have resorted to taking

Figure 1. Change in real average hourly wages, 2009–2011

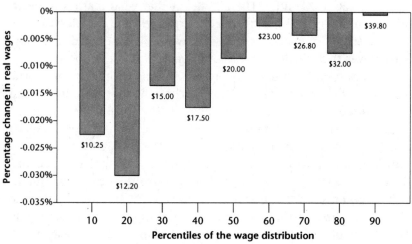

Source: Provided by Armine Yalnizyan, based on Labour Force Survey public use microdata. Used with permission.

Figure 2. Canadian average vs. median yearly earnings, 1976–2010 (in $2011)

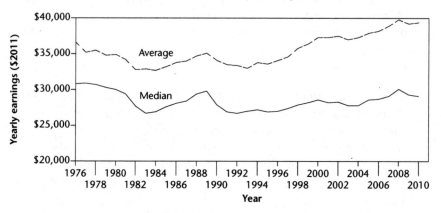

Source: Statistics Canada, CANSIM Table 202-0101.

on higher debt levels. According to the Bank of Canada, Canadians have reached a personal debt ratio of 166 per cent, meaning that for every dollar earned, $1.66 is owed. At this level, Canadian households are now more indebted than Americans were at the peak of their 2007 housing bubble, when the United States reached a staggering debt ratio of 165 per cent.

One manner in which the growing gap and the unnecessary austerity mantra adopted by most levels of government may be confronted is explored by Richard Wilkinson and Kate Pickett in *The Spirit Level*. They cite Richard Smith: "The big idea is that what matters in determining mortality and health in a society is less the overall wealth of that society and more how evenly that wealth is distributed. The more equally wealth is distributed the better the health of that society."[17]

In tracking the correlation between income inequality and social decline in the world's twenty-three richest nations, Wilkinson and Pickett discovered that the country having the greatest income equality is Japan, followed by Finland and Scandinavian countries. Canada falls in the middle of the pack, while the United States and United Kingdom rate as the most unequal on the list. Among the most equal, the rich have less than four times as much wealth as the poor. Infants born in an unequal society like the United States are twice as likely to die in their first year as infants born in an equal society like Japan. The effects of such inequality are well documented in weaker social shock absorbers for the poor; greater levels of social dysfunction, crime, incarceration, mental illness, illiteracy, and teenage pregnancy; and declines in health and life expectancy, civic engagement, social mobility and opportunities, and interpersonal trust.[18]

While some sectors of society tend to ignore such social determinants of health, they cannot escape the fact that widening inequality also results in economic inefficiencies, creating macroeconomic impediments to growth by

- excluding certain groups from the benefits of an expanding economy;
- diminishing the purchasing power of the middle- and lower-income strata that sustain economic growth;
- increasing the social costs of policing low-income groups; and
- having economic and social policy making in the hands of a small number of wealthy groups, whose skewed priorities inevitably lead to misallocations.[19]

There is now a growing consensus among economists that improving socio-economic well-being and reducing income inequality are critical prerequisites for improving economic growth.

The Great Compression

Everything we know about unions says that their new power [after the Second World War] was a major factor in the creation of a middle-class society. First, unions raise average wages for their membership; they also, indirectly and to a lesser extent, raise wages for similar workers, even if they aren't represented by unions. Second, unions tend to narrow income gaps among blue-collar workers, by negotiating bigger wage increases for their worst-paid members. In other words, the known effects of unions on wages are exactly what we see in the Great Compression: a rise in the wages of blue-collar workers compared to managers and professionals, and a narrowing of wage differentials among blue-collar workers themselves.

— Paul Krugman[20]

Famously popularized by Paul Krugman, the Great Compression refers to the period of greater distribution of wealth and prosperity between the 1940s and early 1980s. Labour law, unionization, and the new labour market institutions emerging in this period made an integral contribution to the dramatic dampening of the wide income and wealth disparities that had plagued Canada, the United States, and the rest of the industrialized world before 1940.

Table 1. Share of aggregate incomes received by each quintile of families and unattached individuals (%)

	1951	1961	1971	1981	1991	2001	2011
Top 20% (richest)	42.8	41.1	43.3	41.6	44.4	46.9	47.2
Fourth 20%	23.3	24.5	24.9	25.1	24.7	23.7	23.8
Middle 20%	18.3	18.3	17.6	17.7	16.4	15.6	15.3
Second 20%	11.2	11.9	10.6	11.0	10.0	9.7	9.6
Bottom 20% (poorest)	4.4	4.2	3.6	4.6	4.5	4.1	4.1

Source: L. Osberg, *A Quarter Century of Economic Inequality in Canada, 1981–2006* (Ottawa: Canadian Centre for Policy Alternatives, 2008), 7. Updated to 2011 using Statistics Canada, CANSIM Table 202-0405.

As table 1 shows, between 1951 and 1981, the bottom quintile of income earners in Canada improved their share of aggregate income marginally, while the combined share of the middle three quintiles grew slightly. Over the same period, the richest quintile saw their share decline from 42.8 per cent to 41.6 per cent. The Great Compression's economic boom was distributed in a fashion that reduced the differences in income between the top and bottom quintiles. This compression stayed relatively stable, and the rising tide of economic growth in these years really did lift most boats.

However, in the past three decades, a larger share of total income has gone to the richest Canadians, whose slice of the economic pie has increased from 41.6 per cent to a staggering 47.3 per cent. Table 1 illustrates that the middle quintile saw their share of income drop from 17.7 per cent to 15.3 per cent, while the income share of the second quintile fell from 11 per cent to 9.6 per cent. Clearly, the gains of the few have come at the expense of the middle class. Because there has been no "trickling down" of income from the richest to the poorest, the only boats now being lifted by the rising economic tide are yachts.

The trends in figure 3 are particularly telling. From the onset of both the Great Depression and the current global financial crisis, an increased share of total income in Canada was heavily concentrated with the richest 1 per cent. In comparison, when income distribution was more equal (the Great Compression), Canada experienced decades of economic stability. In fact, the richest 1 per cent saw their share of total income reduced by 45 per cent while the bottom 80 per cent of Canadians increased their share of total income by 1.2 per cent.[21]

Figure 3. Share of total income for the richest in Canada, 1920–2009

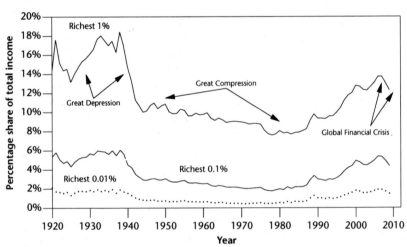

Source: Emmanuel Saez and Michael Veall, "The Evolution of High Incomes in Northern America: Lessons from Canadian Evidence," *American Economic Review* 95,3 (2005), 831–49. Used with permission. Updated to 2009 using data provided by Michael Veall.

A number of analysts have explored the possible links between income inequality, periods of economic crisis, and growth sustainability. Raghuram Rajan points to economic pressures that lead high-income individuals to save and low-income individuals to sustain consumption through borrowing.[22] Michael Kumhof and Romain Rancière argue that the same factors may have played a role in both the Great Depression and the current recession.[23] Common at the onset of both periods was the high concentration of income among the richest 1 per cent.

The Great Compression in Canada was made possible through a combination of dynamic national policy measures such as a progressive taxation system; adequate levels of public spending on education, health, and infrastructure; and protective labour and employment standards.[24] Families were able to earn a decent income and had access to a range of important public programs and services that provided them with greater economic and social security. There was a generational understanding that through taxes and transfers, everyone would contribute towards quality public programs, with enhanced social benefits flowing back. When it was time to retire, it was the next generation who would earn and then contribute back into the system via progressive taxes.

Krugman characterized it as a society without extremes of wealth or poverty, a period of broadly shared prosperity.[25] But due to the resurgence of neoliberalism, taxes on the rich have fallen substantially. As government revenues declined, so did expenditures on quality public services and programs. As the holes in the social safety net grew larger, inequality soared. Krugman labelled this new era of inequality the Great Divergence.

Inequality Divergence

We may have democracy, or we may have wealth concentrated in the hands of a few, but we cannot have both.
— Louis Brandeis, U.S. Supreme Court Justice, 1916–39[26]

In most countries and in many emerging economies, the widening gap between rich and poor grew despite a period of sustained economic growth prior to the 2008–2009 recession, posing a series of economic, political, and ethical challenges while leaving a growing number of people behind in an ever-changing economy.[27]

Growing income inequality has become an international concern, among both policy makers and societies at large. Today in advanced economies, the average income of the richest 10 per cent of the population is about nine times that of the poorest 10 per cent.[28]

A standard measure of income inequality is the Gini coefficient, which ranges from zero to one. When everyone has identical incomes,

Nobel Prize-winning economist Joseph Stiglitz believes inequality hurts economic growth because it is associated with more frequent and severe boom-and-bust cycles. The "hollowing out" of the middle class means that many people cannot afford an education for themselves or for their children, and are also too weak to maintain the levels of consumer spending that have historically driven economic growth.[29]

the Gini is equal to zero; when all income goes to one person, the Gini is one. A national economy with a Gini coefficient below 0.30 would be considered a strongly egalitarian country (e.g., Sweden, Denmark). Countries with a Gini coefficient over 0.35 would be designated as having an unenviable rate of income inequality (e.g., the United States).

The Gini coefficient in Organisation for Economic Co-operation and Development (OECD) countries stood at an average of 0.29 during the mid-1980s. By the late 2000s, however, it had increased by almost 10 per cent to 0.316.[30] Canada, which had relatively stable income distribution up to the mid-1990s, now faces one of the fastest-growing rates of income inequality among OECD countries.

The major political and social transformation of the 1980s laid the foundation for today's growing inequality. Neoliberal champions Ronald Reagan (U.S.), Margaret Thatcher (U.K.), and Brian Mulroney (Canada) pushed their governments to break away from the social contract in favour of a business-friendly vision. They signed free trade agreements that stripped away tariffs and taxes, a key source of government revenues to fund public services. The neoliberal policy framework abandoned the goal of full employment in favour of targeting inflation, primarily to protect the value of financial wealth. Large corporations and the superwealthy came to dominate public policy and legislative decision making, leading to tax cuts, deregulation of finance and other key industries, weakening of labour laws, and massive cutbacks in public spending. As a result, there was a corollary decline in the redistributive effect of taxes and transfers.

Some economists and policy makers assume the rise in inequality was not linked to public policy, but rather could be attributed to technological change and globalization; both, however, were the result of political decisions that greatly enriched the already wealthy. Joseph Stiglitz has argued that while there may be underlying economic forces at play, politics have shaped the market in ways that benefit those at the top at the expense of the rest.[31] If political changes have

Figure 4. Change in the market and after-tax income Gini coefficients and the impact of redistribution policies, Canada, 1981–2010

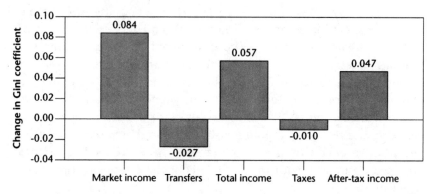

Source: Statistics Canada, CANSIM Table 202-0709; Evan Capeluck and Andrew Sharpe, *The Impact of Redistribution on Income Inequality in Canada and the Provinces, 1981–2010* (Ottawa: The Centre for the Study of Living Standards, 2012).

Figure 5. Canadian inequality trends, 1976–2010

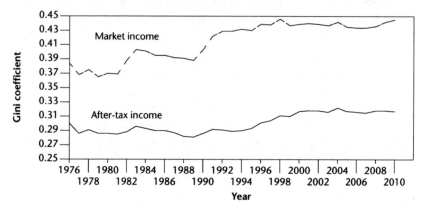

Source: Statistics Canada, CANSIM Table 202-0709.

increased inequality, then reversing these changes through the political process is equally possible.

Figures 4 and 5 map Canadian inequality trends over the past three decades. Evan Capeluck and Andrew Sharpe investigated the impact of Canadian redistributive policies, namely taxes and transfers,[32] and found, as shown in figure 4, the after-tax Gini coefficient increased by 0.047 points or 13.5 per cent. This increase was fuelled by a 0.084 point or 19.4 per cent increase in the market income Gini coefficient; however, 0.037 points or 44 per cent of the increased market income inequality between 1981 and 2010 was offset by changes in the transfer and tax system.

Figure 5 compares Canada's market income and after-tax income Gini coefficients between 1976 and 2010, and reveals the trend of increased income inequality. The only reason after-tax income sits below market income is that taxes and transfers have played an important role in reducing inequality. Policies such as a progressive taxation system mean individuals with higher incomes contribute proportionately more than individuals with lower incomes, thus reducing the rich-poor gap and sustaining social cohesion. However, the positive effects of taxes and transfers have declined as politics trumped economics with the rise of neoliberal policies in the 1980s and 1990s.

Unionization and Inequality

The sharpest increases in wage inequality in the Western world have taken place in the United States and Britain, both of which experienced sharp declines in union membership. Canada, although its economy is closely linked to that of the United States, appears to have had substantially less increase in wage inequality – and it's likely that the persistence of a strong union movement is an important reason why. Unions raise the wages of their members, who tend to be in the middle of the wage distribution; they also tend to equalize wages among members. Perhaps most important, they act as a countervailing force to management, enforcing social norms that limit very high and very low pay. They also mobilize their members to vote for progressive politics.   — Paul Krugman[33]

In recent decades, governments, egged on by the corporate elite, have promoted a neoliberal agenda of cuts to public transfers and taxes. The Canadian labour movement has consistently opposed that agenda, and has been a strong advocate for tax fairness and quality public services. As a result of unions' strong opposition to the neoliberal agenda, they sit squarely in the crosshairs of corporate and government attempts to weaken the house of labour. Governments have weakened labour laws while restricting and, in some cases, eliminating collective bargaining rights. Corporations have unfairly interfered in union drives, threatened unionized workers with plant closures, and lobbied governments both to weaken labour rights and to intervene in private- and public-sector labour negotiations in favour of employers.

Meanwhile, corporate media have been more than willing to negatively portray and denigrate unions. One consequence of this co-ordinated assault is a three-decade decrease in unionization rates, declining from their peak of 41.8 per cent in 1984 to 31.2 per cent in 2011.

Paul Krugman cites strong unions as one of the driving forces that reduced inequality during the Great Compression.[34] From the late 1940s to the early 1980s, organized labour played an important role in the political and social transformation of Canadian society, contributing to a greater distribution of wealth and prosperity. During the Great Compression, gains from economic growth led in turn to higher employment and unionization rates (which rose 32.4 per cent), resulting in better pay for all workers. The rise in incomes, coupled with increases in private consumption and public investment, led to unprecedented economic growth and coincided with a shift towards a more equitable distribution of income.

All citizens now enjoy social rights that have at some point been a central focus of union demands and worker mobilizations, from minimum wages, universal health care, and a public pension plan to improved public services, public education, and progressive taxation. Unions also have a lengthy history of human rights advocacy, working in solidarity with various partners to achieve for all workers – whether unionized or not – workplace health and safety legislation, workers' compensation, employment standards, income support and training for unemployed workers, and equal pay for equal work. Internationally, wherever unions are strong, their beneficial presence is evident in the reduced pay gap between workers and management, men and women, racial minorities and other workers.[35]

The connection between union rates and the levels of inequality is illustrated by figures 6–9, which explore the phenomenon provincially, across Canada, and among a selection of European and Commonwealth nations.

Since the neoliberal assault on labour rights and unions began, income inequality in Canada has been steadily rising. Figure 6 displays the relational trends of Canadian union coverage and Canada's Gini coefficient. Between 1984 and 2010, inequality in Canada increased from 0.357 to 0.395 as union coverage fell from its peak of 41.8 per cent to 31.5 per cent. Clearly, the decreased ability of unions to positively influence the transfer of wealth declined, with the resulting negative social consequences.

When comparing inequality across Canadian provinces, a similar trend to that shown in figure 6 emerges tying falling unionization

Figure 6. Canadian union coverage and Gini coefficient, 1980–2010

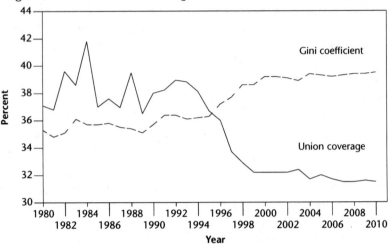

The Gini coefficient data have been multiplied by 100. Data are for workers covered by a collective agreement, which is a slightly greater number than union membership. Industry data are not fully consistent due to changes in classification. Source: Statistics Canada, CANSIM Table 202-0705. For union coverage, J. Visser, Institutional Characteristics of Trade Unions, Wage Setting, State Intervention and Social Pacts database (ICTWSS), www.uva-aias.net/208. 1984 and 1988 data are reported by Andrew Jackson, *Work and Labour in Canada* (Toronto: Canadian Scholars' Press Inc., 2005), 135. 2010 data from Statistics Canada, CANSIM Table 282-0078.

rates to increased inequality. Figures 7, 8, and 9 plot the relationship between provincial unionization rates and their respective Gini coefficients for the years 1980, 2000, and 2010. The relationship between union coverage and inequality varies by province but ideally, it would be desirable to enjoy the lower income inequality and higher unionization rates that are shown on the bottom right portion of figures 7, 8, and 9. However, over the last three decades, Canada has shifted towards the top right corner, which represents higher inequality and lower unionization rates. For the majority of provinces in figures 7 and 8 – Ontario, British Columbia, New Brunswick, Newfoundland, and Nova Scotia – there is a clear association between falling unionization rates and increasing inequality, which is consistent with national data. In figure 7, Prince Edward Island experienced a decrease in inequality, and Manitoba's inequality index remained relatively constant; notably, both provinces saw increases in unionization. The outliers, in figure 9, are Alberta, Saskatchewan, and Quebec.

A number of factors account for the variations across provinces. Alberta and Saskatchewan have both experienced natural resource

Figure 7. Unionization rate and after-tax Gini coefficient, Manitoba, Nova Scotia, Prince Edward Island, 1980–2010

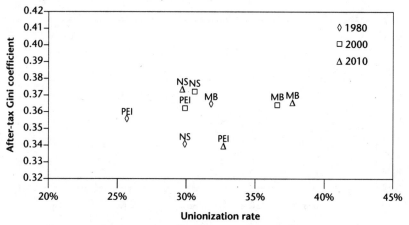

Source: Statistics Canada, CANSIM Tables 202-0705; 279-0025; 282-0078.

Figure 8. Unionization rate and after-tax Gini coefficient, British Columbia, Ontario, Newfoundland, New Brunswick, 1980–2010

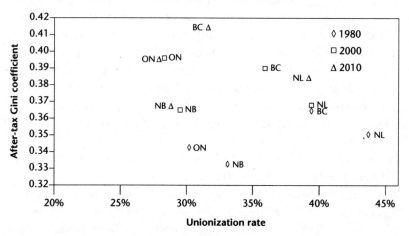

Source: Statistics Canada, CANSIM Tables 202-0705; 279-0025; 282-0078.

booms and dramatic increases in real estate values,[36] while the commodity boom has pushed the value of the Canadian dollar higher, weakening the manufacturing sector. Coupled with falling unionization rates and the implementation of neoliberal policies in most provinces – such as reductions in taxes and cuts in social spending – inequality has been pushed higher.

The negative correlation between declining rates of unionization

Figure 9. Unionization rate and after-tax Gini coefficient, Alberta, Saskatchewan, Quebec, 1980–2010

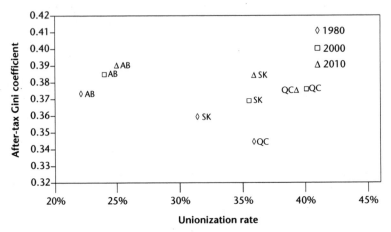

Source: Statistics Canada, CANSIM Tables 202-0705; 279-0025; 282-0078.

and income inequality is not just a Canadian phenomenon. There is broad consensus in qualitative and quantitative international research that confirms increases in inequality have been associated with declining unionization rates in developed and developing countries alike.

Lawrence Mishel, and Daniele Checchi and Jelle Visser, have found that unions' impact on the labour share of income has been positive and redistributive.[37] This trend has been observed worldwide; even the Organisation for Economic Co-operation and Development reported a similar relationship exists between declining union coverage and growing income inequality.[38]

In countries where union density has declined, the top 1 per cent have reaped the gains. As figure 10 shows, the share of income going to the top 1 per cent between 1982 and 2008 has increased in every developed economy that has witnessed a decrease in union density. In countries like the United States and United Kingdom, where unionization experienced dramatic decreases, the income share of the top 1 per cent more than doubled. In more strongly egalitarian countries, the income share going to the very top has been stemmed or sharply reduced.

Table 2 shows that for every country that experienced a decline in union density between 1982 and 2008, the income share of the top 1 per cent increased. The decline in union density and the growth in inequality is no coincidence. In a comprehensive study by economists David Card, Thomas Lemieux, and W. Craig Riddell, the authors conclude that 15 per cent of the growth in Canadian inequality can be

Figure 10. Share of top 1% income recipients in total income, 1982 and 2008

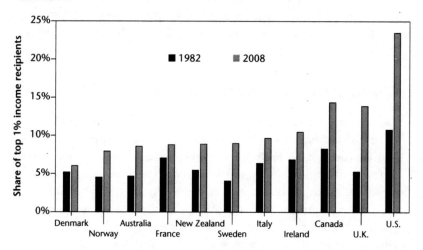

Source: Facundo Alvaredo, Tony Atkinson, Thomas Piketty, and Emmanuel Saez, *The World Top Incomes Database*, http://topincomes.g-mond.parisschoolofeconomics.eu.

Table 2. Percentage change in union density and top 1% income share between 1982 and 2008

	Percentage change in union density	Percentage change in top 1% income share
Norway	-8.3	75.7
Sweden	-13.5	120.3
Denmark	-15.7	16.1
Canada	-23.6	73.3
Italy	-28.5	50.9
Ireland	-39.6	52.5
United States	-42.0	117.6
United Kingdom	-45.6	160.9
France	-55.3	24.4
Australia	-61.7	83.9
New Zealand	-68.4	61.9

Source: Author's calculations based on data from OECD.StatExtracts, http://stats.oecd.org; and *The World Top Incomes Database*.

directly linked to the fall of unionization rates, whereas the numbers are more than 20 per cent in the United States and United Kingdom.[39] The International Labour Organization's *World of Work Report 2008* found a similar correlation in its review of fifty-one countries.[40] The ILO report stated that countries with a higher union density rate had on average lower levels of income inequality. While the precise impact varied from country to country, the trend has been clear: a decline in unionization has been paired with a corresponding rise of income being captured by the very rich.

Declining Unionization Rates and Regressive Labour Laws

> Extreme wealth and inequality undermines societies. It leads to far less social mobility. If you are born poor in a very unequal society, you are much more likely to end your life in poverty.... Social mobility has fallen rapidly in many countries as inequality has grown. When rich elites use their money to buy services, whether it is private schooling or private healthcare, they have less interest in public services or paying the taxes to support them. Those from elites are much more likely to end up in political office or other positions of power, further entrenching inequality.
>
> — Oxfam[41]

Opponents of unions argue that declines in unionization are the result of globalization and technological progress. But Alexandra Mitukiewcz and John Schmitt challenged this argument based on fifty years of data from twenty-one OECD countries.[42] They found that technology did not lead to lower unionization rates and observed that countries with a higher level of globalization have higher levels of union coverage. Instead, they found that a key factor in explaining the observed variation in unionization was the broader political environment in which unions operate.

An important factor within that environment over the past three decades has been governments' diminished respect for and promotion of labour rights. The right to join a union and to bargain collectively has been entrenched in labour relations legislation across the country, but during the past three decades governments have restricted this fundamental right with the passage of regressive labour laws. As table 3 shows, between 1982 and 2013, federal and provincial governments passed 204 restrictive labour laws that suspended or denied collective bargaining rights. While the courts have occasionally ruled that government rollbacks of statutory labour rights have violated the *Charter of Rights and Freedoms,* they have more often given a narrow and illiberal reading of the *Charter* and upheld the anti-worker actions, or inactions, of governments.

Table 3. Summary of labour laws restricting collective bargaining and trade union rights, 1982–2013 (as of Sept. 2013)

Type of Legislation	Jurisdiction											
	Fed	BC	AB	SK	MB	ON	QC	NB	PE	NS	NL	Total
Back to work – dispute sent to arbitration	11	4	–	3	–	14	3	2	–	2	–	39
Back to work – settlement imposed	8	6	4	3	–	5	17	4	–	1	3	51
Suspension of bargaining rights – wage freeze or rollback imposed	6	12	–	1	2	7	6	2	2	4	3	45
Restrictions on certification process	1	1	–	1	1	2	1	–	–	–	1	8
Denial of workers' right to join a union	–	1	2	–	–	3	2	–	–	–	–	8
Restrictions on scope of bargaining & other union activities	4	15	4	6	4	6	3	4	1	3	3	53
Total	30	39	10	14	7	37	32	12	3	10	10	204

Source: Canadian Foundation for Labour Rights, "Restrictive Labour Laws in Canada," www.labourrights.ca.

Government interference in labour relations has become more prevalent, and the number of restrictive laws enacted in the past three decades is higher than any other period in the history of Canadian labour relations.[43] Both the federal government (with nineteen pieces of legislation) and provincial governments (seventy-one times) have relied heavily on back-to-work legislation. These laws not only force workers back to work after they have taken legal strike action, but also arbitrarily impose settlements on them.

In addition, federal and provincial governments have passed forty-five pieces of legislation that suspended the bargaining rights of workers and imposed wage freezes or rollbacks. Derek Fudge has pointed out that since 1982, unions' ability to organize has been restricted by sixty-nine amended federal and provincial labour laws, with eight of those pieces of legislation denying groups of workers the right to form a union, and eight restricting the certification process.

As table 4 shows, a comparison of key U.S. and Canada labour market indicators is illuminating. Canadian union density rates are more than twice that of the United States despite both having experienced similar market forces over the past three decades. Canada's high unionization rate and more extensive collective bargaining system have led to significant social benefits, with less extreme income inequality and poverty compared to south of the border (although in recent years income inequality is growing at a faster rate in Canada than in the United States). Canadians also have the comfort of knowing that they do not have to worry about upfront costs for health care. Unions in Canada, through collective bargaining and their ability to influence public policy and legislation, have contributed to these positive outcomes, which have benefited all Canadians.

Table 4. Selected labour market and social indicators, Canada and the U.S.

	Canada	U.S.
Unionization (union coverage as share of employed non-agricultural workforce, 2011) (%)	31.2	11.8
Unemployment rate (unemployed as share of labour force, 2012) (%)	7.1	8.1
Population below poverty line (%)	9.4	15.1
Income inequality (Gini coeffcient, 2010)	0.395	0.469
Absence of health coverage (proportion of population without health insurance, 2011) (%)	n.a.[a]	15.7

a All citizens and permanent residents in Canada are entitled to comprehensive public health insurance.

Source: Statistics Canada, CANSIM Table 282-0078; Barry T. Hirsch and David A. Macpherson, Union Membership and Coverage Database from the CPS, www.unionstats.com; Bureau of Labor Statistics, Current Population Survey Database and International Unemployment Rates and Employment Indexes, www.bls.gov/data. Definitions of poverty vary considerably among nations. Canada 2008 and U.S. 2010 est. retrieved from CIA, *The World Factbook*, www.cia.gov; U.S. Gini coefficient from U.S. Census Bureau, Current Population Reports, P60-239, *Income, Poverty, and Health Insurance Coverage in the United States: 2010*; income, poverty, and health insurance coverage data from Current Population Reports, P60-243, *Income, Poverty, and Health Insurance Coverage in the United States: 2011*.

A critical target of Canadian labour law reform is the legislative framework that governs how unions organize workplaces and the certification process unions must carry out to become the bargaining agent on behalf of workers. Traditionally, unions in Canada were certified once a majority of people in a workplace signed a union card. This card-check certification system was a fair and efficient measure of workers' true wishes for unionization, as it minimized employer influence and enhanced the ability of workers to join unions. In the 1970s, all eleven jurisdictions in Canada – the federal government and the ten provinces – employed the card-check system as the statutory gateway to unionization.

Over the past three decades, many governments have abandoned card-check models in favour of mandatory voting, regardless of whether the majority of workers signed union cards. Today, five jurisdictions – British Columbia, Alberta, Saskatchewan, Ontario, and Nova Scotia – have enacted the automatic certification vote procedure. This has led to increased incidences of employer interference in union organizing drives, from anti-union propaganda, limiting communication between union organizers and employees, and threats to dismantle and shut down workplaces, to various other unfair labour practices as defined by provincial labour boards.

In June 2013, a Conservative backbench member of Parliament from Alberta introduced Private Member's Bill C-525, deceptively titled the Employees' Voting Rights Act. It sought to amend the *Canada Labour Code*, the *Public Service Labour Relations Act*, and the *Parliamentary Employment and Staff Relations Act*, thereby imposing undemocratic conditions on all certification and decertification votes held by unions within the federal jurisdiction.

Currently, any union within federal jurisdiction that demonstrates it has 50 per cent plus one support of employees in a workplace can be certified without having to conduct a mandatory vote. Bill C-525 would change that process and require a mandatory vote for all organizing drives, regardless of whether the union is able to demonstrate that it has union cards signed by the majority of the employees. Bill C-525 further states that in order for the union to be certified, a majority of the workers "in the bargaining unit" must have voted in favour of joining the union. This is quite different from the standard process for all democratic election votes, in which a majority is determined based on the number of persons voting. If this bill were implemented into law, those employees who did not participate in the certification vote would automatically be assumed to have voted against the union.

The same undemocratic principle would also be applied in all decertification votes, except that those union members who did not vote would automatically be assumed to have voted in favour of decertifying the union. Even if a majority of employees who voted cast ballots against decertification, the union could still be decertified if that majority were less than 50 per cent of all workers (including those who did not vote). This undoubtedly would lead to a concerted push for decertification votes throughout the federal sector, as union busters would benefit from undemocratic voter suppression techniques similar to those used by the Conservatives in the last federal election. Research by Susan Johnson shows that mandatory voting can reduce certification success because, unlike the card-check process, it increases the amount of time required for certification campaigns, thus allowing employers more opportunities to interfere with union drives. Johnson found that mandatory voting reduced certification success rates by approximately nine percentage points compared to what would have occurred under card check.[44]

Craig Riddell investigated the impact of union suppression within a mandatory voting regime in British Columbia, discovering a 20 per cent decrease in the success of union organizing drives.[45] This is consistent with what has occurred in other provincial jurisdictions when mandatory voting came into force. Throughout this period of deteriorating labour rights, both public- and private-sector union members in Canada have faced suspension and/or restrictions, with one common irritant being the use of legislation to unilaterally impose contracts that favour the employer's bargaining position. In 2011, the Harper government intervened and suppressed labour rights for both Air Canada and Canada Post workers.

In the first nine months of 2013, four labour laws passed in Canada further restricted the collective bargaining rights of Canadian workers.

In January, Dalton McGuinty's Ontario Liberals introduced the notorious *Putting Students First Act* (Bill 115), which denied the basic and fundamental rights of 155,000 teachers and education workers by imposing a two-year contract. Needless to say, the repercussions were felt by all Ontarians.[46]

In June, the federal government passed its 2013 omnibus budget legislation (known as Bill C-60, the *Economic Action Plan 2013 Act*), which contains a small section granting the federal Cabinet the right to direct a Crown corporation to have its negotiating mandate approved by the Treasury Board. Now, Crown corporations can only agree to a new collective agreement that has been approved first by Treasury Board. The provisions also give the Treasury Board the power to directly set wages, working conditions, and all other employment terms of non-union employees of Crown corporations.

On June 30, another piece of restrictive labour law was passed in an extraordinary Sunday sitting of the Quebec National Assembly, forcing an end to a two-week construction strike. Bill 54, *An Act Respecting the Resumption of Work in the Construction Industry*, forced 77,000 construction employees and their employers to resume work by July 2 or face fines from $100 for an individual offender to $125,000 for a union or an employers' association. The legislation extended the current expired contract for one year and gave the workers the same annual pay increase of 2 per cent this year that was agreed to by another 98,000 construction workers who had negotiated an end to their strike the week before. The legislation forbids strikes and lockouts during the period of the contract extension. Only Québec Solidaire, the left-leaning party with two Assembly seats, opposed a legislated end to the strike.

In July, Nova Scotia's NDP government held a special one-day sitting of the provincial legislature to pass its first-ever restrictive labour law, one aimed at averting a pending strike by ambulance workers. Bill 86, the *Ambulance Services Continuation Act*, takes away ambulance workers' right to strike during their current round of bargaining. The legislation also forces the dispute to final offer selection arbitration. Both the union and the employer will now have to submit their final offers to a mutually agreed-upon arbitrator who will choose one option within ninety days.

Unions in the United States have also been weakened by regressive and ineffective labour legislation. In the 1960s, the United States and Canada had unionization rates hovering around 30 per cent, but since then, unionization rates have diverged dramatically due in large part to differences in labour law and public policy.

Kris Warner studied the impacts of two labour law provisions that explain the divergence in Canadian and American unionization rates – card-check certification and first contract arbitration (FCA).[47] Because there is no card-check process in the United States, it takes longer to hold a union certification vote, which gives the employers an upper hand when organizing anti-union drives. In the United States, the period between a union petition and the election to unionize often stretches to months, and sometimes to more than a year. This has allowed employers to commit illegal acts of intimidation and fire workers in an attempt to discourage employees from voting to unionize.[48] Simply put, the longer it takes unions to organize workers, the longer employers have to organize anti-union campaigns. Since U.S. enforcement of penalties for unfair labour practices is weak, employers have gone largely unchecked, and continue to trample on labour rights.

American workers also face the disadvantage of having no provisions for employers to negotiate a first contract when union certification does occur. Recent research states that half of newly certified unions in the United States are unable to negotiate a contract two years after certification.[49] If unions cannot achieve gains for their members through bargaining for a fair contract, they cannot be fully effective. Due to the lack of effective U.S. labour laws, Warner states that unfair labour practices have continued to rise and led to a burgeoning union avoidance industry made up of lawyers, consultants, industry psychologists, and "strike management" firms that continue to weaken labour rights. In contrast, Canadian unions are in a relatively better position, as eight Canadian jurisdictions currently include FCA provisions in their labour legislation: British Columbia (1974), Quebec (1978), the federal jurisdiction (1978), Manitoba (1982), Newfoundland and Labrador (1985), Ontario (1986), Saskatchewan (1994), and Nova Scotia (2012). If there is a bargaining impasse in Canada, the first step is for the employer and union to apply for mediation. If mediation fails, a Labour Relations Board assigns an arbitrator who could impose a first contract. This arbitration process is rarely pursued and contracts are rarely imposed,[50] but allowing for FCA provisions can encourage the negotiation process.

"Right-to-Work" Laws Are Wrong

> In our glorious fight for civil rights, we must guard against being fooled by false slogans, such as "right-to-work." It provides no "rights" and no "works." . . . Its purpose is to destroy labor unions and the freedom of collective bargaining. . . . We demand this fraud be stopped.   — Martin Luther King, Jr.[51]

The biggest blow to Canadian unions may soon be in the offing with American-style right-to-work laws that have been touted by conservative leaders federally and in Alberta and Ontario. Contrary to what the name suggests, right-to-work has nothing to do with paid employment. A core principle of Canadian labour relations has been the Rand formula, which ensures that all those who benefit from a workplace union must contribute to the costs of the union's operation. Right-to-work laws undermine that principle, essentially allowing workers to receive all the benefits that a union provides through collective bargaining and workplace representation without having any obligation to contribute union dues. Giving workers the right not to join a union is one thing, but allowing them to freeload by not paying their fair share is another.

The public musing about right-to-work laws forms part of the backdrop to an ongoing attack on labour rights. In June 2013, the Harper government used its majority to support and pass through the House of Commons Private Member's Bill C-377, which will impose strict and excessive financial reporting measures on unions that would add costs and time-consuming administrative requirements to their normal activities. Unions already provide financial information to their members through financial audits, reports, and regular membership meetings. Bill C-377 blatantly discriminates against unions, as it excludes similar requirements for employer bargaining associations. Like unions, these associations are referenced in provincial labour legislation, are formed for the purposes of collective bargaining, pay dues which they deduct from their taxable income, and also engage in advocacy, political lobbying, and public relations activities.

The Conservative government's divide-and-conquer strategy to undermine union organizing and mobilizing will likely play out in two parts. First, Bill C-377 was designed to encourage union members to identify political causes they don't support but that their unions advocate for (a strategy that was partially played out in a series of well-placed 2013 newspaper stories about union donations to potentially hot-button political causes, such as Palestinian rights). Second, having stoked the discontent of union members, the Harper government is reportedly set to introduce right-to-work legislation that would outlaw the Rand formula.

While Bill C-377 passed the House of Commons in December 2012, it surprisingly underwent significant changes in the Conservative-dominated Senate following weeks of debate in the spring of 2013. It was subsequently sent back to the House of Commons with amendments prior to Parliament being prorogued until October 2013. Unlike government bills, private member's bills do not die on the order paper. Therefore, Bill C-377 will return to the Senate for first reading in the form it was passed by the House of Commons in December 2012. The expectation is that along with Bill C-377, there will be an attempt to introduce a right-to-work law in the second half of the Harper government's mandate, legislation for which corporations have lobbied fiercely in an effort to increase profits by driving down wages and offering reduced benefits for both union and non-union workers.[52]

In American states with right-to-work laws, workers annually earn an average of $1,500 less and have lower rates of employer-sponsored health and pension plans.[53] Furthermore, right-to-work laws do not create jobs and, in some states, like Oklahoma, jobs have been lost to lower-wage countries like China and Mexico.[54] Meanwhile, among the numerous Canadian conservative canards backstopping their right-to-work push are claims that unions are responsible for job losses. However, these fly in the face of data proving that relatively union-friendly Canadian labour laws do not come at the cost of jobs.

For example, Ontario and Quebec have traditionally dominated industrial production in Canada and have distinct labour laws, but Quebec's 2010 unionization rate in manufacturing was 37.4 per cent, close to double that of Ontario's 19.8 per cent. Moreover, the manufacturing unionization rate in Quebec is almost unchanged from 2000, when it stood at 41.7 per cent, while the rate has fallen sharply in Ontario from 31.1 per cent over the past decade. Between 2000 and 2010, Ontario lost 301,000 (28.9 per cent) of the province's manufacturing jobs while Quebec lost 120,000 (19.9 per cent).[55] Even with a higher rate of unionization in the manufacturing sector, Quebec experienced relatively fewer manufacturing job losses than Ontario.

A comparison with the U.S. yields similar results, with Canadian labour market performance significantly stronger than in the U.S. for several years (even though Canada's unionization rate is more than twice as high). Canada's unemployment rate is also significantly lower than that of the United States, and Canada's employment rate (the proportion of working-age Canadians holding jobs) has been higher as well. In fact, the empirical evidence from both countries shows that unionization does not have a negative impact on unemployment rates.[56] In this context, arguments in favour of right-to-work or similarly restrictive labour laws simply do not hold water. Rather, the factual record serves as an argument to strengthen labour rights.

Reducing Income Inequality through Collective Bargaining and Union Activism

> Strong, responsible unions are essential for industrial fair play. Without them, the labor bargain is wholly one-sided.
>
> — Louis Brandeis[57]

As member-driven organizations, unions represent workers' interests to management by making their collective voices heard not only during bargaining, but also in the day-to-day operations of the workplace. The strength of unions at the bargaining table leads to improved wages and benefits for workers. In Canada, the wage premium for union workers for comparable jobs has been 7–14 per cent, holding constant for other factors that determine wages.[58]

Beyond improving the economic return to their own members, unions raise the wages and benefits of non-unionized workers in related industries, in part because non-unionized employers seek to dampen the appeal of unionization.[59] Data in U.S. cities have consistently proven that in areas of high-wage, unionized industrial jobs, workers in nearby non-union industries benefit from higher bargaining power for their own jobs as well.[60]

Traditionally, unions have played a significant role in public policy and legislative decisions that affect the distribution of income. Working in coalitions across a spectrum of groups, unions have been able to push policy makers to address issues of rising inequality, bringing to the table an admirable track record of lobbying efforts for minimum-wage laws, public pension plans, unemployment insurance, and occupational health and safety legislation. Unions have also supported the fight for gender equality along with initiatives to reduce poverty, combat racism, advance social inclusion and human rights for equality-seeking groups, and advocate for healthy communities. With a tool chest that includes everything from organizing education events to holding mass rallies, unions have mobilized the broader society to resist the erosion of human rights.

Political scientists Jacob Hacker and Paul Pierson argue that it is the role of organized labour on issues of economic and social policy that matters most in the political economy.[61] They find that the decline of organized labour has greatly diminished the pressure on policy makers to sustain or refurbish commitments to social provisions made during the Great Compression. When politicians and corporations remain silent on gross violations of human rights, unions remain a strong line of defence to advocate for equality, especially on the international front.

Indeed, unions have often assisted the transition from dictatorship and corruption to democracy and the rule of law. Whether it was opposing Latin American military dictatorships in the 1970s, supporting Solidarność and the Polish pro-democracy movement during the 1980s, leading the boycott against South African Apartheid, or supporting recent struggles for democracy and social justice in the Arab countries, unions have been on the front lines of struggles and solidarity campaigns. This counterweight provided by organized labour is essential as policy makers bend over backwards to accommodate the unending demands of corporate power.

Unions and Democracy

> The haves are on the march. With growing inequality, so grows their power. And so also diminished are the voices of solidarity and mutual reinforcement, the voices of civil society, the voices of a democratic and egalitarian middle class.   — James Galbraith[62]

Unions have been, and continue to be, an important force for democracy, not just in the workplace, but also in the community – locally, nationally, and globally. While valuable research on the importance of unions tends to focus on how unions improve wages for both union and non-union workers, it often tends to overlook the critical role unions play in making democracy work better. Even though less than one-third of all Canadian workers are currently union members, unions help boost political participation among ordinary citizens and convert this participation into an effective voice for policies that benefit the great majority of Canadians.

A just and democratic society depends on a healthy and free labour movement. It is no coincidence that in countries where there are free and active trade union movements, there are more democratic, transparent, and representative forms of government. In those countries where there is no union movement or the movement is vulnerable, the vast majority of citizens continue to be trapped in poverty. It is in these conditions that instability and extremism thrive at the expense of democracy.

The democratic structure of unions affects attitudes and behaviours of workers outside the workplace. Researchers Alex Bryson, Rafael Gomez, Tobias Kretschmer, and Paul Willman found that union membership in Canada is associated with a roughly 10–12 per cent increase in the propensity to vote.[63] They point out that if workers are involved within the democratic structure of their unions, they will have an increased sense of attachment to democratic governance elsewhere. Their research, showing greater voter turnout of union members, was further confirmed even when controlling for other factors that could affect voter participation.

When looking at voter participation in Canada (figure 11), it's clear that union density acts as a complement to voter turnout. The decline of unionization rates over the past three decades reflects a similar trend in voter turnout. Through awareness and participation, unions have mobilized voters and brought them to the polls.

Bryson et al.'s research is reinforced by studies on voter turnout

Figure 11. Canadian federal elections, voter turnout, 1979–2011

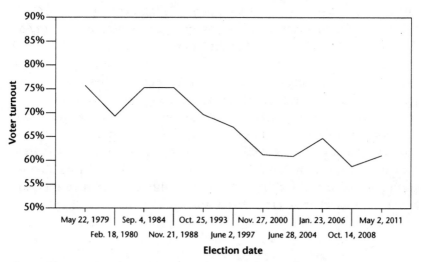

Source: Elections Canada, *Voter Turnout at Federal Elections and Referendums*, www.elections.ca.

conducted by the Organisation for Economic Co-operation and Development and the Institute for Democracy and Electoral Assistance. Their findings show that countries with higher unionization rates have higher voter turnout. Looking at average voter turnout data between 2000 and 2010, they found that the top ten unionized countries have a 77.9 per cent voter turnout, while the bottom ten countries have a 61.8 per cent voter turnout.[64] As union density declines, this otherwise positive influence on democracy is similarly reduced.[65]

The Challenge Ahead

> The different sorts of equality are finally inseparable but up to a certain point they are sufficiently distinguishable, and one may speak of political equality, equality before the law and economic equality. Without the last, the first and second exist only measurably, and they tend to disappear as it shrinks.
>
> — William Dean Howells (1837–1920), American literary critic and former *Atlantic Monthly* editor[66]

Over the past three decades in Canada and throughout the world, massive inequality and social exclusion have grown in direct proportion to the increasing collusion between governments and corporations. The values of an egalitarian society based on the common good and common wealth – compassion, sharing, and caring – are in danger of being extinguished by the corporate elite's notions of individual responsibility and survival of the fittest.

Balance must be restored to the scales of economic equality and social justice. The only democratic counterweight to the power of corporations and the superwealthy is an agenda that supports and promotes strong labour rights and unionization. These are key components to a functioning democracy and an equitable and sustainable economy. It is only by making such connections that Canada's labour movement and its progressive allies will be able to push back against the rising tide of inequality and improve the economic and social well-being of all Canadians.

Two

Income Inequality in Canada

History and Trends

Armine Yalnizyan

INCOME INEQUALITY HAS BECOME A HOT TOPIC since the global economic crisis erupted in 2008, and as debate escalates over its economic, political, and social significance, it's becoming a defining issue of our era. How inequality is understood and discussed will shape its evolution, and it's therefore crucial to examine which factors historically and currently drive the income gap, define key intergenerational and interregional differences, and explore the role of democracy and collective processes in offsetting market trends.

While all societies have some degree of income inequality, assessing the nature and extent of the problem and ascertaining if and how a society is becoming more unequal are important questions that rely on a variety of measurements. A typical measure of income inequality marshalled by both sides of the debate is the Gini coefficient. This statistic calculates a number that ranges from zero to one, where zero equals total equality (everybody has the same income) and one means a single person has all the income. The bigger the number, the more inequality exists in society. Figure 1 shows that after-tax income inequality is higher in Canada than at any time in the past 35 years, though most of its acceleration happened before the year 2000.

Figure 1. Gini coefficients, Canada, 1976–2011 (all family units)

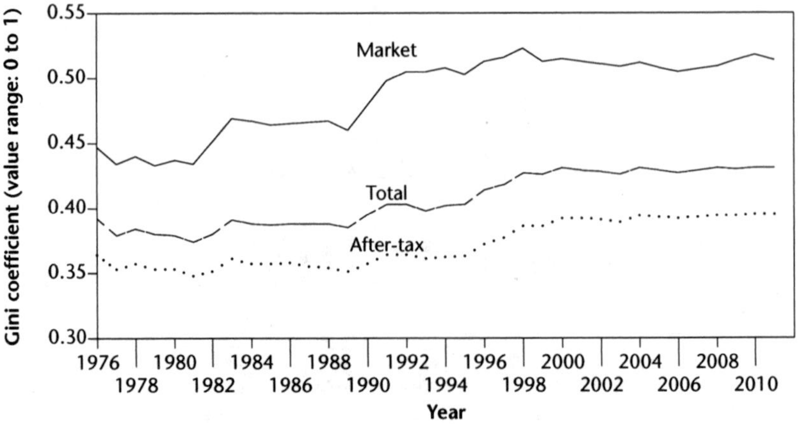

Source: Statistics Canada, CANSIM Table 202-0705.

Each definition of income shows an increase in income inequality over the course of a generation, and each provides a different insight. Market income (the top line) measures earnings from employment and self-employment, returns on investments (including rent), and private pensions. Inequality in market incomes increased dramatically between 1976 and 1996. After 1996, even a decade of unusually rapid economic growth and high rates of job creation did little to reduce market income inequality. Notably, market income inequality typically rises after recessions, with swelling ranks of the unemployed and underemployed – fewer hours of paid work, or paid work that does not make use of higher skills.

Total income (the second line) shows that government programs significantly lower inequality by raising incomes at the bottom of the distribution. These statutory income supports kick in when people are temporarily unemployed (Employment Insurance), unable to work (parental benefits, sickness benefits, social assistance, and workers' compensation), retired (elderly benefits), or raising children (child benefits and allowances).

The bottom line in the graph shows after-tax income inequality isn't increasing as rapidly as it once did, but it's still on the rise. Progressive taxation of incomes closes the gap further, primarily by lowering top incomes. (The lower down the income spectrum, the less likely one will pay income tax. In 2011, 34 per cent of Canadian tax filers paid no income tax.)

Irrespective of the definition of income, income inequality has been increasing over most of the past thirty-five years, most rapidly after each recession. The fact that the Gini coefficient registers little change since 2000, however, does not mean that there is no cause for concern.

The Rich-Poor Gap Is Still Widening

No less an authority than the Conference Board of Canada has pointed out that the rich-poor gap has been accelerating over time. Between the mid-1970s and mid-1990s, a dramatic increase in market income differentials between the average incomes of people in the top and bottom quintiles was virtually offset by Canada's tax and income transfer system. (Each income quintile represents 20 per cent of the population. Figure 2 looks at individuals, not families.)

Figure 2. After-tax income gap between top and bottom quintiles, Canada, 1976–2011 (in $2011)

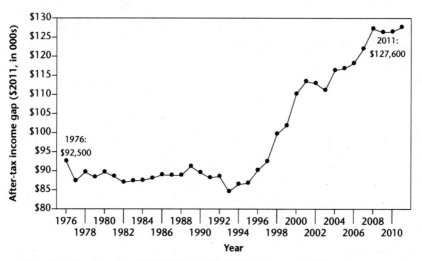

Source: Statistics Canada, CANSIM Table 202-0706. Update of unadjusted series used in Conference Board of Canada, "Canadian Income Inequality: Is Canada becoming more unequal?" www.conferenceboard.ca.

Since the mid-1990s, that gap has grown. Taxes and many income supports were cut while the earned incomes of people at the top grew far more rapidly than those at the bottom. Measured as the average amount of income that separates the richest and poorest Canadians, income inequality has grown more rapidly in recent years than in earlier times, precisely the opposite finding of the Gini coefficient graph.

The significance of income inequality trends in Canada has been dismissed by some observers – call them the inequality deniers – who like to point out that what really matters is not whether the rich are getting richer, but whether the poor are getting poorer. They then point to statistics that suggest poverty trends may not be a cause for concern, either.

Figure 3 shows that using the old way of measuring poverty, the incidence of poverty since the mid-1990s has declined for all age groups in Canada, with record lows for seniors and children. It is based on data that were the most common way to track poverty in Canada until a few years ago: Statistics Canada's low-income cut-off (LICO) rate, calculated on after-tax income. However, a strong, evidence-based argument about declining poverty is railroaded by using the LICO, as it is an out-of-date measure, based in 1992 and not updated since.

Figure 3. Poverty rates, by age, Canada, 1976–2011, measured by low-income cut-off (1992 base) after tax

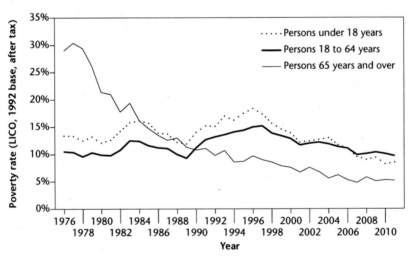

The old way of measuring poverty shows it's falling. Source: Statistics Canada, CANSIM Table 202-0802.

The most dramatic reduction in poverty rates is among seniors, the combined result of public policies that improved public pensions and elderly benefits, enhanced private sector pensions over time, and the steady rise in women's labour force participation rates. In the mid-1970s, relatively few women aged 65 or older relied on paid employment in their pre-retirement years, and those who did rarely had jobs offering pensions. That situation was reversed by the 1990s, when both earnings and pensions steadily rose for most women, pushing down poverty rates among retirees when measured by their ability to cover the necessities of life – food, clothing, and shelter – based on the amount those items cost the average family in 1992 prices.

Using the after-tax LICO as a measure, poverty rates among working-age adults (18–64) rose and then fell over the course of the thirty-five-year period. Poverty rates usually go up after a recession, and the recessions of 1981–82 and 1990–91 were harsh. LICO numbers show poverty reduction since the mid-1990s has been almost continuous for working-age adults, despite massive job losses associated with the global economic crisis of 2008. The after-tax LICO suggests poverty rates among working-age adults are among their lowest levels in thirty-five years. Similarly, the after-tax LICO measurement indicates children's poverty rates have dropped to the lowest rates on record, falling most rapidly since the mid-1990s, when Statistics Canada stopped updating the measure.

Once the gold-standard for measuring poverty in Canada, the LICO has become an out-of-date measure that no longer does what it was intended to do. It was supposed to define low-income households both by their income levels and the proportion of their incomes spent on the absolute necessities of food, shelter, and clothing. LICO never included other basics like transportation, communication, health care, or postsecondary education, and the spending component is still based on 1992 levels of spending on housing, food, and clothing, period.

Should the LICO be recalculated to account for increases in the cost of housing, food, and clothing, poverty rates would rise, but Statistics Canada says it will not be updating this measure, and urges analysts to use a new mechanism, the Low-Income Measure. The Low-Income Measure (LIM) doesn't include any calculation for how incomes are used. It simply counts the proportion of the population that lives on an income less than half of the after-tax median. Unlike the LICO, there is just one LIM, irrespective of where one lives. It's not sophisticated, it's easy to compute, and it's what the Organisation for Economic Co-operation and Development (OECD) and others use to track international comparisons. It's also the basis for tracking success or failure in those Canadian provinces and territories that have committed themselves to poverty reduction strategies (eleven are working on or developing such a plan).

In stark contrast to the LICO results, the Canada-wide after-tax LIM, figure 4, shows that the incidence of poverty is increasing for seniors, falling for children since the mid-1990s (but not back to mid-1970s levels), and increasing for working-age adults. It's clear when viewed through the lens of this internationally accepted, official measurement that reductions in Canadian poverty have been reversed or stubbornly resistant to economic growth over the past thirty-five years.

Figure 4. Poverty rates, by age, Canada, 1976–2011, measured by Low Income Measure, after tax

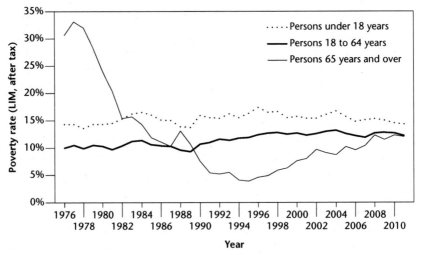

How we measure poverty now: it's not falling. Source: Statistics Canada, CANSIM Table 202-0802.

The Fall and Rise of Canadian Incomes

Having dismissed concerns about income trends at the top and the bottom of the income distribution, the inequality deniers point to trends for the vast majority, and note that average incomes of all income groups have been rising since the mid-1990s (see figure 5). While this is true, that growth comes on the heels of twenty years of dropping average incomes for all income quintiles, triggered by the big recessions of 1981–82 and 1990–91. This argument also fails to note that the most affluent 20 per cent lost ground at roughly the same pace as most Canadians until the mid-1990s, but their income gains roared ahead of the pack after 1997. That's when Canada entered a decade of robust economic growth and job creation unparalleled since the 1960s.

Figure 5. Gains in after-tax income compared to 1976, by quintile, average income, individuals, Canada, 1976–2011 (1976 = 1)

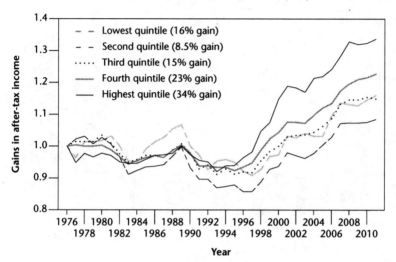

Source: Indexed series based on Statistics Canada, CANSIM Table 202-0706.

The poorest income quintiles saw steady growth in average incomes since the mid-1990s because from 1993 to 2007, unemployment rates plunged from their highest rate in postwar history to their lowest rate since the 1960s. On average, those at the bottom added more hours of paid work while those at the top did not, but this did not lead to a reduction in the income gap. Instead, despite solid improvement in the rate of income growth for every income quintile, the biggest gains from economic growth in dollars and cents went to the top 1 per cent.

The Top 1 per cent versus the Rest of Us

Figure 6 shows what's been happening to the share of income going to the top Canadian 1 per cent as far back as the Roaring Twenties. In the decade preceding the 2008 recession, Canada saw the most rapid job growth since the 1960s, outpacing the rate of employment and

GDP growth in every G7 nation.[1] But instead of broad-based prosperity, the top 1 per cent captured almost a third of all income gains from economic growth. That's four times the share of growth they enjoyed in the 1960s, a similarly robust period of economic expansion, and almost double the share of the Roaring Twenties, a period of transformative industrialization.

Figure 6. Share of income gains captured by top 1%, Canada, 1920–2007

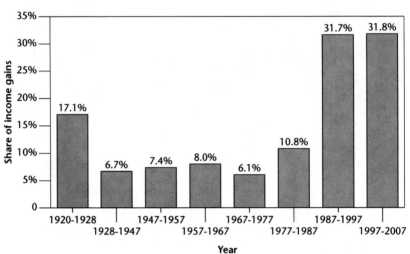

Source: Original tax file data custom-ordered by Michael Veall, McMaster University; calculated by author for Armine Yalnizyan, The Rise of Canada's Richest 1% (Ottawa: Canadian Centre for Policy Alternatives, December 2010), www.policyalternatives.ca.

The data show a changing relationship not previously seen in almost a century of statistics, which has led to talk of the 99 per cent and the 1 per cent. This terminology is not about envy, but rather expresses an emerging consciousness of a new dynamic between the many and the few, an awakening that old expectations are being replaced by new ones.

It's said that a rising tide lifts all boats. But economic growth has not translated to broad-based income growth. The Canadian economy is more than twice as big as it was in 1976, but median incomes, shown in figure 7, have barely budged (comparisons of dollar figures over time are adjusted for inflation). Importantly, median incomes are not average incomes, but rather represent the absolute middle of the income spectrum: half of all workers earn less than this amount, half earn more.

Reducing Income Inequality through Labour Rights

Figure 7. No gains in median earnings in 35 years, Canada, 1976–2011 (in $2011)

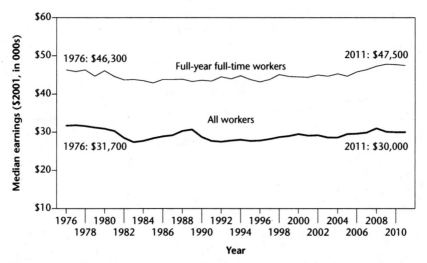

During this period, the economy grew 2.5 times bigger, and workers became more educated. Source: Statistics Canada, CANSIM Table 202-0101.

Stuck in the Middle

In 2007, median earnings of full-time, full-year workers were at the same level as in 1976. They've risen slightly since, but while the median full-time, full-year worker makes $1,200 more today than a worker in the mid-1970s, the economic pie has more than doubled, and this generation of workers is far more educated.

Median earnings for the whole labour force – including those who did not work for the full year, or had part-time hours – are below the 1976 level. In other words, half of all Canadian workers are making less today than they were almost forty years ago, and there are fewer earning opportunities in the upper middle of the income distribution.

Indeed, while people usually climb up and down the income ladder over the course of their lives, statistics show that the rungs are getting farther apart. Figure 8 shows that compared to 1976, fewer people now have annual earnings (measured in constant dollars) between $30,000 and $60,000. Half of Canada's workers earn less than $30,000 today, a higher share than in the mid-1970s. The group making over $60,000 has grown, but not enough to offset the decline in the middle range.

It may come as a surprise to learn that the biggest job growth over the course of a generation has been in the low-income (less than

Figure 8. Share of Canadians with low, middle, and high annual earnings, Canada, 1976–2011 (in $2011)

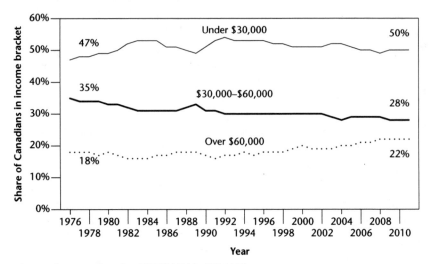

Source: Statistics Canada, CANSIM Table 202-0101.

$30,000 a year) category, as there are far more part-year and/or part-time positions available. The combination of where job growth and job decline has occurred bodes poorly for this generation of workers.

Greater Intergenerational Inequality

Figure 9 documents income changes for different age cohorts of workers. It does not track the same people from 1976 to 2011. Rather, it shows how pre-tax income has changed over time for each age group. Many of the people who are in the 55–64 age cohort today were in the 25–34 age cohort in the early 1980s. (Data on median earnings or market income are not available in CANSIM tables by age group.)

The 45–54 age group had the highest incomes over the decades. But after the fall and rise of incomes due to deep recessions, today's 45- to 54-year-olds are scarcely earning more than their counterparts of the late 1970s. Median earnings of this age cohort are only up 3 per cent compared to thirty-five years ago. For people aged 35–44, median incomes nudged up 2 per cent compared to a generation ago (that is, 2–3 per cent above inflation).

By a large margin, the 55–64 age cohort saw the biggest improvement, with median earnings up 12 per cent since the mid-1970s. This age cohort has lower median earnings than 45- to 54-year-olds

Figure 9. Inflation-adjusted median pre-tax income, by age, Canada, 1976–2011 (in $2011)

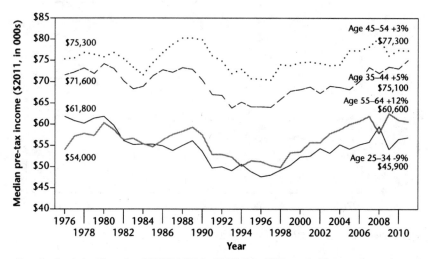

Source: Statistics Canada, CANSIM Table 202-0404. All household units by age, total income.

because while some people in this age group are at their peak earning years, others who lose their jobs at this stage in life suffer major earning declines, and some take early retirement.

The biggest story in this chart is that the youngest prime-age workers (aged 25–34) have seen the greatest decline in their incomes, despite the fact that this group has more than doubled its investments in postsecondary education since the 1970s. They earn 9 per cent less than their counterparts in the mid-1970s, even though the economic pie is more than twice as big in inflation-adjusted terms.

Interregional Income Inequality

As international comparisons show, inequality isn't a one-size-fits-all story, and there are important differences within Canada as well. In figure 10, the Atlantic provinces are grouped together, and Manitoba is excluded, because of small sample sizes. As measured by after-tax Gini coefficients, the Atlantic region has consistently had the least inequality in Canada since 1976, followed by Quebec. British Columbia is currently the most unequal jurisdiction, and has shown the most rapid inequality growth since 1986.

While all jurisdictions except for Quebec reduced inequality from

Figure 10. After-tax Gini coefficients, Canadian regions, 1976–2011

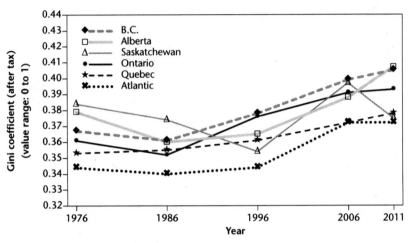

Source: Statistics Canada, CANSIM Table 202-0705.

1976 to 1986, all have witnessed inequality increases since then. Saskatchewan is the only jurisdiction that has reduced its level of inequality since 2006, but its economy was barely touched by the economic crisis of 2008. (These data also undoubtedly understate the level of income inequality in Saskatchewan, since Statistics Canada doesn't assess with this survey the incomes of the on-reserve Aboriginal population, which accounts for about one in six people in both Saskatchewan and Manitoba.)

Inequality has flatlined in the Atlantic region since 2006. Some provinces in Atlantic Canada saw continued economic growth right through the recession, while some suffered setbacks. Alberta, Quebec, and Ontario, all hard-hit by the recession, have recovered, but with higher levels of inequality.

Every province and region of Canada shows higher rates of inequality than a generation ago, but each jurisdiction has arrived there by a different trajectory. Most of these data are driven by what is happening in big cities, because that's where most Canadians live. Whether they are rich or poor, people move to big cities for opportunities, and that's also where most newcomers settle.

Path-breaking research at the University of Toronto shows a distinctive, predictable pattern emerging in Canada's big cities over the past thirty years: there are fewer middle-income neighbourhoods, and more neighbourhoods with high or low incomes. Income polarization is translating into spatial polarization. Figure 11 shows that the once-dominant middle-income neighbourhood in Toronto is an endangered species. Low-income neighbourhoods are becoming predominant and, in a pattern that is being replicated across all big Canadian cities, the fastest-growing type of neighbourhood has either very low or very high incomes.

Figure 11. Change in neighbourhood income distribution in the city of Toronto, 1970–2010

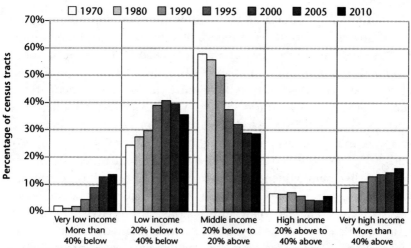

Income is measured as census tract average individual income relative to the Toronto census metropolitan area average income. Individual income is for persons 15 and over, from all sources, before tax. Census tract boundaries correspond to those that existed in each census year. Income for 2010 is based on all taxfilers for 2006 CT boundaries. Source: from J. David Hulchanski, *Three Cities within Toronto: Income Polarization among Toronto's Neighbourhoods, 1970–2005* (Toronto: University of Toronto, Centre for Urban and Community Studies, December 2010), www.NeighbourhoodChange.ca. Updated by Hulchanski. Used with permission. Based on Statistics Canada, Census Tract Profile Series 1971–2006; Canada Revenue Agency Taxfiler Data 2010.

It's also clear that there's trouble brewing in cities where poverty can be predicted by postal code, as erosion of the middle decreases the incidence both of commonly shared experience, and of the ability to identify shared purpose. This concerning trend is documented by epidemiologists Richard Wilkinson and Kate Pickett in their book *The Spirit Level*,[2] which examines how rising inequality is associated with rising stress, resulting in everything from lower life expectancy and higher rates of disease to greater crime and incarceration rates along with higher private and public expenditures. Clearly, inequality affects and costs everyone in the community.

Impact of Government on the Growing
Income Inequality Gap

Such inequality is not inevitable or irreversible, and income gaps can be offset both through labour market practices and policy changes that affect the distribution of wages, and via the taxation system, which collects revenues that redistribute income or offer more opportunity through social wages in the form of better pensions, education, or health care.

Both Statistics Canada and the Conference Board of Canada have noted how taxes and transfers reduce income inequality, but since the mid-1990s their impact has eroded in Canada.[3] The state is today more redistributive than it was in the late 1970s and early 1980s, but after-tax income inequality is also much higher today than it was then. Figure 12 shows the degree to which government policies are making less of a difference today than they once did. Taxes and transfers were most effective in reducing income inequality between 1976 and 1996. Since the mid-1990s, however, the retrenchment of income supports like employment insurance and social assistance, combined with the escalation of tax cuts, have become ubiquitous public policy thrusts across all Canadian jurisdictions, irrespective of political stripe. While new income supports such as the Canada Child Tax Benefit and the Working Income Tax Benefit have been introduced or enhanced since the mid-1990s, they have not offset the shrinking role of government in mitigating income inequality.

The View from the Top: Make That a Double

Those at the top of the income distribution have benefited doubly from such trends, enjoying the biggest portion of income gains in the labour market and the largest share of income flowing from tax cuts. It is not possible to present a single national picture of trends in the top marginal income tax rate, since every province has a different tax regime that combines with federal rates. Ontario has the largest population, and figure 13 shows the top marginal tax rate on personal incomes going back to 1920. (The top tax rate has kicked in at different income thresholds over time, and the number of tax brackets has also changed. This chart simply shows the rate of income taxation applied at the top bracket, over time.) In Ontario, the top marginal tax rate on personal incomes reached 95 per cent during the First World War, and subsequently dropped dramatically to a low of 46 per cent.

Figure 12. Impact of the tax and transfer system on after-tax income inequality, 1976–2011

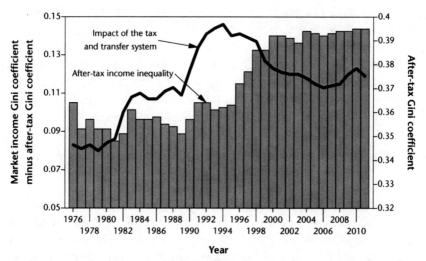

Until the mid-1990s, the tax and transfer system grew, offsetting income inequality. Its impact is smaller today, and after-tax income inequality is higher. Source: Statistics Canada, CANSIM Table 202-0705. All families, Canada, as measured by the Gini coefficient.

Figure 13. Top marginal tax rate, Ontario, 1920–2012

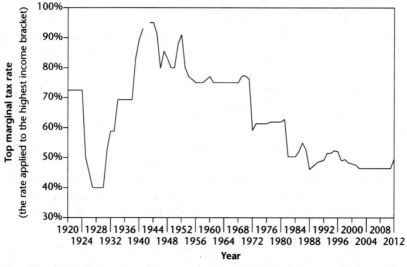

Source: Updated from Armine Yalnizyan, *The Rise of Canada's Richest 1%* (Ottawa: Canadian Centre for Policy Alternatives, December 2010), www.policyalternatives.ca.

The small uptick at the end of the graph is the hotly contested sur-tax on incomes over $250,000 that was added as an amendment to Ontario's 2012 budget as a result of opposition pressure on a Liberal minority government seeking to avoid an election. Other jurisdictions have also recently increased the top marginal rate, but nowhere in Canada are the top marginal rates even close to their historic levels. In Ontario, the top marginal rate during the Second World War applied to incomes above $1 million (about $5 million in today's dollars); the current top rate kicks in for incomes over $250,000.

The View from the Bottom: Less Protection from the Economic Storm

Another important factor driving income inequality in Canada has been the concerted campaign to undermine the protections of the Employment Insurance (EI) system, with changes that have restricted access to middle-class and low-income workers during periods of massive economic downturn. All Canadian employees pay EI premiums, but as shown in figure 14, EI coverage is near historic lows, with fewer than four in ten unemployed Canadians currently receiving jobless benefits (a far cry from the previous two recessions, when the vast majority of Canada's unemployed received income support from EI benefits). The Harper government continues to introduce changes that further restrict unemployed workers' eligibility for EI benefits.

A less generous EI system is not the only reason people are scrambling to find work, thus lowering the "reserve" wage, the pay rate at which one will give up a job search in hopes of higher wages or a better fit with one's skill set. Another labour policy that shapes income inequality and increases competition at the low-wage end of the job market is the growing use of temporary foreign workers.

A Temporary Recovery?

In figure 15, permanent economic immigrants are compared to the census of temporary foreign workers as of December 1 of each year. This chart compares the number of temporary foreign workers presently working in Canada, but not their entry into the country, which would better match immigration numbers. However, the census of those present as of December 1 is a more appropriate measure, because statistics on entries include those who enter multiple times a year, and rule changes since 2006 permit most migrant workers to

Figure 14. Proportion of unemployed Canadians in receipt of regular jobless benefits

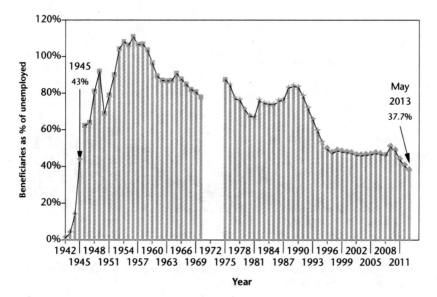

Regular beneficiaries as percentage of unemployed, seasonally adjusted: the number today is lower than it was in 1945.

Notes:
1) There is no publicly available administrative data regarding the number of people in receipt of unemployment insurance benefits from 1971 to 1974.
2) A round of expansionary reforms to the Unemployment Insurance system in the 1950s caused the coverage of unemployment insurance benefits to exceed the total number of unemployed. This is because new rules a) extended the provision of supplementary benefits to those who did not qualify for regular benefits and self-employed fishermen, b) permitted workers to earn up to 50% of benefits (i.e., roughly 25% or less of their earnings before job loss) without penalty, and c) extended benefits for those who became ill (and who were consequently not counted as in the labour force). Maximum benefit levels were adjusted to reflect higher wages, and the duration of benefits was extended to fifty-two weeks.

Source: Armine Yalnizyan, *Exposed: Revealing Truths About Canada's Recession* (Ottawa: Canadian Centre for Policy Alternatives, April 2009), www.policyalternatives.ca (updated). For those in receipt of unemployment insurance benefits there are three data series, two of which overlap. From 1942 to 1970, Statistics Canada E166–171; there is no administrative data from 1971 to 1974; from 1975 to 2012, Statistics Canada CANSIM Series 276–0001; from 1997 to date, CANSIM Table 276-0022. For number of unemployed there are three overlapping data series: Series 1, from 1920 to 1960, Statistics Canada Catalogue No. 11–516-X; Series 2, from 1946 to 1976, Statistics Canada Catalogue No. 11-516-X and D146–159; and Series 3, from 1976 to date, Statistics Canada, CANSIM 282-0087.

Figure 15. Temporary foreign workers and permanent economic immigrants, Canada, 1987–2012

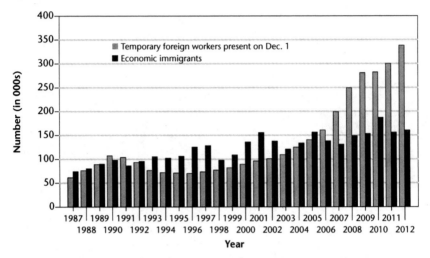

Source: Citizenship and Immigration Canada, *Facts and figures 2012 – Immigration overview: Permanent and temporary residents,* www.cic.gc.ca.

work on multiyear permits, though the vast majority cannot become citizens.

Taking stock of the number of temporary foreign workers present in Canada on December 1 avoids counting most of the migrant workers who enter under the Seasonal Agricultural Workers Program. The biggest growth in the Temporary Foreign Worker Program is through the Low Skilled Pilot Project, whose use has exploded since 2006. As of April 2011, temporary foreign workers can work in Canada for up to four years for the same employer. By law, they cannot work for someone else. In order to count their presence in the labour market, they must be counted through administrative data that document their exit. These data do not include undocumented workers whose temporary work permits have expired.

The number of official temporary foreign workers has tripled in the last decade, with the most rapid expansion occurring since the 2008 recession. The only way temporary foreign workers arrive in Canada is if the government approves the employer's application, based on the claim that they are facing a labour shortage that impairs their ability to meet the demand for their products or services. Until recently, regulations allowed the employer to pay temporary foreign workers up to 15 per cent below prevailing wages. While that regulation was repealed in 2013, public service cutbacks have reduced the bureaucratic capacity to establish, monitor, and enforce payment of the prevailing wage. Deportation is the most common response to workers who complain about non-compliance with employment standards or their employment contracts.

Flooding the low-skill job market with disposable workers exacerbates difficulties faced by young people and immigrants competing for entry-level positions. The Temporary Foreign Worker Program, as it is currently being used, is lowering the wage floor.

The Role of Social Wages in Mitigating Income Inequality

While some public policies make income inequality worse, others can close the gap. Social wages are supports governments provide through taxation to make affordable and accessible more of the basics of life. While these supports improve everyone's standard of living, the poorest benefit the most.

Jobless benefits, welfare, and public pensions are all types of social wages, but not all social wages are primarily income-based. Some just improve the quality of life and opportunity for all citizens. For example, publicly insured health care is the biggest redistributive program that exists in Canada. It is funded by taxation, which is progressive (on balance, affluent Canadians pay a higher proportion of their incomes in tax, and more gets spent on lower-income Canadians). This system helps to both close the income gap and improve the health and quality of life for everyone. It could do so even more if public insurance were extended to prescription drugs and dental and vision care.

Funding improvements in transportation infrastructure and public transit are another way public revenues get converted into social wages. Both programs can offset stagnant and falling incomes by saving money and creating huge efficiencies for a community, moving people, goods, and services in a timely way.

The social wage can also include the provision of affordable housing options. In 1993, Canada became the only advanced economy without a national housing strategy.[4] Since housing takes the biggest bite out of incomes, and shelter costs have risen far more rapidly than incomes since the 1990s, a key way to reduce poverty and enhance economic security is to use public programs to create a bigger stock of affordable housing or offset market prices. Price regulation (rent control, mortgage rules, even development charges) can also play a role.

High-quality, regulated, and affordable child care is yet another aspect of the social wage.[5] In the mid-1970s, over two-thirds of women with children under the age of six stayed at home to raise their children. By 2012, over two-thirds (68 per cent) of women with children under six were in the paid workforce, but there has been no federal policy response to this social revolution.[6] Quebec's experiment with seven-dollar-a-day childcare shows this public policy more than pays for itself: higher household incomes have resulted in higher public revenues, and more children from low-income and immigrant households are entering school learning-ready.[7]

Similarly, both individuals and society benefit from affordable postsecondary education and skills upgrading. In recent years, the high cost of learning has soared past income increases, and many young people are experiencing difficulty finding paid work, or juggling school and work to offset mounting levels of debt. Enrolments in every category of postsecondary education are rising, but so too are attrition rates. Given the well-documented benefits of higher learning, a bigger collective investment could easily pay for itself while levelling the playing field of opportunity.

Governments are uniquely positioned to offset inequality, setting rules of the road in the paid workplace and regulating markets through employment standards, pay equity, employment equity, or immigration legislation. Governments can also reduce income inequality through direct provision of income supports and services, but in this post-recession environment, government expenditures are often viewed as costs to be constrained, not expanded.

Is the Public Sector Too Big?

Quality public services are a key component to reducing income inequality, but right-wing critics claim too much is spent on social programs and the people who provide them. As figure 16 shows, Canada's public sector is nowhere near the size it was in the 1970s, despite higher and rising demand for health and education services. The public sector is poised to shrink more in the coming years as a component of government plans to lower deficits. Regardless of the sector's size, however, it is not the only venue for addressing income inequality.

Markets can also reduce inequality in individual workplaces, by lowering the gap between the compensation of top executives and other employees, or strengthening career ladders. There are work-

Figure 16. Share of employees in the public sector, Canada, January 1976 to August 2013

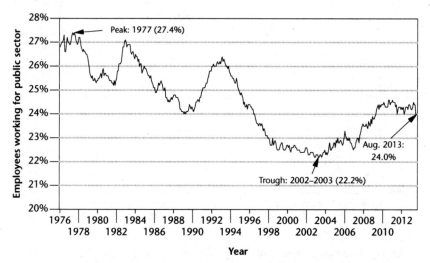

Source: Statistics Canada CANSIM Table 282-0089. Seasonally adjusted monthly data.

places committed to such practices, but all business managers are tasked with maximizing profits, and in the aggressively competitive, slow-growth post-recession world, enhancing the bottom line is increasingly synonymous with lowering labour costs.

Collective bargaining is the chief market-based mechanism for achieving broader distribution of the benefits of growth or, conversely, for minimizing potential lost ground in bad times. There will always be some individuals who can successfully negotiate improvements to their wages and working conditions, but the post-recession wave of corporate consolidation has strengthened the hand and bargaining power of employers. Fewer employees can win a share of growth these days – or prevent losses – without the power of collective action. Not surprisingly in this context, businesses and some politicians portray unions as an impediment to economic success for individual firms and for the economy as a whole.

Are Unions the Problem?

At the same time that they are decried as too powerful, unions are described as a yesterday's answer to yesterday's problems, or a spent force that protects the interests of only a handful of people. Union density figures, shown in figure 17, are one way of reaching beyond

Figure 17. Union density, Canada, 1921–2012

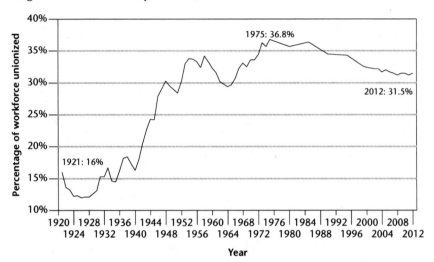

Source: Data come from three Statistics Canada series. 1997 to current: CANSIM Table 282-0078; 1975–1997: Labour Force Survey, Table 7; pre-1975: Historical Statistics of Canada, "Labour Unions and Strikes and Lockouts" (Series E175-197).

the rhetoric and determining the role and significance of the labour movement.

Canada's rate of unionization is lower today (31.5 per cent) than at its peak in 1975 (36.8 per cent). While union density dropped until 2008, it has remained surprisingly stable since the recession, hovering around 1950s and 1960s levels. What has changed dramatically since the 1960s, however, is the composition of organized labour, from a primarily male-dominated industrial and trade union movement to one with significantly greater female participation that's driven by the public service. By 2012, in a reflection of the shrinking share of manufacturing in the Canadian economy, only 18 per cent of the private sector was unionized, down from over 21 per cent in 1997. In comparison, the share of the unionized public sector has held steady around 75 per cent since 1997 (the year such data started being collected).

Perhaps these figures explain why public sector unions are in the crosshairs of those who seek to reduce the influence and power of a collective voice in the economy. Indeed, without a collective voice organized through democratically elected governments or unions (which many tend to forget are also democratic organizations that hold elections), the chances of reversing the trend to growing inequality, in good economic times and bad, are virtually nil.

Reducing Income Inequality through Labour Rights

How Will Income Inequality Evolve in Canada?

Income inequality has been forestalled over the past three decades through increased individual investment in education and through the expanding role of women in the workplace. These two developments have produced mixed results until now, and cannot be advanced to the same degree for future generations.

Today's young workers are better educated than any previous generation of Canadians, but they are having a tougher time entering a post-recession labour market than their counterparts in the 1980s and 1990s. When they do launch, the majority are getting paid less than those entering the 1970s workplace.

Since the 1980s, women have played a major role in preventing the hollowing out of the middle of the income distribution for households. Women have increased their participation in the paid labour market, upped their hours of work, and moved into a broader range of better-paying occupations. But today's generation of young women are already working almost as much as men. The next generation of Canadian households simply can't count on deploying a similar increase in paid work time as the strategy for families to get to, and stay, in the middle.

Between 1997 and 2007, just before the global economic crisis hit, Canada was one of the ten biggest economies in the world, and enjoyed the fastest GDP and employment growth in the G7. Yet income inequality became more accentuated in Canada during this decade, even as many of our peer democratic nations in the OECD – with both bigger and smaller economies – managed to close the gap. Such facts lead to a troubling question: If everything from more jobs and a thriving economy to enhanced education and more time in the labour market are not reducing the income inequality gap, how will the next generation prevent further lost ground?

Dismissing poverty and inequality won't reverse the trends, nor will attacking unions and reducing the role of governments result in a more widely shared prosperity. Individual effort is a necessary but insufficient condition for economic growth to translate to broad-based improvements in incomes and/or quality of life of a society. Real change requires democratic, collective processes which introduce different points of view to the developing economic and cultural narrative that would otherwise be shaped solely by the already dominant and powerful. That tension between the privileged few and the grass-roots democratic clamour for a more just economy helps situate what's at stake in the post-2008 world.

The Need for Countervailing Voice and Power

In the wake of the biggest global economic shock since the 1930s, Canada's economy is witnessing the rapid growth of two- and even three-tier workplaces, greater substitution of permanent jobs with temporary and outsourced forms of employment, and the accelerating use of low-wage, low-skill temporary foreign workers. The global economy is no longer in recession, but growth is sluggish and corporate competition has become increasingly aggressive. If business strategies to contain labour costs in order to boost profits become accepted as the inevitable new normal in this economic climate, expect the pace of widening income inequality to quicken. That's because all these strategies strengthen the hand of the employer, and erode the ability of workers to bargain for something better.

Individuals and households are peddling faster than ever to stay in place, but individual effort won't get one far without the commitment of democratic institutions to ensure that we all share in the prosperity we create together. However, the strategy voiced most prominently by many business and political leaders in 2013 is to reduce the role of collective instruments such as democratically elected governments and unions.

Unions are particularly important because their organized response to growth and decline consistently delivers better outcomes for their members than markets deliver for similar workers who aren't organized. Unions help define the architecture of improved living conditions for all workers, and unionized workers and their families provide vivid examples of how individuals gain economic clout through collective heft. They also voice a counternarrative about the purpose of the economy and the source of wealth creation. Ironically, those who don't like what they have to say are also organizing. They're organizing to silence or mute union voices. As business lobbyists recognize more clearly than most workers: lose voice, lose choice.

Without vigorous countervailing opinion shaping the big public debates of the day, those who profit from the growing concentration of income and wealth will control and shape a message whose sole purpose will be further concentrating income and wealth. Ultimately, the manner in which society collectively defines how wealth gets generated and shared is just as important to future well-being as economic growth. It's not just about economics. It's also about culture and meaning. That's what makes income inequality another inconvenient truth of our time, a defining issue of our era.

Three

Increasing Inequality

The Challenge to Canadian Unions

Lars Osberg

The Impacts of Unions on Inequality

IN CANADA, THE LAST THIRTY YEARS have seen increasing inequality of income distribution coupled with a decline in the membership, economic power, and political influence of trade unions. Are these trends connected?

As Jelle Visser and Daniele Checchi have noted, "Throughout their existence, trade unions have been an important force tempering inequality."[1] Fostering norms of fairness and equality has been essential for the labour movement to build solidarity and bargain successfully – and these values are a large part of why people form unions in the first place. Labour economists such as R.B. Freeman have also long recognized that the influence of unionization goes well beyond wages. An improved level of, and greater equality in, fringe benefits, working conditions, and workplace rights are crucial objectives in collective bargaining. However, because these attributes are difficult to summarize in a way that can be compared over time or across countries, most analysis has focused on issues that are easier to quantify, such as wage levels and pay differentials.

Determining the impact of unions on wage inequality could, in principle, go either way. Unionization is partly equalizing, because collective agreements equalize pay for workers of similar qualifications, and because wage differentials between types of workers in the same bargaining unit tend to be compressed in collective agreements. Clearly, the greater the fraction of workers covered by collective agreements, the greater the impact of these equality-enhancing aspects of unionization. The potential inequality-enhancing aspect of unionization is that it creates a differential between the wages of union and non-union workers. That differential decreases when, as in many continental European countries, union membership is not necessary for union coverage, and when unions can bargain on behalf of large regional or national industry-level bargaining units.

As Visser and Checchi note, unions play very different roles in different countries. There are large institutional differences – for example, European collective bargaining is often done on an industrial basis, while workplace bargaining is typical in Canada and the United States. There is also substantial variation in the percentage of workers covered by collective agreements (ranging from over 80 per cent in Scandinavian countries to only 11 per cent in the United States). These differences imply that it is unrealistic to expect a single country's estimate of the impact of unions on wage inequality to be universally valid. However, in both Canada and the United States, the collective bargaining framework is that of a sole bargaining agent at a defined workplace bargaining unit for a defined contract period, which has been called the Wagner Act model.[2]

American researchers, including David Card and Bruce Western, have investigated the extent to which rising hourly wage inequality can be linked to declining union density. At present, the consensus estimate is that between a fifth and a third of the rise in U.S. wage inequality can be attributed to the eighteen percentage point decline in U.S. union coverage (from 29.6 per cent in 1970 to 11.3 per cent in 2012[3]). Not only does this leave four-fifths to two-thirds of the rise in U.S. wage inequality unexplained by the truly massive drop in U.S. union density, it also suggests that the much smaller decline in Canadian union density over the same period (from 33.6 per cent to 32.0 per cent) cannot possibly explain much of the rise in Canadian wage inequality.

Moreover, hourly wages are only part of the inequality picture. The total disposable annual money income of households also depends on

- the weeks of work and hours per week of labour supply of individual household members;
- the correlation of annual labour earnings among household members; and
- the income from capital and the net impact of taxes minus transfer payments for all household members.

To examine inequality in a broader sense, one should also add in each household's access to public services such as health care, education, social housing, transit, or other services. Because public services often are basically delivered per person, the impact of public spending tends to be fairly equally distributed. A repeated lesson of cross-country comparisons of inequality is the huge importance of public sector social spending in mitigating inequality in market incomes.[4]

Cross-national comparisons of household income inequality at a particular point in time also take the structure of the economy and social policy as givens, but both are in fact partly the product of past political choices. In the political economy of policy choices, the presence or absence of unions may make a significant difference. Both the level of unemployment (which is sensitive to macroeconomic policy decisions) and the level of public services have often been influenced by the political voice of the union movement. When unions use their political presence to argue for higher minimum wages, better unemployment insurance protection, high-quality public services, or the importance of full employment as a macroeconomic objective, they are advocating policy decisions that can have substantial impacts in reducing economic inequality for union members and non-members alike. Such impacts will not, however, show up in breakdowns of the union/non-union differential in hourly wages.

Inequality Trends in Canada

Canadian income tax records indicate that the big news of the last thirty years in income inequality is the rapid rise of the top 1 per cent's income share. Figure 1, based on data from *The World Top Incomes Database,* shows the increased income share of the top 1 per cent in recent years in Canada and the United States, but many authors (such as Mike Veall, and Thomas Piketty and Emmanuel Saez)[5] have noted that the top 0.1 per cent and the top 0.01 per cent of the income distribution have seen even greater gains. Indeed, as figure 4 will show, the further up the income distribution one goes, the more rapid is the rate of increase in incomes.

Canadian readers may be somewhat comforted that the increase in top-end income shares in Canada appears to be somewhat less than in the United States, but those differences may be deceptive. To get a long span of comparable historical data, figure 1 omits income from capital gains, and since available Canadian data only goes up to 2010, it also omits the recovery of Canada's top 1 per cent from the recession of

Figure 1. Top 1% income share, United States and Canada

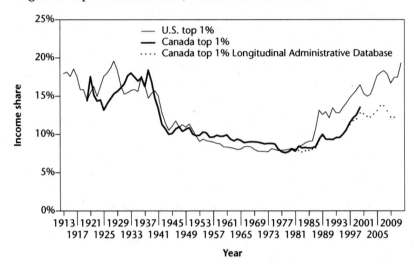

Source: Facundo Alvaredo, Tony Atkinson, Thomas Piketty, and Emmanuel Saez, *The World Top Incomes Database,* http://topincomes.g-mond.parisschoolofeconomics.eu.

2008. As well, Veall cautions that income tax data[6] in the two countries is based on different definitions of taxable income. In Canada the retained earnings of Canadian-Controlled Private Corporations (CCPCs) are not attributed back to individual income tax filers, while in the United States, the net revenues of comparable private personal corporations flow through directly and immediately to the personal tax return of the owner or owners. Hence, the apparent difference in income share trends in recent years is at least partially due to the greater ability of very wealthy Canadians to shelter income from income tax through the use of CCPCs.

As figure 1 illustrates, the income share of the top 1 per cent was similarly high in the early part of the twentieth century, but from 1940 to 1980, the concentration of income share fell. However, this did not happen because the incomes of the top 1 per cent fell in an absolute sense; rather, it happened because the incomes of everyone else grew faster than theirs. As the North American economy moved from 1930s depression to the 1940s wartime boom, declining unemployment and a rapid rise in wages combined to produce strongly growing family incomes for middle- and working-class households. Throughout the 1950s and 1960s, the union movement was relatively strong and some major structural trends – urbanization, higher education, and greater female labour force participation – also pushed up

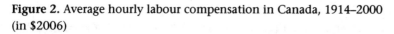
Figure 2. Average hourly labour compensation in Canada, 1914–2000 (in $2006)

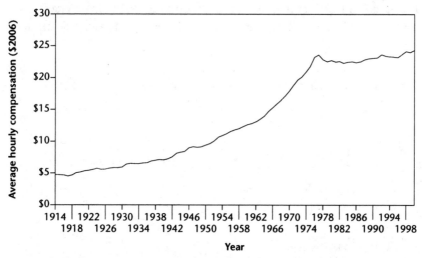

Source: 1914–1960: M.C. Urquhart and K. Buckley, eds., "Historical Statistics of Canada," Statistics Canada cat no. 11-516-XIE, Table series E198-208 – Index numbers of wage rates, wage rates and salaries; 1961–2000: Statistics Canada, CANSIM I series I603501 (matrix 9467) [CANSIM II series V717706 (table 383-0003)], CPI – CANSIM I series P100000 matrix 9940 [CPI – CANSIM II series V735319 table 3260001].

the incomes of working families. In the 1970s, the income share of the top 1 per cent stabilized, as their incomes and those of the other 99 per cent grew at about the same rate.

However, as figure 2 indicates, Canada's long tradition of rising average real hourly wages came to an end around 1980. Prior to that, policy makers attempted to find a balance between minimizing unemployment and controlling inflation, but since the early 1980s, inflation control has been the sole priority of Canadian governments. Unemployment is hardly mentioned anymore in Canada's official macroeconomic pronouncements,[7] and the national unemployment rate, which rarely exceeded 6 per cent before 1979, has only rarely been below 7 per cent since 1980. High unemployment means that with many people chasing a few jobs, there is little competition among employers for workers, and therefore, as figure 2 indicates, no reason for market forces to push up real wages.[8]

In both Canada and the United States, the last thirty years have seen remarkably flat real incomes for family units at most points in the income distribution ladder. Figure 3 shows the total real income of Canadian households at specific points in the income distribution

– specifically the 20th, 40th, 50th (median), 60th, and 80th percentiles. Over this period, only the 80th percentile has noticeably
increased in real income.[9] There has been remarkably little change at
most points in the distribution of real pre-tax household money
income.[10]

Figure 3. Total income of Canadian family units, 1976–2011 (in $2011)

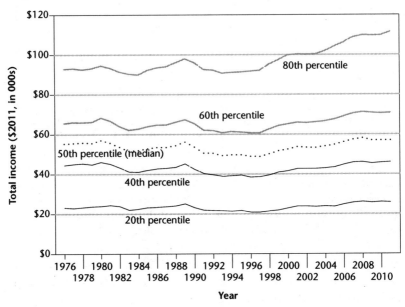

Source: Statistics Canada, CANSIM Table 202-0405 (v25731821, v25731822, v25731823,
v25731824); CANSIM Table 202-0411 (v25739992).

When most household incomes stagnate but the incomes of the
top few percentiles of the distribution grow strongly, the income
share of the top few must necessarily grow. Figure 4 shows the differential in income growth rates that drives the changing income shares
of Canada's income elite.

Why is the share of the top 1 per cent the big news of inequality
trends in Canada? It's because the shifts involved are very large by
historical standards. Table 1 presents the longest data series available,
which compares quintile shares (i.e., how much of household income
each fifth of the total population of family units receives).[11] The available survey data indicate that the top 20 per cent have gained six percentage points in share of total income since 1981 (which implies that
the other quintiles have lost that much income share). Previously,

Figure 4. Average real income compound annual growth rate, Canada and United States, 1984–2010

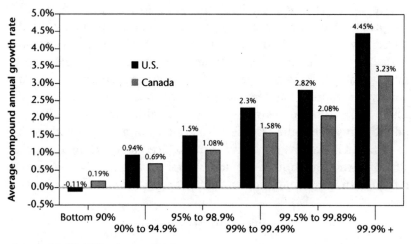

Source: *The World Top Incomes Database.*

Table 1. Income shares of Canadian family units (%)

	1951	1961	1971	1977	1981	1986	1991	1996	2001	2006	2010
Bottom 20%	4.4	4.2	3.6	4	4.6	4.7	4.5	4.4	4.1	4.1	4.2
Second 20%	11.2	11.9	10.6	11	11	10.4	10	9.7	9.7	9.7	9.6
Middle 20%	18.3	18.3	17.6	18	17.7	17.1	16.4	16.1	15.6	15.7	15.3
Fourth 20%	23.3	24.5	24.9	25.5	25.1	24.9	24.7	24.7	23.7	23.8	23.6
Richest 20%	42.8	41.1	43.3	41.5	41.6	42.9	44.4	45.2	46.9	46.8	47.3

Statistics Canada, CANSIM V1546461 to V1546465, Table 202-0701; Statistics Canada, *Income Distribution by Size in Canada,* Catalogue No. 13-207, 1998; J.R. Podoluk, *Incomes of Canadians* (Dominion Bureau of Statistics, 1968).

movements of a percentage point or so would have been considered large shifts, but the shift to the top in the last thirty years has dwarfed prior changes. Indeed, the income *gain* of the top 1 per cent is substantially greater than the total share of the bottom fifth of the population.

Over the last thirty years, there have been huge changes in American and Canadian labour markets. The labour force has become, on average, older and much better educated, and has been reallocated across industries and regions. Cohorts of new immigrants have arrived. Compared to the situation in 1980, Canadians now work with many new technologies and considerably more capital in a much more deregulated labour market, with much less protection through unions, minimum wages, and tariff barriers. Implicit guarantees of continuing employment have withered away for many workers while contingent work, on call, and subcontracting arrangements have proliferated. Compared to thirty years ago, Canadian households now supply significantly more weeks of work to the paid labour market (particularly at the lower end), and the variance of weekly work hours has also increased. A general increase in education levels (particularly for women) has been accompanied by a marginal increase in spousal correlation of earnings. However, although these changes undoubtedly have shifted the relative position of many individuals in the earnings hierarchy, they have not produced much of an aggregate shift at all, certainly nothing remotely approaching the six percentage point growth in income share of Canada's top 1 per cent.

Trends in Union Density

In recent years, Canadian private sector union density (i.e., membership as a percentage of the work force) has trended down – declining from 20.7 per cent in April 1998 to 17.8 per cent in March 2013. In Canada's public sector, union density is much higher and steadier – rising, in fact, to 75.0 per cent from 74.2 per cent over the same period.[12] The modest decline in overall union density (from 33.4 per cent to 32.0 per cent) thus masks a mixed story. Public sector unionization is holding its own in Canada, but growth in private sector union membership has not kept up with growth in private sector employment, so union density in Canada's private sector is slowly slipping (at about 0.2 percentage points per year since 1998). Nevertheless, the role of unions in Canada is today nowhere near as limited as it is in the United States, where overall union density in 2012 was only 11.3 per cent.[13] In the U.S. private sector in 2012, union members constituted only 6.6 per cent of the workforce, while the U.S. public sector unionization rate (35.9 per cent) was less than half that of the Canadian public sector.

These Canada/U.S. differences have emerged gradually over the last thirty-five years. Craig Riddell notes that throughout the 1940s and 1950s, union density in the United States was in fact substantially greater than in Canada. As late as 1965, 29.7 per cent of the non-agricultural workforce in Canada were union members, compared to 30.1 per cent in the United States. However, by 1980, U.S. union membership had slipped to 23.2 per cent, while Canadian density had risen to 37.1 per cent. Throughout the 1980s, Canadian union density remained at this level, but U.S. union membership

Reducing Income Inequality through Labour Rights

continued to slide (to 16.1 per cent by 1990), and the descent continues.

What explains these differing trends in union density? Riddell concluded "much of the Canada-U.S. unionization gap can be attributed to inter-country differences in the legal regime pertaining to unions and collective bargaining and to differences in overt management opposition (itself possibly a consequence of differences in collective bargaining laws and their administration)."[14] Riddell found no empirical support for the idea that differences in underlying social attitudes to unions could explain the Canada/U.S. union density gap, as American workers were just as likely as Canadian workers to want trade union membership and representation, but much less likely to be able to get it.

Since political actors determine the legal regime surrounding union recognition and collective bargaining, the political strength of the trade union movement is crucial to its long-term survival. When the trade union movement is politically weak, changes in collective bargaining details can be pushed through (for example, governmental efforts to erode or eliminate card-only bargaining unit certification, first contract arbitration, or the Rand formula). As the continuing rollback of union rights across the United States has shown, these changes then have a gradual impact on union membership and political strength that makes it even easier to push through subsequent adverse changes to collective bargaining legislation and regulation.

The Dilemma for Canadian Unions

Ultimately, the long-term impact of unions on Canadian trends in economic inequality is primarily through their political action (or inaction) – and only secondarily through their direct impact on wages. For most of the population, the level of public services and transfers is crucial for effective equality of real income, economic security, and opportunity. A key determinant of the level of public services is the tax revenue available to pay for it. Strong union movements play a crucial public role in political debates on taxation and on the quality and level of public services, as they do in debates on the minimum wage, public pensions, labour regulation, and much else.

Virtually every aspect of economic policy – from regulation of the environment to financial market supervision and consumer protection legislation – also has a distributional impact, and to the extent that unions make the case for low-income Canadians, they influence drivers of economic inequality. Historically, strong union movements have also influenced macroeconomic priorities, particularly the relative importance of full-employment policies, which also matter hugely for inequality.

However, the main event in Canadian inequality trends in recent years is the growing incomes and rising income share of the top 1 per cent – a trend that collective bargaining does not directly address, even if (as argued by Western) the strength of the union voice in political debates may directly influence corporate governance and CEO compensation by helping to set some implicit bounds on corporate excess.[15] Although collective bargaining could, in principle, help some Canadian resource sector workers get higher wages, the main event in the resource sector is not the level of wages paid to a fairly small number of directly employed workers.[16] The crucial issue is the royalty and taxation regime that decides what share of the surplus generated in Canada's resource extraction boom will stay in Canada to pay for the public services that benefit all Canadians, and what amount will either be exported as profits or absorbed domestically by Canada's top 1 per cent.

Canada's biggest trend to greater inequality is the rising share of the top 1 per cent – something that unions in Canada cannot directly bargain over in standard contract negotiations at individual unionized workplaces. A business unionism model in which unions limit their attention to workplace bargaining issues therefore will not influence much the trend to greater concentration of income and wealth at the very top. However, the top 1 per cent are very active politically and it is clear that they have very different political values and attitudes than the rest of the population[17] – so their rising income share will eventually affect business unions. The political influence of the top 1 per cent already is substantially more than that of average Canadians, and it grows with their growing wealth and income. If their voices are the only ones being heard, one can expect ever growing pressures for labour law reforms along the lines already implemented in many U.S. states – which will imply, with a lag, downward pressure on the membership of all unions, including those with only a workplace focus.

Canada's unions thus face a dilemma. The framework of current labour law in Canada gives unions a mandate to negotiate the terms and conditions of work at individual workplace bargaining units – but if that is all that unions do, they will have little impact on the biggest economic inequality trends and they can eventually expect a more and more marginal existence. The top 1 per cent have been major beneficiaries of recent public policies such as lower marginal tax rates in the income tax system and looser regulation of banking and finance and corporate governance and CEO compensation – and Canada's top 1 per cent are pushing strongly for more of the same. Canada's union movement has to decide if it wants to push back.

Four

Labour Law and Labour Rights

The Wagner Act in Canada

Michael Lynk

A Labour Rights Framework

IN 1935 AND 1944, RESPECTIVELY, the United States and Canada adopted the same comprehensive legislative approach to entrenching labour rights in the North American workplace. Known as the Wagner Act model of labour law,[1] this approach protected the right of employees to join unions, required employers to bargain with unions in good faith and to refrain from committing unfair labour practices, granted legal status to collective agreements, and ensured the mandatory adjudication of workplace grievances. To supervise and enforce these rights, it established neutral labour relations boards and arbitration tribunals made up of expert adjudicators. In exchange for these guarantees, unions surrendered their broad right to strike, and accepted instead a limited and conditional window of time during which they could legally withdraw their labour.

The Wagner Act model was a major advancement for labour relations, as the legislation it inspired became a principal tool to reduce the uneven playing field between unions and employers. This legal framework differed in secondary details between the two countries and among the eleven Canadian jurisdictions, but the core framework was essentially the same across the northern continent. The legislators and jurists who shaped the Wagner Act legislation accepted three fundamental assumptions about the North American workplace:

- Bargaining power between employers and individual employees was inherently unequal.[2]
- The purchasing power of workers needed to be strengthened to spur economic growth and forestall business cycle failures.[3]
- Enabling workers to organize into unions and bargain collectively over working conditions was necessary to offset the dominant power of employers and to provide a measure of social stability against the spectres of deep inequality and want.[4]

Social reformer and U.S. Supreme Court Justice Louis Brandeis was alive to these assumptions, noting, "Strong, responsible unions are essential to industrial fair play. Without them, the labor bargain is wholly one-sided."[5] With their respective enactments of the Wagner Act model, legislators in both countries affirmed that collective bargaining was a positive social good and an integral part of modern public policy.[6]

During the Wagner Act's first forty years, the model proved to be a social and economic success. With labour rights embedded in the North American workplace, unions and collective bargaining experienced spectacular growth. In Canada, for example, unionization levels rose from 18 per cent of the non-agricultural workplace in 1941 to 28 percent by 1951, a jump of 55 per cent. This, in turn, contributed meaningfully to the lengthy North American boom of postwar prosperity and rising social egalitarianism – the so-called Great Compression – that lasted into the 1980s. Through this period, the modern middle class was born; the egregious income and wealth inequalities that had scarred the United States and Canada through much of the previous century were significantly reduced; the state assumed a more activist role in the economy as public spending on education, health programs, and infrastructure grew substantively; and social mobility became more open and fluid.[7] In the North American workplace, this new collective voice created a dynamic form of industrial democracy, where workers acquired the ability to shape their own employment conditions and also, for the first time, play a meaningful role in broader national debates on labour legislation, taxation levels, budgetary spending, political platforms, and international affairs.[8]

Despite such positive changes, serpents were alive in this garden. In the United States, an unsympathetic judiciary, mounting employer opposition, and repeated congressional failures to reform and modernize the legislation combined to whittle away the *National Labor Relations Act*, the formal title of the American Wagner Act.[9] Unionization levels in the United States tumbled from 30 per cent of the labour force in 1960 to 18 per cent in 1985. By 2012, they had fallen all the way to 11 per cent, their lowest levels since the early 1930s, and among the lowest in the industrial world.[10] The decline in American union numbers was matched by weakened influence in Congress and state legislatures and, more importantly, in the court of public opinion. Recently, four midwestern industrial states that had once been heavily unionized – Wisconsin, Ohio, Indiana, and Michigan – have elected Republican governors who then stripped private and public sector workers of their core labour rights. Falling unionization rates also contributed to the rightward drift of American politics and widening economic disparities that have left the United States among the most unequal of countries in the West.[11] Indeed, the American economic gap between the rich and everyone else – the ratio between the richest and poorest 10 per cent in terms of income – stood at 16:1 in 2008.

In contrast, intense consultations with unions and employers ensured Canadian labour legislation was regularly updated by Parliament and provincial legislatures between the 1950s and the 1990s. This steady stream of labour law reform helped to boost unionization levels from 28 per cent in 1960 to 38 per cent by 1985. But after the mid-1990s, as the postwar political consensus on the activist liberal state began to fray, labour legislative initiatives virtually dried up in Canada. In turn, Canadian unionization levels steadily declined, falling to 29 per cent by 2012. As Canadian unionization rates began to contract, domestic levels of economic inequality started to rise: the ratio of the richest and poorest 10 per cent of Canadians in 2008 stood at 9:1, a level above the medium for Organisation for Economic Co-operation and Development member states (the OECD, commonly known as the rich countries' club).[12] Like the United States, but in a less dramatic fashion, Canadian unions have seen their political voice weaken at the federal level and in many provincial capitals over the past thirty years, while labour's share of GDP has steadily eroded to its lowest levels in half a century. Although Canada is not doomed to follow the American path, neither can it avoid this spectre should governments at the federal and provincial levels continue to dilute the vitality of Canadian labour laws through active reversal or benign neglect.[13] Countries around the world have developed a variety of labour law models and approaches to guaranteeing labour rights and regulating management-union relations. Where the Wagner Act model as practised in Canada has been permitted to flourish through a genuine political commitment to collective bargaining, as it was between the 1960s and the 1990s, it has proven to be one of the more stable, effective, and successful approaches to labour law among the modern liberal democracies. The Canadian model has not resulted in the Scandinavian countries' high levels of unionization, but it has also not witnessed the significant tumble experienced recently by many Western European countries that have historically relied upon a more laissez-faire approach to workplace regulation.

A sober review of the Wagner Act model's contemporary Canadian balance sheet reveals both a range of successful accomplishments and a pattern of urgent problems. The former are significant and have made a measureable difference in the lives of many Canadians, but they are unlikely to be sustainable if the institutions of collective bargaining become targets of attack rather than affirmative instruments of public policy. The problems of the Wagner Act model are visible both through the bitter experiences south of the border, and the as-yet-confined but growing clamour among the Canadian right to import the worst features of American labour law into domestic legislation. A contextual understanding of the Wagner Act model's successes and problems helps illustrate why Canadians need to defend this signature prototype from such attacks.

Successes of the Canadian Model

Stability, Durability, Predictability

Canada's present labour law model has remained intact and highly functional for almost seventy years, a major accomplishment among liberal democracies. The industrial relations systems in many countries – the United Kingdom, Australia, New Zealand, Spain, France, and Italy, to name a few – have gone through significant political and legislative upheavals over the past thirty years, with right-of-centre governments overhauling their labour law systems, sometimes more than once. Almost always, the consequence of these changes has been a significant drop in labour protections and union membership. In the United Kingdom, for example, unions represented more than twelve million workers in 1979, the year Margaret Thatcher was elected. Her government substantially degraded British labour legislation in the 1980s, and these structural setbacks have largely remained in place ever since; by 2012, unions in the United Kingdom represented fewer than six million workers.[14]

The durability of Canada's model results from a broad political consensus among unions and employers to support the fundamental tenets of the Wagner Act model, even as debates and struggles continue over some of its secondary features. As a result, extensive legislative protections for unions have endured through the years, notwithstanding the political stripes of the party in power. This assurance has enabled unions, at least until recently, to focus their energies on collective agreement improvements and broader political issues, without having to regularly expend their limited resources to defend the fundamental legislative rights that they had already achieved. The Wagner Act model has also proven to be a flexible and adaptable system that has been extended to the unique circumstances of artists and cultural workers, professional athletes, and construction workers. However, this labour-management consensus has held primarily because unions have been strong enough to assert their place at the table; as they weaken in numbers and political voice, the consensus will almost certainly unravel, and employers will increasingly advocate both weaker labour protections and, possibly, even the end of the Wagner Act model.

A Labour Law System That Has Worked

The primary purpose of any industrial relations system that seeks to protect labour rights is to promote a process of free collective bargaining which meaningfully improves the working conditions of employees. This is why most workers have sought to belong to trade unions. The other fundamental labour rights recognized by international labour law – the right to create and join trade unions, and the right to strike – are foundation stones that undergird the ultimate goal of the right to bargain collectively. Thus, the legal and political freedom accorded to free collective bargaining is invariably the most telling measurement of the effectiveness of any industrial relations system.

By this litmus test, Canada's Wagner Act model has been a considerable success, at least up until the late 1990s. The core of the Canadian model has been the enactment of a number of legislative protections that have given substance to the right to collectively bargain: the broad right to join a union, meaningful legal status for collective agreements, the obligation to bargain in good faith, strict penalties for unfair labour practices, and high-quality labour tribunals to supervise the legislative provisions. Equally important is the Wagner Act's majoritarian, exclusive, and democratic approach, with a union being certified as the sole representative of a unit of employees if it can demonstrate the support of a majority of the workers. Because of these statutory and bargained rights, the power of unionized employees is significantly greater than that of their non-unionized counterparts.

Significantly, unionized workers enjoy meaningful protections against unjust discipline and dismissal, and have ready access to industrial justice forums. They have also achieved greater wages, benefits, and pension settlements, and their concerns about important workplace concerns such as health and safety, harassment, gender equality, and human rights must be listened to by governments and their employers. When it works best, the Wagner Act model not only delivers these protections to unionized members, but also positively influences the availability of employment protections for non-unionized employees.

A Truly Expert and Neutral Adjudication System

The system of expert and neutral labour adjudicators who decide upon the basic and secondary rights of unions and their members forms a centrepiece of the Canadian model. The Wagner Act's purpose in establishing this separate administrative system was to remove legal decision-making authority from the judiciary – whose innate sympathies invariably sided with employers and property rights – and to create a new system based on legal experts who understood the workplace culture and could demonstrate true neutrality. The stability of the Wagner Act model has meant that the political parties in power – whether right, centre, or left – have almost always adhered to the prevailing consensus that made it unacceptable to politicize labour relations board appointments. The same is true for the community of labour arbitrators who adjudicate union-management disputes over the application of collective agreement provisions. This, in turn, has enhanced the respect of these boards among unions and employers, the courts, and the broader public.

Over the years, the quality of these neutral bodies' decision making has ensured that unions have ready access to a fair, knowledgeable, legally autonomous, and relatively speedy adjudication process. Just as important, these labour board chairs and arbitrators have produced a rich body of case law that has progressively entrenched or widened a variety of labour issues into the law, including privacy rights, human rights and the accommodation duty, free speech at work, important procedural protections during the discipline process, and restrictions on the scope of management rights. Many of these new rights have been subsequently extended to non-unionized employees, inevitably creating a much fairer Canadian workplace.

The Emergence of Human Rights Law and the Accommodation Duty

Perhaps the most positive recent development within Canada's Wagner Act model over the past twenty-five years has been the emergence of human rights law as an integral part of this country's collective agreements and labour law system. Unions have long fought for human rights at work, and their advocacy has resulted in what is now probably the most advanced human rights legal culture in the world. Labour arbitrators and human rights tribunals regularly adjudicate important workplace issues on disability, family status, gender, sexual orientation, and the rights of religious employees at work. While less progress has been made on race and age issues, these areas are nonetheless improving. As a result, the Canadian workplace has become more diverse, more accessible, more accommodating, and more tolerant than ever, with employers and governments forced to respect these deeply entrenched, core human rights.[15]

Disability rights in particular have become the most litigated human rights ground in the Canadian workplace, setting high legal standards that now apply to other human rights.[16] These advancements are important because of the pervasive discrimination that persons with disabilities have traditionally suffered and continue to experience at work and in society at large. As recently as the late 1980s, persons with disabilities had few legal rights protecting their ability to enter into, or remain in, the Canadian workplace. Now, as a result of Canada's human rights revolution, governments and employers have extensive obligations to ensure that workplaces are barrier-free, employees can readily access necessary accommodations, discriminatory employment assumptions are challenged and eliminated, and workplace rules, including collective agreements, are fully compliant with human rights obligations.

Freedom of Association and International Labour Rights

Since 2001, trade unions have won several significant constitutional victories at the Supreme Court of Canada and other legal forums that have breathed life into the freedom of association guarantee (section 2(d)) in the *Charter of Rights and Freedoms*. Reversing what had been a sterile and inert approach towards fundamental workplace constitutional rights that had begun with its rulings in the so-called labour trilogy in 1987,[17] the Supreme Court stated in the 2001 *Dunmore* case that freedom of association includes the right of dispossessed employees to have a collective voice.[18] The 2007 *B.C. Health Services* case affirmed public employees' right to have significant collective bargaining gains respected by their legislative employers.[19] The Court has since reverted to a more conservative and hesitant approach to freedom of association guarantees in its 2011 *Fraser* judgment,[20] but the door remains open, based on some comments in recent Court rulings, that the *Charter* may yet become a dynamic tool that will protect fundamental rights in the workplace.[21]

One intriguing feature of this recent, if cautious, constitutional breakthrough has been the Supreme Court's endorsement of international labour law as an interpretive tool when reading the *Charter*. International labour law – made up of guarantees found in the leading international human rights covenants and the International Labour Organization's conventions – lays out a liberal vision of fundamental employee rights, including the rights to organize, collectively bargain, and strike, coupled with the right of unions to be free from government interference and repression. In short, these international documents clearly place labour rights within the family of universal human rights. In *B.C. Health Services*, the Supreme Court declared, "Canada's current international law commitments and the current state of international thought on human rights provide a persuasive source for interpreting the scope of the *Charter*."[22] In other words, the protection of freedom of association in Canada should be consistent with the broad and purposive spirit that has animated the foundational documents of international labour and human rights law. Among other consequences, such a resolute reading of section 2(d) would restrict the ability of Canadian governments to interfere with fundamental labour rights unless a substantial justification (such as a real threat to public health and safety) could be established.

Challenges

The Representational Limitations of the Wagner Act Model

The Wagner Act model arose in a now-distant era, when a largely male labour force worked predominantly for large industrial employers that each employed thousands of workers. The backbone of the mid-twentieth-century labour movement was composed of workers in the enormous auto, steel, and other manufacturing plants, the mines, the craft and construction unions, and the transportation industries. Later, in the 1960s and 1970s, public sector employees won the right to collective bargaining across the country. The Wagner Act model, with its majoritarian and exclusive representation approach, enabled unions to organize these enormous workplaces, while it had been historically much less successful in organizing the service, financial, and retail industries in the private sector, where smaller workplaces, more tightly competitive economic imperatives, and more hostile employers proved to be significant obstacles.

Today, the Canadian economy and labour force have been transformed. Manufacturing as a percentage of the GDP has significantly declined and, in the face of the technological revolution, global economic competition, and the rise of more knowledge-based work, the industrial workplaces where Canadian unions established their beachheads have dramatically shrunk in size and employment numbers. Taking its place as the engine of Canada's private sector economy are the service, financial, retail, and information technology industries, where union representation has rarely risen above 10 per cent. In the early 1960s, Canadian unions represented around 45 per cent of the private sector; they now represent only 16 per cent. The labour movement is kept afloat today because the public sector (which makes up about 22 per cent of the Canadian labour force) is about 75 per cent unionized. The existential question facing advocates of the Wagner Act model is whether it is capable of flourishing only in an "old economy" characterized by large industrial workplaces, or whether it's sufficiently adaptable to the new economy's shifting focus on smaller service-oriented and highly skilled workplaces. The age-old need for an effective collective voice in the workplace has not gone away, but creating an appropriate entity for this new paradigm remains a significant challenge.

An abiding strength of the Wagner Act model has been its legislative adaptability and flexibility. Once the basic model was transplanted north to Canada in the 1940s, both Parliament and provincial legislatures accepted collective bargaining as an important public policy commitment, enacting a regular infusion of legislative reform measures. The 1960s witnessed the adoption of public sector collective bargaining laws, followed by health and safety legislative reform throughout the 1970s, gender equality statutes in the 1980s, and the entrenchment of human rights laws into the unionized workplace during the 1990s. Throughout these decades, labour relations statutes were regularly reformed and updated to enhance the right to collectively bargain, and included first contract legislation, increased protections for striking and picketing workers, stronger remedies for employer breaches, and a more liberal definition of who constitutes an "employee." A crucial lesson from the Wagner Act experience in both the United States and Canada is that the legislation needs to be regularly refreshed and improved to remain dynamic and relevant.

Over the past fifteen years, Canadian labour law reform has been missing in action. During the 1990s, Ontario, British Columbia, and Saskatchewan all enacted significant labour law reforms to strengthen access to collective bargaining. All three reforms were undone by the subsequent election of conservative governments, and have not been reinstated. More modest legislative reforms were adopted in the federal sector (1997) and Manitoba (2002), but they marked the last successful attempts by governments in Canada to enhance their Wagner statutes. Rather, when Canadian governments have introduced labour law initiatives over the past two decades, they have been designed to restrict access to collective bargaining, from replacing the card-check union certification process with mandatory votes and decreasing access to first contract arbitration, to weakening the bargaining power of essential service workers.

More alarming has been the governmental trend towards enacting back-to-work legislation that has either ended a legal strike or forestalled its occurrence.[23] Over the course of 2011–12, the federal government passed six such statutes in disputes involving Canada Post and Air Canada, a record for such frequency and a signal of intolerance for the operation of the long-standing industrial relations system. Given the intricate relationship in Canada between the strength of labour legislation and the size and power of the labour movement, it is hardly surprising that, during the past two decades, the demise of the legislative reform spirit has been accompanied by the steady decline of unionization levels.

The American Experience with the Wagner Act: From Model to Threat

Canada directly borrowed its labour law legislative model from the extraordinary American reform initiatives in 1935, when the federal government in Ottawa was pushed to institute a fair system that would satisfy the aspirations of an increasingly militant Canadian labour force and ensure a period of greater industrial peace.[24] From the 1940s until the 1980s, Canadian courts and tribunals regularly looked south of the border for legal innovations in labour law and human rights decisions by the United States Supreme Court and the National Labor Relations Board. But as U.S. labour law began to atrophy by the 1980s, Canada paid increasingly less attention to the American experience and devised its own home-made legal innovations to Wagner Act model statutes and case law. The principal legal problems that had come to plague the American Wagner Act model – "right-to-work" laws that strangle union financing, widespread prohibitions on public sector collective bargaining, intrusive legislative oversight over internal union affairs, inadequate remedies for unfair labour practices, the unavailability of the card-check method in the union certification process, the permanent replacement of striking employees, and highly political appointments to the National Labor Relations Board that have undermined its institutional neutrality and integrity – did not arouse much interest from Canadian political figures or from industry.

Ironically, the American experience with the Wagner Act has recently attracted renewed attention in Canada, but not by Canadians interested in the promise of collective bargaining. The Canadian right, anchored in the country's conservative parties, corporate media, and right-leaning think tanks, has become enchanted with these harsher elements of American labour law, and now seeks their adoption on this side of the border. The Ontario Progressive Conservatives, the province's official opposition party, issued a policy statement in 2012 that endorsed a significant revision of the province's labour laws, drawing its inspiration and examples directly from the United States.[25] The House of Commons in December 2012 passed a Conservative backbencher's private member's bill, C-377, that would impose stringent financial reporting obligations on unions, but not on employer organizations or professional associations (it was eventually stalled by Senate amendments in June 2013). Other conservative governments (Saskatchewan) and provincial opposition parties (Alberta's Wildrose Party) have drawn similar policy inspiration from the American Wagner Act experience to consider substantive revisions of their own labour legislation.

A Model Worth Defending

The Wagner Act model in Canada is shrinking, in both its protection of collective rights at work and its coverage of working Canadians. What was once widely accepted as a solid political commitment to an enlightened act of public policy is now diminishing in importance, scope, and respect. This decline is neither inevitable nor irreversible, but Canada's labour law system will not regain its promise or restore its vitality until trade unions can effectively demand that Canadian legislatures recommit themselves to the institutions of collective bargaining.

Such a process is easier said than done: Canadian labour legislation has always been the result of the particular balance of power between workers, employers, and governments at critical historical turning points. Unions achieved strong labour laws because they were sufficiently mobilized and powerful enough to demand them. Now, as their bargaining power wanes and their influence in Parliament and in most provincial legislatures contracts, the ability of unions to protect their legislative achievements is eluding them precisely because of their weakened political power in a globalizing economy and a hostile political environment.

But this is not an obituary. Labour law, as an integral feature of modern human rights, will always remain an ongoing project and never a settled accomplishment. The Wagner Act model, notwithstanding its flaws and imperfections, is well worth defending. It remains a viable legislative system for protecting labour rights that, with imagination and political commitment, can ensure that the collective voice of employees remains a vibrant tool – indeed, the single most effective and proven tool we have yet devised – for enforcing rights at work.

Part 2

Promoting Democracy, Economic Equality, and Social Rights

Five

Unions and Democratic Governance

Empowering Participatory Citizenship

Nathalie Des Rosiers

DURING A PERILOUS TIME FOR UNIONS – when media pundits and politicians alike pose questions about the relevance and value of organized labour – it is useful to dig beneath the headlines and surface conclusions to analyze the myriad ways in which these unique organizations have contributed to Canada's democratic social fabric. While many acknowledge the role unions have played to equalize our society and diminish the gap between rich and poor, few recognize their substantial contribution to the practice and theory of democracy. Even if unions had not been so successful in achieving economic justice for employees, they should still be maintained because they contribute directly to the techniques and ideas essential in a democracy. Recognizing this fact is crucial in the face of a perverse critique of unions that employs the language of democracy to herald a right to choose, a right to work, or a right to have access to information that would subsequently be manipulated to control and weaken unions.[1]

In many respects, any effort to destroy unions will destroy a little bit of our democracy. Indeed, unions act as motors of democracy because they stimulate the emergence of new ideas and concepts about democratic governance and create the tools to enflesh these concepts. This is not to say, of course, that unions are beyond reproach, could not improve, or are always well managed or truly democratic. Some unions have been infiltrated by the mafia or have acted in a discriminatory fashion,[2] just as political parties or religious groups also inherit a history marked by scandals and mismanagement. In the same manner that Winston Churchill famously remarked, "It has been said that democracy is the worst form of government except all the others that have been tried," unions may not be the best form of human organization, but their absence would leave society with a significant democratic deficit.

Democratic Participation beyond the Right to Vote for Government

Unions exist to protect workers and to advocate on a range of issues, from improvements to working conditions and wages to ensuring the maintenance of health and safety. They accomplish their goals through a range of participatory activities designed to hold employers accountable and to ensure that employees' needs are considered in the organization of the workplace, from making demands and requesting information to brandishing the threat of strikes, withdrawal of services, or other collective action. In essence, the combined power of a cohesive group and the solidarity of workers can confront the power of the purse and the shelter of ownership while arguing for democratic management of the workplace.

In light of these relationships, it's stimulating to realize that democracy is not only about controlling governmental abuse of power, but also about monitoring power exerted by private sector owners. It's also a revolutionary concept that unions recognize the inherent dignity of all and presuppose that the representative participation of everyone in decisions directly affecting them will enhance the legitimacy of decision making and ultimately lead to better outcomes. To extend democratic ideals outside of the confines of politics opens the doors of empowerment in many areas of life. Challenging a tyrannical boss by seeking accountability in the same way one might seek to hold governments in check expands the concept of democratic demands into the private sphere. The subsequent discovery that concentrated decision-making power can only be counteracted by collective action is a revelation, as is the recognition that a horizontal grouping of individuals is better equipped to respond to the vertical concentration of power.

Democratization is ultimately about giving voice to people who are institutionally and economically silenced. The manner in which unions reconfigure workplaces from zones of exploitation, individual pain, and arbitrary rules to places where decisions must be rational, predictable, able to be questioned, and accountable to employees is a model for transforming other potentially abusive relationships. Prisons are less dangerous if inmates can participate in decision making, religious orders increasingly value the opinions of their parishioners, and even large corporate actors benefit from consumer representation.

In addition to providing a vehicle for workers' voices, unions also try to model democracy themselves. In general, union leaders are elected and owe an equal duty of representation to all members, and strike actions are decided by votes. Indeed, respect for the decision-making capacity of workers inherent in this process supports larger claims about citizenship. As Michael Ford suggests, a "fuller understanding of citizenship, originating with de Tocqueville [. . . suggests that] it is only through democratic participation in small-scale voluntary associations that individuals come to acquire the cognitive and moral qualities they require in order meaningfully both to exercise their democratic powers in the larger political sphere, and to understand the legitimacy of democratic government."[3] In other words, because workers experience, test, and use democratic tools in the workplace, they are better positioned to participate in democracy at large. This understanding is in stark contrast to governmental efforts to denigrate unions by questioning their transparency and accountability.

In practising the tools of democracy, unions provide a training ground for leadership skills, including the arts of politics, negotiation, positioning, and public and media relations. Indeed, union leaders have run for and been elected to public office, expanding the notion of who, exactly, is fit to govern.

Protests and Rallies as Democratic Techniques

The right to protest is one that inevitably disturbs and disrupts. It is meant to. It disturbs ordinary people who may be delayed, inconvenienced, or unable to conduct business as usual. It disturbs businesses for which any change in scheduling may mean additional costs. It should also disturb governments.

When protests disturb and paralyze traffic, what should be done? During the 2012 Quebec Spring, the government initially ignored student protests against proposed tuition increases. But as the protests grew larger, some people sought court injunctions, leading to a chain reaction of arrests, violent interaction between police and protesters, further court challenges and arrests, tear gas in the streets, and broken shop windows. The Quebec government then enacted a special law that significantly curtailed the right to protest, but it was rejected by a broadening of support for the protest movement and, eventually, by an election that saw the newly elected Parti Québécois revoke the legislation.

Protests are legitimate forms of political expression and while they do disturb, so do road construction, street parades, fundraising races, and motorcades. All are part of living in a democracy, and unions have played a significant role in strengthening the capacity to imagine collective actions, protecting such gatherings from physical and legal assaults, and providing them an air of professionalism through the development of logistical and organizational competencies to guarantee effective and well-run protests. While governments have sought to criminalize protests, obtain injunctions to stop blockades, and impose back-to-work legislation and hefty fines on unions that defy them, the labour movement has continued to insist on its right to be heard and to fully participate.

Democratic Ideas, Group Rights, and Freedom of Association

Democratic life is founded on a series of ideas, among which are the right to vote and to be governed by elected representatives. In addition, respect for the rule of law and the idea that all power should be accountable are essential underpinnings for true freedom of expression, due process rights, and the need for proportionality between punishment and misconduct. Mature democracies appreciate the needs for constant vigilance against abuses and for the empowerment of the vulnerable. Indeed, a democracy is a fragile ecosystem whose equilibrium is easily disturbed and can rapidly disintegrate. Union advocacy and insights often provide the oxygen needed to replenish and refresh sclerotic political systems, especially in nourishing new concepts of freedom of association.

The idea of freedom of association as a fundamental element of democracy has not been sufficiently theorized. Most analyses have a rather defensive and restrictive perspective on group rights that exhibit a fear of this particular freedom; they could benefit from an understanding of how unions manage the difficult line between protecting individual members and acting for the collective. While the judicial ambivalence with respect to freedom of association appears rooted in individualistic notions of civil liberties, it also seems to grow from a generalized fear posed by the potential dangers of extending unlimited freedom to various groups. Individualized concepts of civil liberties are based on protection of the individual's right to be who she is, to believe what she wants, and to say whatever she feels. The protection of freedom of expression is related to a sense of self-fulfillment, the possibility of self-reflection, the pursuit of one's own ideas, and efforts to deepen knowledge and seek the truth.

In that context, a strong protection of freedom of association has often been seen as antagonistic to the protection of the individual, given a fear that the community can be just as exploitative or oppressive as a government. The 1984 U.S. Supreme Court case of *Roberts* v. *United States Jaycees*[4] demonstrates a potential adversarial relationship between equality and freedom of association. In that instance, freedom of association was argued as a shield against the application of the *Minnesota Human Rights Act*, which prohibited discrimination against women. While the Jaycees argued that freedom of association allowed them to exclude women from the club, the Court concluded that such grounds could not be used to justify discrimination. But left unanswered are significant questions: Is the status of that association free from court supervision? Do groups enjoy associative rights that override other rights? Is it better to narrow the protection of freedom of association, or to accept that at times potentially conflicting rights (freedom of association and equality) may need to be reconciled in a manner that limits the freedom of association?

Of particular concern is the freedom of non-association, a concept that could threaten a large number of compulsory membership arrangements that are deemed socially beneficial. Could a robust protection of freedom of non-association undermine marketing boards or compulsory membership in professional organizations or student associations? While it is true that some compulsory arrangements impose a burden on individuals, they may need to be justified under *The Canadian Charter of Rights and Freedoms* as a "reasonable and demonstrably justified" limit on the right to freedom of association.

It is not surprising that a restricted version of freedom of association has emerged, nor that the Supreme Court of Canada limited the scope of section 2(d) of the *Charter*. In the 1987 trilogy of labour cases, the Court viewed freedom of association as the right to form an association, to belong to a group, and to collectively exercise individual rights and freedoms, but did not extend it to any activity that was essential to the full functioning of the organization.[5] According to Justice Sopinka, the purpose of section 2(d) "commands a single inquiry: has the state precluded activity because of its associational nature . . . ?"[6] This limited vision of freedom of association prevailed for many years, and while recently the Supreme Court has moved away from this reasoning,[7] there nevertheless remains a hesitant approach to[8] and only a piecemeal expansion of the freedom.[9]

It would therefore appear timely to develop a more affirmative notion of freedom of association that protects a priori collective activities and enjoys the expansive interpretation already afforded freedom of expression. There is no reason that freedom of association cannot be interpreted in the same broad manner as other freedoms. In fact, there are numerous advantages to rejecting a piecemeal approach and developing a broad definition of freedom of association. Not only would it provide internal consistency to section 2 of the *Charter*, but it would also support the development of collective rights enshrined in Canadian constitutional law. It is particularly instructive that while freedom of expression enjoys a broad and purposive interpretation, there exists no threat to existing legislative limits. Indeed, prohibitions against child pornography and hate propaganda have survived constitutional challenges, so one could presume that challenges to the limits on freedom of association or non-association would still, even with a broader interpretation, be dealt with judiciously and in sync with the *Charter*.

Courts always grant a large margin of discretion to lawmakers in socioeconomic matters. While one can imagine that mandatory union dues would survive a challenge under section 1 of the *Charter* (which references reasonable limits that can be justified in a free and democratic society),[10] it is at times scary to accept that the judiciary may weigh in to evaluate legislative interventions designed to benefit workers. Many have argued that courts are fundamentally incapable of understanding workers' struggles and always lean towards employers. Nevertheless, as the political climate shifts towards undermining unions' roles in workplace and society, it might be worthwhile to investigate how a properly framed judicial role could be helpful.

At the very least, a stronger protection of freedom of association will be required, and the onus of proving otherwise will be on government. The battle is far from won, but at least a discussion can take place not so much on the legitimacy of the right to engage in strike activity or in collective bargaining, but on what would be viewed as reasonable limits on such activities. Forcing the government to explain its choices often exposes their irrationality. It may ultimately be necessary to reconcile the exercise of freedom of association, the right to strike, and the right to collective bargaining with various personal freedoms, whether the right to vote or the right to dissent. This reconciliation between diverse perspectives is the hallmark of a mature democracy that recognizes multiple interests are often at stake and should not be feared.

A more generous approach to freedom of association would also provide stronger intellectual foundations for collective rights. Justification for the collective rights of linguistic minorities or Indigenous communities recognizes their guarantee of equality: it is not possible, for example, to truly live as an Aboriginal person without the constitutional recognition of an Aboriginal identity and the associated collective rights that flow therefrom. Freedom of association can also support the development of collective rights in a broader context that recognizes the importance of community participation for all human beings. It is not possible to have access to adequate pay and recognition of equality as workers without a collective exercise of negotiations.

Modern defenders of civil liberties recognize that growing inequality and the rapid development of neoliberalism have shrunk the space for making demands and the exercise of freedom. In this precarious age, power is distributed unfairly, and abuse of that power is certainly not limited to the excesses of governments. In the private sector, large corporations continue to sue their critics for libel in an effort to impose silence.

The choice to work in a judicial framework and to argue for expansive definitions of rights is controversial. However, some groups are boxed in to this realm when governments work deliberately to minimize collective capacity and action as they have done with Quebec's Bill 78 (severely restricting the right to demonstrate) and Ontario's Bill 115 (allowing for the imposition of a collective agreement on teachers). The game is dangerous because the courts are not always in a position to recognize and understand the plight of workers. Other forms of political resistance and engaged democracy are often more effective than court battles, but it is untenable to allow the government to argue in the judicial arena for an impoverished vision of the freedom of association without an alternative vision being presented.

Socioeconomic Rights and Freedom

One of many early union contributions to the world of ideas is the connection between democratic participation and socioeconomic conditions. Before the international community decided to move beyond political rights to embrace socioeconomic rights, unions had paved the way. Their central claim was and remains that people should not have undue constraints placed on the right to live and engage freely in political action, nor on the rights to political thought, expression, and religion. But those very rights pale in a context of raw economic inequality, exploitative working conditions, and abusive workplaces. Indeed, disembodied freedom – freedom in the abstract, understood separately from the context of unequal distribution of wealth – is a hollow freedom. It is a freedom that belongs to the very few, and one that can legitimize abuse and oppression. Liberty cannot be discussed only in a dematerialized state. Such decontextualized discussions provide little relief to the hungry and the sick, and may also mask their suffering. The idea that democracy demands a consideration of economic welfare as a matter of right, and not only as a political choice, is a significant contribution. This certainly explains the opposition to unions, given their long-standing role as outspoken supporters of economic justice.

The attempts by union opponents to render the labour movement toothless through false concepts of democratic rights recall the words of Mahatma Gandhi, who asked, "What difference does it make to the dead, the orphans, and the homeless, whether the mad destruction is wrought under the name of totalitarianism or the holy name of liberty or democracy?"

Given unions' role in maintaining the health of the democratic state, such ongoing attacks have profound ramifications. As with all organizations, unions must be reflective and engage in critical discussion about self-improvement, but it is dangerous to tolerate a world without them.

Six

Advancing Human Rights for All Canadians

The Struggle for Equality

Paul Champ

EQUALITY IS A FUNDAMENTAL VALUE for any truly democratic society. As strong and progressive institutions, trade unions have played a primary role in promoting equality in Canada, not only through collective bargaining and litigation, but also through education, social action, and lobbying for legislative change. Their efforts, combined with those of other social movements, have made securing and protection of equality rights an increasingly important social objective since the Second World War. As a result, federal and provincial governments have passed human rights legislation to redress and prevent discrimination in the areas of employment, services, and accommodation.

This chapter provides a brief review of trade union efforts to advance human rights in Canada since the war. Unions have frequently been in the vanguard of equality rights, helping tackle everything from racial and sex discrimination to sexual orientation and accommodation of persons with disabilities. In many cases, unions have raised such important social issues in collective bargaining and grievances, long before legislative changes followed. Unions have played an important part in pushing for the passage of human rights laws, seeking amendments and improvements to those laws and, when necessary, securing their enforcement. By doing so, unions have successfully advanced human rights and equality on behalf of all Canadians.

This review also demonstrates that labour rights and equality rights are mutually reinforcing. In the postwar period, trade union leaders recognized that the purveyors of economic injustice often exploit discriminatory attitudes and beliefs to divide the labour movement. Not willing to play this divide-and-conquer game, however, unions increasingly employed the strength and stability that came from labour rights protections after the Second World War to become more proactive in promoting wider societal change. Many scholars have observed that Canadian unions have provided critical support and resources to equality-seeking groups, with some expressly attributing this union strength to the postwar settlement that secured important labour rights such as legal recognition, the right to strike, the right to collective bargaining, and the right to negotiate Rand formula[1] union dues. Clearly, the protection of labour rights empowered Canadian unions to advance equality rights for all Canadians.

Racial Discrimination

Discriminatory practices towards racial and ethnic minorities in Canada remained largely unchallenged until after the Second World War. Refusing to hire members of minority groups, declining to rent them lodgings, and denying them service in restaurants or entry to dance halls or skating rinks were all deemed matters of private business in which the state had no right to intervene. Following the war, however, views on these issues began to change.[2]

The Jewish Labour Committee became an important group that organized for social change in this period. Originally established in 1936 with the goal of rescuing Jewish and socialist refugees from Nazi Europe, the group was formed by unions in industries with large numbers of Jewish workers at the time, such as the garment and needle trades. After the war, however, the Jewish Labour Committee built strong bonds with the broader Canadian trade union movement, and jointly organized campaigns for racial equality.[3] The Jewish Labour Committee was successful in persuading other trade union leaders to understand that racism was often used by labour's enemies to weaken the labour movement.[4] In times of economic hardship, racism was a ready scapegoat to mask and distract from the real problems within the prevailing economic system.

The Canadian labour movement suffered many divisions in the first half of the twentieth century. Often, trade unions could be hostile to racial minorities, who were viewed as threats to jobs and higher wages. There was also a major schism between industrial and craft unions, with no single organization representing unions such as exists today with the Canadian Labour Congress (CLC). By the time of the Second World War, there were two competing organizations, the Trades and Labour Congress (TLC) and the Canadian Congress of Labour (CCL). While co-operation between these two organizations was not unheard of, it was certainly rare, with conflict more often the norm.[5]

In Canada and around the world, the horrors of the war caused many to re-evaluate and question previously held beliefs on a range of issues, with decidedly progressive views on race emerging from the global conflict. Canadian trade unionists were no exception. In 1944, the Trades and Labour Congress set up a permanent National Standing Committee on Racial Discrimination to "promote the unity of Canadians of all racial origins, and to combat and counteract any evidence of racial discrimination in industry in particular and life in general." A resolution introduced at the 1947 Canadian Congress of Labour convention called for "vigorous action" in "the fight for full equality for all peoples, regardless of race, colour, creed, or national origin."[6] These kinds of activities may seem familiar to unions today, but it must be remembered that, before the war, unions were often governed by the same racist values as the majority of Canadians.[7]

The Jewish Labour Committee was largely responsible for working with both the TLC and the CCL to put forward these anti-discrimination resolutions and initiatives. In 1947, the Jewish Labour Committee was even successful in bringing these two bodies together in collaboration, establishing the Joint Labour Committee to Combat Racial Intolerance in Toronto.[8] Chapters were later established in cities across Canada, including Vancouver, Winnipeg, Windsor, Hamilton, Montreal, and Halifax.[9] Later called the Labour Committees on Human Rights, these committees' executives were drawn from influential labour leaders belonging to both the TLC and CCL.[10]

These Labour Committees on Human Rights developed a comprehensive approach to social justice through education, legislation, and social action, convincing union members to fight against prejudice and discrimination through massive education campaigns. The approach included the distribution of pamphlets on racism and discrimination, lectures at trade union meetings and labour institutes, and networking with other educational bodies.[11] In providing training to trade union officials and leaders, the committees encouraged discussion of human rights questions, and published a monthly bilingual bulletin, *Canadian Labour Reports*, that was sent to local presidents and secretaries across Canada. Editors ensured that articles about discrimination were authored by leaders from both the TLC and the CCL.[12]

As part of a broader public education strategy, the committees promoted films and radio dramas with anti-discrimination themes and monitored newspapers for biased reporting. For example, a 1949 *Financial Post* article about a strike at Massey Harris identified the local president as being Ukrainian, implying that the strike was the work of foreign agitators. Letters to newspaper editors slowly began to curb the practice of regularly identifying individuals in news stories by their ethnic or racial background.[13] The Labour Committees on Human Rights also encouraged unions to establish fair employment practice committees to involve rank-and-file members in these campaigns. These committees would push for anti-discrimination measures in collective agreements and initiate human rights resolutions at union conventions.[14]

Unions also played an important role in lobbying for legislative change, pushing for the adoption of municipal anti-discrimination bylaws, and maintaining a significant presence in the coalition that met with Ontario Premier Leslie Frost in 1949 and 1950 to lobby for human rights legislation. These efforts led to the adoption of the 1951 *Fair Employment Practices Act* and later the *Fair Accommodation Practices Act* in Ontario.[15]

For unions and the Joint Labour Committees, direct action often involved publicizing blatant acts of discrimination. The United Auto Workers (UAW) engaged in important work exposing and protesting several instances of discrimination against black Canadians in southern Ontario hotels and barbershops during the late 1940s and early 1950s. Meanwhile, pressure from the UAW forced the Windsor Chrysler plant in 1953 to change its policy and end its refusal to hire black Canadians.[16] Unfortunately, racist hiring practices did not significantly diminish after the passage of human rights legislation because provincial enforcement was often lacking or non-existent. In response, the Toronto and Windsor Joint Labour Committees decided to adopt a new tactic to address this problem: the test case.[17]

Generally, a test case refers to an individual who challenges – or tests – the validity, application, or interpretation of a law, and the labour committees had no shortage of ideas to test the new anti-discrimination laws. In one example, a woman using the name Ethel Greenberg would respond to a job advertisement. If she was rejected because "the position was filled," another woman using the pseudonym Janet O'Connor, claiming similar or lesser qualifications, would apply. When O'Connor was offered the job, it would be reported to the authorities as a case of anti-Semitism. In other cases, a black unionist would enter a barbershop, followed shortly thereafter by a white union member. If the former was refused service and the latter offered a haircut, they would go together and report the situation to the authorities.

In the most famous case, the Toronto and Windsor labour committees jointly organized a campaign in Dresden, a town in the heart of southwestern Ontario.[18] In the 1950s, segregation in Dresden was flagrant and widespread, and one could be forgiven for confusing the small Ontario town for one in the southern United States.[19] The Toronto and Windsor committees filed numerous complaints on behalf of black people in Dresden when several restaurants, barbershops, and other establishments openly flouted the new fair practices laws. The owner of one restaurant, Kay's Cafe, made his views well known, publicly declaring that he would not respect the law and would never serve black people in his restaurant. While local authorities were reluctant to prosecute, pressure from the labour committees, and evidence from black and white union volunteers, finally resulted in a 1956 conviction for Kay's Cafe.[20]

As noted by human rights historian Ross Lambertson, "The story of Dresden helps illustrate the significant contribution of trade unionists, especially the Jewish Labour Committee, to the Canadian post-war human rights struggle."[21] In his general history of human rights activism in Canada from 1930 to 1960, Lambertson observed that trade unions were able to pursue human rights issues in the postwar period due to recent governmental protections of labour rights. According to Lambertson, "By the late 1940s, the trade union movement had been strengthened by legal recognition of the workers' right to form unions, go on strike, and bargain collectively, as well as the adoption of the 'Rand Formula,' which encouraged union membership."[22]

The union movement continues to play a very important role in fighting racism in Canadian workplaces and communities. The Canadian Labour Congress released an Anti-Racism Task Force report in 1997 documenting the experiences of racial minorities. The report's framework for action includes recommendations for internal structural changes to unions to address issues of racism while focusing on racism in society more broadly in areas such as immigration, education, housing, the political process, the legal system, and the media. Unions responded to this report by developing anti-racism initiatives, policy statements, educational programs, and anti-racism committees that continue to operate in many unions.[23]

Women's Rights

The labour movement's vigorous action to combat racial discrimination in the postwar period did not extend to fighting for women's equality rights. At that time, many in Canada still believed that women were in fact not equal, and certainly should not enjoy workplace equality. Above all, women were expected to be mothers and to concentrate on their families, and not to "take" jobs that could be occupied by men. Unfortunately, union activists with deep convictions on racial discrimination remained blind to sex discrimination.

From a twenty-first-century perspective, it's difficult to imagine the profound discrimination faced by Canadian women in the 1950s workplace. Paying men and women differently for the exact same job was common and was justified by the argument that men were expected to support a family while women were not. Generally, it was understood that a woman was in the workforce on an exceptional and temporary basis, namely until she fulfilled her proper societal role and got married. To further reinforce the prevailing social norms of inequality, sexism, and gender roles, many employers in the 1950s, including the federal government, maintained a policy of dismissing women who chose to become married. Needless to say, views about pregnancy and the workplace were similarly unenlightened.

Attitudes began to shift from the mid-1950s to the late 1960s as women entered the workforce in much greater numbers, with female membership in trade unions growing as well. Only 4 per cent of married women worked outside the home in 1941. This number grew rapidly to 22 per cent in 1961 and 30 per cent in 1968.[24] By 1981, more than 50 per cent of women, including married women, were in the Canadian paid labour force.[25]

This shift in labour force participation also changed the face of the labour movement, albeit more slowly. In 1962, women were 16 per cent of Canadian union membership, growing to 28 per cent by 1977 and 40 per cent in the 1990s.[26] Working-class women with unions to back them up became some of the most assertive opponents of both marriage and pregnancy prohibitions in the workplace. In most cases, this meant fighting for equality one grievance at a time. A review of all reported labour arbitration decisions from 1948 to 1969 reveals that over half of discharge cases dealing with female employees concerned dismissals for reasons related to matrimony or pregnancy.[27]

Despite many setbacks, unions persisted in grievances seeking basic equality for women. In one notable 1965 case, a Pacific Western Airlines flight attendant with the Canadian Airline Flight Attendants Association (CALFAA) grieved her employer's policy of automatic dismissal for marriage, one followed by most airlines of the day, including government-owned Air Canada. Airlines wished "to maintain the image of the young, attractive flight attendant," and therefore kept a firm marriage bar and fired stewardesses at thirty-two years of age.[28]

At her arbitration hearing, grievor Dianne Konderat and her union argued that any term of employment that required termination upon marriage was "void and unenforceable as being contrary to public policy." The union cited several European cases in support of this position, but the arbitration board chose instead to rely on American cases that upheld the marriage bar. In rejecting Konderat's grievance, the arbitration board stressed that a woman's proper social role was to be "home with her husband" and found that a stewardess's marriage might be "jeopardized" by her job.[29]

While the *Konderat* decision was disappointing, it articulated in clear language the entrenched discriminatory attitudes and rationalizations that were common at the time. But it was not the end of the issue, as it illustrated how the grievance system provided an avenue for women to challenge these kinds of harmful stereotypes, especially with the resources of a union behind them. It also provided a useful organizing tool for a union-led public campaign. After the *Konderat* decision, CALFAA contacted the B.C. Federation of Labour and the Canadian Labour Congress to help exert public and political pressure on the airline industry. The public campaign achieved results, as Air Canada relaxed its marriage bar the following year. Within a few years, other airlines also dropped the archaic policy, and the pernicious practice of marriage as a barrier to employment ended in Canada.[30]

With a large number of women members, it was unsurprising that CALFAA would challenge issues that directly affected women. But other unions also took up the cause of equality. When the United Auto Workers, for example, held its first conference for women workers in 1964, it called for full equity. In 1965, the Ontario Federation of Labour set up its first women's committee. Responding to increasing pressure from their members, other unions began to hold conferences, educational sessions, and training programs. Women's committees and caucuses were established at the national and local levels to help identify priority concerns and to develop strategies and tactics to advance those issues.[31]

In the 1960s, trade unions were also negotiating collective agreement terms that benefited women, including pay equity and maternity leave. These advances for unionized women through collective bargaining were later extended to all women workers by different provincial statutes.[32] Unions also played a role in the federal government adopting maternity benefits in the Unemployment Insurance (UI) program in 1971. Discussion about women's entitlement to UI during pregnancy and after birth was debated as early as 1954 at a Trades and Labour Congress convention, and while unions did not consistently lobby for maternity benefits in the 1960s, the issue was certainly raised periodically; for example, unions made submissions to the Royal Commission on the Status of Women calling on the UI system to allow for maternity benefits.[33]

It would be inaccurate to portray the union movement's support for women's issues as fully committed and unflagging throughout its history.[34] Academics have sometimes described early union support for women's issues as "reluctant,"[35] and the Royal Commission on the Status of Women carried out studies showing that many male unionists in the late 1960s had "an ambivalent attitude towards women in the work world."[36] Women unionists who made a presentation to the royal commission on behalf of the Canadian Union of Public Employees (CUPE) felt it was important to state for the record that the labour movement could be doing better:

> CUPE does not feel that the labour movement does enough to fight discrimination against working women. . . . The majority of female workers who fight for true equality do so without the wholehearted support of their fellow trade unionists, male and female.[37]

In the 1970s and 1980s, many unions and labour organizations adopted proactive steps to be more responsive to women's issues, from hiring full-time staff to study and co-ordinate equity issues and organizing national conferences on women's issues to adopting affirmative action measures within their organizations. For example, the Canadian Labour Congress designated a minimum of six women vice presidents, and many unions have embraced women- and family-friendly policies such as free child care at union conventions.[38]

Perhaps most importantly, trade unions have consistently expended significant resources over the years litigating women's issues and creating a range of landmark legal precedents. There are many, but a few significant ones include the following:

- In the 1987 *Robichaud* case, the Supreme Court of Canada redefined the meaning of sexual harassment, and set out an employer's strict duty to maintain a harassment-free workplace.[39]
- In the 1989 *Brooks* case, a union was responsible for backing three part-time grocery store cashiers all the way to the Supreme Court of Canada and establishing the principle that discrimination on the basis of pregnancy is sex discrimination. Significantly, the union persuaded the Supreme Court to overturn a judgment from ten years earlier where a less enlightened Court stated, "Any inequality between the sexes in this area is not created by legislation but by nature."[40]
- With the 1999 *Meiorin* case, the Supreme Court of Canada tossed out a fitness test for a female firefighter because the employer could not show the standard was a "bona fide occupational requirement" and essential to the job. The case established the "duty to accommodate" test which protects all women and people with disabilities in the workplace.[41]
- The Public Service Alliance of Canada (PSAC) won the largest damages award in Canadian legal history with its $3.6 billion pay equity case against the federal government.[42]

Different academics have suggested that unions have been able to take a leading role on equality cases due to the stability associated with labour rights protections. Joan Sangster observed that stronger collective bargaining protections in the postwar period offered women new avenues to challenge the law and social norms concerning work and pregnancy.[43] One study of the *Meiorin* case observes that "the financial and political support of her union and the fact that the general membership was sympathetic to the equality dimension of her claim, were both crucial to her success."[44]

While there may have been some bumps in the road, there can be little doubt that unions have been on the front lines fighting for working women's rights for fifty years. From early grievances involving dismissal for pregnancy or marriage, to more recent cases requiring employers to modify work schedules to accommodate parental obligations,[45] unions have continued to advance women's rights up to the present day.

Disability

Human rights statutes enacted across Canada from the 1940s to the 1960s largely prohibited racial, sexual, and religious discrimination, but they did not address physical or mental disability until 1976, when provinces started amending human rights legislation.[46] While unions were already negotiating protections for disabled workers through collective bargaining, the rights of persons with disabilities seemed to be a low priority for the labour movement until the 1990s. As a result of advances in the jurisprudence, union litigation for disabled workers exploded during that decade. Increased awareness of workplace disability issues led to an environment in which every local steward in the country now likely knows the phrase "duty to accommodate."

Prior to the 1980s, disability discrimination cases generally involved disputes about fitness for work and whether an employee with a disability could safely perform the duties of a particular position. However, there was no consideration of situations where employees' disabilities prevented them from doing a job without assistance of some kind.[47] The duty to accommodate – that is, the concept that an employer should modify a position, schedule, or workplace rule so the impact of an employee's disability on his or her capacity to perform a job was minimized or eliminated – was relatively unknown.

The emergence of the duty to accommodate in human rights jurisprudence reflected "an extraordinary sea change" for the rights of persons with disabilities. Their legal position was transformed "from sufferance to status" as Canadian law embraced substantive equality.[48] Following the Supreme Court of Canada's clarification of the duty in 1990, unions brought a huge number of disability accommodation cases to labour arbitrators, reshaping the modern workplace for persons with disabilities. Law Professor Michael Lynk describes this profound change:

An employee with a disability is still required to productively perform the core aspects of her job in order to maintain the employment relationship, but that has now become subsumed by the considerable obligations acquired by the employer through the accommodation duty. To satisfy these new legal responsibilities, an employer has to be prepared to make changes to the organization of work, to the tools required to perform the particular job, to the assignment of duties for the work position, to the content and application of work policies, and even to the attitudes of the workforce. And the pace of change triggered by all this has been profound. Human resource practices have been revolutionized as disabilities and capacities in the workplace have become understood in an entirely new light.[49]

Since 1990, unions have been responsible for bringing a large number of grievances to arbitration, creating the body of case law that has defined – and continues to define – the parameters of an employer's responsibility to employees with disabilities. These sorts of grievances are often the most expensive to litigate, usually requiring medical experts and complex legal arguments. Yet unions have continued to provide the resources to fight these cases, aggressively protecting the rights of disabled employees.

The most important Canadian case in disability law and the duty to accommodate is *Meiorin*, a 1999 decision that actually involved sex discrimination. As explained above, Ms. Meiorin was a female firefighter who could perform the job, but was unable to pass a newly imposed aerobic capacity test designed for men. Fully supported by Ms. Meiorin's union – the B.C. Government and Services Employees Union – this grievance began in labour arbitration, went through the B.C. courts, and ended up at the Supreme Court of Canada.[50] The Supreme Court's judgment made it clear that the duty to accommodate employees was a heavy one, requiring employers to take all steps necessary to the point of "undue hardship." The *Meiorin* standard is now the law of the land, positively affecting employees in unionized and non-unionized workplaces alike.

Unions have also become more assertive in promoting the rights of disabled workers through collective bargaining and public education and campaigns.[51] Most unions have established committees that develop strategies to promote disability rights within the union movement and in the workplace.[52] In 1994, the Canadian Labour Congress formed a Disability Rights Working Group, and in 1999 it created a new position on its executive council, vice president (person with disabilities). The CLC later held its first National Disability Rights Conference in 2000, and launched its MORE (Mobilize, Organize, Represent and Educate) campaign the following year. In 2004, the CLC published *The MORE We Get Together: Disability Rights and Collective Bargaining Manual*, which contained pertinent information, self-audit checklists, and sample collective agreement clauses.[53]

As with the areas of racial and sex discrimination, scholars have linked union support for disability rights with the strength that unions enjoy from labour rights protections. Lynk has suggested that unions are in a position to be strong advocates for disability rights because of their statutorily protected presence in workplaces. As a result, he says, "unions have the resources to litigate a broad spectrum of disability accommodation issues, and the staying power to police the implementation of disability accommodation settlements and orders."[54]

Sexual Orientation

Nearly twenty years before the last province in Canada finally added protection for sexual orientation to its human rights legislation,[55] a Canadian Labour Congress convention in 1980 passed a resolution calling for the inclusion of sexual orientation in all provincial human rights codes, the *Canadian Human Rights Act*, and the *Canadian Charter of Rights and Freedoms*.[56] Trade union support for lesbians and gays later extended to collective bargaining for "no discrimination" and spousal benefit clauses in collective agreements, litigating grievances and court challenges, and funding educational programs and community groups. Today, most unions and labour organizations in Canada have Pride committees and conferences dedicated to equality issues for the LGBTQ community.

Following the CLC's call to action in 1980, a number of unions tried to negotiate the inclusion of sexual orientation in the non-discrimination clauses of their collective agreements. The few that were successful in the early 1980s included public employers such as Canada Post, universities, and libraries.[57] Governments, however, proved more difficult. The Public Service Alliance of Canada, for example, tried to add sexual orientation to its collective agreements with the federal government for six years before the addition was finally obtained through binding conciliation in 1986.[58]

Negotiating for spousal benefits proved even more difficult for unions. Some employers seemed content to add sexual orientation to the "no discrimination" language in collective agreements, provided the benefits provisions included a definition for "spouse" that could not encompass same-sex couples. In other words, equality was fine so long as it did not cost any money. Unions tried to get around this bargaining tactic by filing grievances for spousal benefits anyway, arguing that the "no discrimination" clause should supersede the narrow definition of "spouse" in the employer's benefits plan. While these grievances routinely lost in the late 1980s and early 1990s,[59] unions continued to pursue them until, finally, they started winning.[60]

While in 1990 the Canadian Labour Congress urged all unions to make bargaining for same-sex benefits a priority, in reality, negotiations seldom achieved that result and litigation was required.[61] With the changes to human rights legislation in the 1990s, employers started to routinely lose these cases, and same-sex benefits finally became the norm in collective agreements. Notably, unions also helped fund litigation on equality for same-sex couples that did not relate directly to their members or workplaces. For example, CUPE instigated a court challenge to the exclusively heterosexual definition of "spouse" in the *Income Tax Act*.[62] In other cases, unions donated money to EGALE (a lobby group originally known as Equality for Gays and Lesbians Everywhere) to participate in rights litigation.[63]

Unions have also contributed to broader campaigns of consciousness raising, funding community groups and educational programs on topics such as homophobia and AIDS.[64] Many unions organized Pride or Pink Triangle committees to monitor and enhance union commitment to gay and lesbian equality.

Homosexual rights in Canada have become commonplace and uncontroversial, and same-sex marriage is broadly accepted. But in the 1980s, it was a very different story, with lesbians and gays often facing serious harassment, stigma, and legal discrimination. In that environment, unions at bargaining tables were asking employers for "no discrimination" clauses and same-sex benefits and, while change did not always occur through negotiation, a multipronged approach also saw the labour movement put their resources behind legal battles, from grievances for spousal benefits to constitutional challenges.

A History of Solidarity

In Canada, unions have adopted an expansive view of their role in improving the well-being of their members. As the courts have recognized, unions are not limited to advancing the economic interests of their members through the negotiation and administration of collective agreements. Unions are expected to "be players in the broader political, economic and social debates in society" and end discrimination towards their members.[65]

It is in this broader role that unions have pushed for social and legal change for equality-seeking groups such as racial minorities, women, persons with disabilities, and gays and lesbians. Over the past sixty years, unions have often provided critical support to these disadvantaged groups in achieving, securing, and protecting important gains. Unions have also leveraged their strength to lobby for legislative changes, and then have engaged in litigation to create important legal precedents. While unions have played an important part in achieving social justice for their more vulnerable members, these precedents have often had ripple effects for all members of society, regardless of union membership.

Many authors have separately attributed the active role of Canadian unions in broad societal issues to the strength and stability they enjoy from the postwar settlement that established many legal rights and protections for organized labour.[66] Canada's experience is in contrast with that of the United States, where legal changes have rolled back labour rights and limited the ability of American unions to similarly engage in issues beyond the workplace. U.S. labour scholars have lamented these differences with Canada, with some suggesting laws such as the infamous Taft-Hartley Act have "pushed unions into narrowing their horizons from broad social visions to the more modest goals of servicing their existing members."[67]

Given this history of solidarity, equality-seeking groups should be very concerned about recent efforts to attack or erode labour rights, a strategy that has undermined U.S. unions over the years. Indeed, the weakening of unions is but one part of a broader attack on the capacity of progressive communities to organize, negotiate for and, when necessary, litigate on behalf some of Canada's most vulnerable people. As history shows, rights won by labour inevitably become rights enjoyed by the whole population. The old labour movement slogan that never seems to lose its currency certainly applies here: an attack against one is an attack against all.

Seven

A Changing Union Tide Hurts Vulnerable Workers

A Case Study on Migrant Workers

Naveen Mehta

IN NORTH AMERICA TODAY, income inequality is the highest it has been in almost a century.[1] This state of affairs takes place amid ongoing attacks on union members by governments and employers in both the United States and Canada.[2] At the same time, corporations, even after the devastation of the 2008 recession, are reaping record profits.[3] These realities do not operate in isolated silos; they are no mere coincidence. They are, instead, the yin and yang of broad social and economic decay.

In contrast, for almost thirty years after the Second World War, the union tide rose, raising many social and economic boats along with it. Unfortunately, the reverse applies as well. When the union tide is in decline, the social and economic requirements of a thriving society suffer.

One boat that rises with an ascending tide is the ability of unions to protect, promote, and advocate for the most vulnerable people in our society: those who have generally been forgotten or disregarded by the state. For over a century, the labour movement has worked on behalf of the most vulnerable workers. This work spans wars and domestic conflicts, and raises fundamental questions of the role that class and other markers of inequality play in our society and our unions.

A poignant Canadian example of a group that has been fundamentally abandoned by the state at all levels, and to some degree by civil society, is migrant workers.[4] Arguably, no group better exemplifies workers in the most precarious and vulnerable of employment situations. Only in an environment where unions thrive can essential supports begin to be made available to them. My analysis is that the predicament of many so-called low-skilled migrant workers in Canada is, at best, modern-day indentured servitude. At worst, it has been described as modern-day slavery.

As of December 2011, there were an overwhelming 300,000 migrant workers in Canada.[5] The number of migrant workers has almost tripled over the last decade. At the same time, Canada has stagnated at approximately 0.7 per cent of the population arriving as permanent residents.[6] In 2011, approximately 250,000 permanent residents were admitted.[7] These two groups form the new Canadian workforce, with migrant workers serving as the commodified, more easily exploitable, and just-in-time disposable workforce. The influx of migrant workers into Canada takes place at the cost of nation building and of a robust and sustainable immigration regime.

Over the past five years, many Canadians have heard about the perils migrant workers face. But they may not be aware of the critical role that unions play in protecting those in precarious work, social, and economic situations. In the courts, at the workplace, in the fields, in traditional and social media, on the internet and on the streets – the labour movement and, in particular, UFCW Canada have been crucial in shaping the dialogue relating to migrant workers in Canada.

Settlement agencies, by aiding migrant workers in their adjustment to temporary life in Canada, have undoubtedly lowered the level of suffering they experience. Settlement agencies provide supports such as teaching English as an additional language (EAL), offering guidance about where to find services, and encouraging employers to not exploit those who are so easily exploitable. But while these agencies play a considerable and positive role, my analysis begins with some elementary questions: What effective protections are there for migrant workers in their workplaces, where they are arguably the most vulnerable? After all, work is the reason for migrant workers being in Canada in the first place. Moreover, who is policing the employers who employ hundreds of thousands of migrant workers annually?

The Realities of Migrant Workers

Migrant workers are among the most vulnerable workers in our society, and the way our governments continue to allow some employers to commodify them is despicable. It is not just greedy; it is mean-hearted. Migrant workers are too often exploited in almost every aspect of their lives – even by the government. For instance, they cannot effectively collect their Canada Pension Plan benefits, because the federal government does not make the workers aware of their eligibility. Nonetheless, migrant workers pay tens of millions of dollars annually into the program. Similarly, Employment Insurance premiums are deducted from the paycheques of seasonal migrant workers. These workers receive marginal benefits in comparison to permanent residents or Canadian citizens. One might say that migrant workers make an involuntary biweekly donation to the Canadian taxpayer.

The Temporary Foreign Worker Program was designed to ensure that migrant workers would lack the effective mobility to leave one job and seek another. The work permits issued by Citizenship and Immigration Canada securely fasten them to a single employer. In thousands of cases that we have documented in the UFCW Canada Human Rights Department, the single-employer work permit allows unscrupulous employers to use this power as either a stick, forcing migrant workers to work below the limits of their often minimal contracts, or as a carrot, promising immigration to Canada where it is unattainable. Linguistic barriers, employer-provided housing – sometimes similar to the shantytowns of the developing world – and severe racial discrimination are just a sprinkling of the hardships faced by migrant workers living in communities across Canada.[8]

UFCW Canada Responds

UFCW Canada's engagement with migrant workers began with legal and settlement matters for migrant agricultural workers. Many agricultural workers in Ontario are migrant workers, under the Seasonal

Agriculture Workers Program. In the 1990s it became clear that the legislative barrier for farm workers in Ontario to join a union and to collectively bargain – a legislative right available to almost all other workers – had no rational basis in law and was fundamentally unjust. Since farm workers could not join a union, UFCW Canada responded by establishing ten Agricultural Workers Support Centres to help deal with the myriad of problems they faced.

UFCW Canada also fought the unreasonable ban on collective bargaining to the Supreme Court of Canada in a case called *Dunmore*.[9] There were some successes.[10] The Conservative regime of the day, however, enacted legislation that did not adequately protect farm workers in the process of collective bargaining, thus defeating one of the primary benefits of unionization. UFCW Canada then went back to the courts in *Ontario (Attorney General)* v. *Fraser*.[11] Although this case was successful at the Ontario Court of Appeal, UFCW Canada did not have the same success at the Supreme Court of Canada, and the union did not achieve the unfettered collective bargaining rights for farm workers that we had hoped for.

Currently, UFCW Canada is litigating the alleged blacklisting of migrant farm workers in British Columbia, which involves an unfair labour practice complaint that initially named the Mexican government. A recent victory in Quebec successfully challenged section 21 of the *Quebec Labour Code* dealing with agricultural workers, many of whom are migrant workers from the global South. This section stipulated that agricultural workers were excluded from collective bargaining on farms that have three or fewer employees working on a year-round basis.[12] UFCW Canada has been able to do all of this with very little financial input from migrant workers. It is a strategy based on vision: the union has taken the strategic road of advocating for those who could not effectively advocate for themselves.

Out of our membership of over 250,000, several thousand are migrant workers who are employed outside of agriculture in industries such as fisheries, hospitality, health care, and food processing. We have therefore developed some ingenious programs to aid these workers not only at their workplaces, but in society as well. This approach recalls the origins of the labour movement, where a union was not limited to the four corners of the factory but was a fundamental social support system.

One of UFCW Canada's significant successes has been negotiations with large employers to effectively make the draconian Temporary Foreign Worker Program into a permanent immigration program. Several UFCW Canada local unions negotiate with employers so that every person arriving to work in these unionized workplaces has the potential to be entered into the relevant Provincial Nominee Program – typically the Alberta or Manitoba programs. Since 2004, the union has helped thousands of migrant workers out of the wrong immigration line, and placed them in the right line on their way to permanent residency and citizenship.

If you get a job in a UFCW Canada meatpacking plant as a migrant worker, the union ensures you are placed on the road to permanent residency. Your counterparts in non-unionized settings are more likely – especially given recent legislative changes – to be on the road home by the end of four years or sooner. And in many of the unionized workplaces, it is the union, not the employer, that greets migrant worker when they get off the plane.

These workers are covered by strong and mature collective agreements and receive the wages, benefits, and working conditions of all other unionized workers in those plants. It is an equity-based approach to counteract the exploitive foundation of the Temporary Foreign Worker Program. A robust union provides fundamental protections not only in the workplace, but also in the area of immigration.

UFCW Canada polices health care, financial, and education issues. The union files Employment Insurance and Canada Pension Plan benefits, prepares and files income tax returns, and organizes social events to celebrate, for example, Jamaican Independence Day or Cinco de Mayo. The UFCW Canada/Agriculture Workers Alliance Support Centres allow migrant workers free calls home and connect workers to faith groups, emergency health care, dental treatment, union scholarships for their children back home, and even advice on where milk, bread, and eggs are on sale.

UFCW Canada extends its protective services to housing as well. Local union representatives often inspect housing before new migrant workers arrive to ensure it meets with municipal housing codes and that the housing is appropriate given the number of workers who are to live there. Contemplate the following situation: You are new to Canada. You do not speak English or French. You have no family here and only new acquaintances from your home country. You are alone. You are paid, but you may not know if you are being paid the right amount. You have no idea what laws are available to protect you, much less how you would utilize those laws. Housing is deducted directly from your cheque.

UFCW Canada has found situations where, in a four-bedroom

house, workers are charged as much as $500 per month per worker as rent. Some workers ended up with less than $600 per month after all of their bills had been paid. One example of how much greed is possible occurred in this same four-bedroom house. Four men slept in each bedroom, and two men slept in the living room: eighteen men in a house with two washrooms and only two showers. These men worked the day shift. When they went off to work, the night shift returned, and a separate group of eighteen men slept in the same beds. There were thirty-six men living in a four-bedroom house, paying a total of $18,000 per month rent for a house with an estimated purchase price of $110,000. The employer was unconcerned by the situation. But through the help of the union, this abuse was ended.

On the international front, UFCW Canada has numerous bilateral agreements and mutual support pacts with a variety of state and municipal governments across Mexico, as well as with non-governmental organizations in Canada and in the global South.

Concerning education, the union introduces workers to English as an additional language education so that they fit the criteria for the Provincial Nominee Program. In fact, UFCW Canada Local 832 in Manitoba is one of the largest providers of EAL education in the province, and has training centres to meet the needs of its migrant worker members.

In 2012, UFCW Canada established (on the initial suggestion of my eight-year-old daughter Tara) the Migrant Worker Family Support Fund to help the survivors and families of the victims of the horrific Hampstead tragedy that killed eleven workers and severely injured three others on a rural road in Ontario. In a period of four months, with the support of the labour movement, community groups, advocates, and working people from coast to coast to coast, the fund was able to raise and disperse $226,000.

And the list goes on. From showing migrant workers how to bank to creating community associations, UFCW Canada operates as an established settlement agency, as a successful immigration advocate and, of course, as a union at the workplace. Only in an environment where a robust labour movement thrives can there be meaningful reductions in the destitution and despair faced by migrant workers. These are the types of things that a vigorous trade union movement is capable of. These are the boats that rise in the union tide.

All this is accomplished with almost nothing from the pockets of the most vulnerable – or from government. This is ironic, given that many companies and individuals behave as if migrant workers represent an opportunity for exploitation and maximizing profits, whether at the workplace or at the grocery store. Sadly, the irony continues when we look at the role of some governments, such as the federal Conservatives in Ottawa, who have fine-tuned the skill of looking away from the pleas of migrant workers for basic protections and essential legislative enforcement.

Now contemplate where migrant workers in Canada would be without unions such as UFCW Canada. The most vulnerable and the most exploited are those who are most easily forgotten. When left unchecked, an increased Temporary Foreign Worker Program with individuals who have no path to permanent residency will inevitably exacerbate economic inequality and social dysfunction. UFCW Canada has learned that Canada does not require a robust Temporary Foreign Worker Program. It requires, rather, a return to a robust and sustainable immigration regime.

The Steps Forward

An engaged and motivated union movement working for the benefit of migrant workers has allowed thousands to be brought in from the periphery. In this area, the union movement not only does what it should do but also supports a longer-term strategic plan of quantitative and qualitative growth. The strategies and actions described in this chapter allow the union movement to renew itself and to create a more robust, diverse, and inclusive movement. The labour movement continues to evolve into a force that has the voices, experiences, and expertise of a wider range of perspectives.

Challenges will undoubtedly continue. We must continuously develop an insightful vision and pursue bold steps. Whether the labour movement thrives or only survives will depend on whether it brings those on the periphery of society, and very importantly, those who are on the margins of the movement, into a more inclusive, reflective, and diverse labour movement.[13] Based on their history, unions have the propensity and ability to empower working people – whether they are migrant workers or members of other historically oppressed groups – to obliterate barriers. That continues to be our greatest challenge going forward.

Part 3

Constitutional Protection of Labour Rights

Eight

Who Owns *Charter* Values?

A Mobilization Strategy for the Labour Movement

Fay Faraday and Eric Tucker

AN IMPORTANT COMPONENT of any successful mobilization strategy is a compelling story about why something is worth fighting for. Sometimes an issue touches such a raw nerve that it activates the broad public support and deep commitment needed to sustain the fight. But often it does not. In those latter cases, linking the particular struggle to a larger vision that explains or amplifies the issue's significance helps build support and sustain mobilization. For example, while it is important to oppose a demand at the bargaining table for yet another concession – even while the employer's profits are healthy – or to protest against legislation that strips away yet another piece of protective labour law or erodes collective bargaining rights, it is also important to explain how that specific fight advances a particular vision of a just workplace and society. Without that broader vision, it is more difficult to mobilize people to win the immediate fight. Equally important, it also leaves unchanged the ideological context in which employer and government attacks on workers' rights occur, making it easier for them to continue.

Central to any compelling story are certain core values. The

Canadian Foundation for Labour Rights has adopted the motto that "labour rights are human rights" and identifies democracy, economic equality, and social justice as three key norms that labour rights promote. On a practical level, how can that vision be spread among trade union members, working people, and social movement allies so that they are mobilized to struggle for its realization? How can that vision gain the broader public acceptance required to shape the moral economy so that employers, politicians, and maybe even judges feel that they cannot ignore it without suffering a loss of legitimacy?

Among possible answers to these questions is an exploration of how to employ democratic or popular constitutionalism as a mobilizing strategy. The values expressed in the *Canadian Charter of Rights and Freedoms* have the potential to frame a compelling narrative of social justice. Can *Charter* values create a space to build alternatives to dominant political and legal narratives? Can *Charter* values help bridge progressive social movements in order to broaden alliances and find common cause? Can these values highlight what is at stake in a struggle? Who gets to control the meaning of fundamental rights and freedoms in a free and democratic society? By understanding the concept and history of democratic constitutionalism and how it has been engaged by a variety of social movements, it is possible to envision how incorporating this approach could help tell the compelling story needed for successful mobilization.

What Is Democratic Constitutionalism?

Democratic constitutionalism may be described as the use of constitutional discourse or language by social movements to establish that the claims they make are supported by the fundamental and widely shared norms of a just society, all of which governments are obliged to respect. This definition is intentionally open-ended because it aims to encompass a range of practices in different times and places.

This concept illuminates the fact that constitutional rights and values do not live exclusively – or even most importantly – in the realm of litigation. As Canada's current Chief Justice has written, "The *Charter* is not some holy grail which only judicial initiates of the superior courts may touch. The *Charter* belongs to the people."[1] Hence, constitutional rights and values are equally the stuff of daily political struggle, and social movements can wrap their claims in the mantle of constitutional values, even if those claims are not judicially recognized. While this may be done in part in the hope of influencing legal outcomes, adopting the language of constitutional values also endows claims and movements with a higher level of democratic legitimacy and leverage – perhaps even entitlement – all of which can help mobilize support.

Notably, democratic constitutionalism doesn't have any pre-set content. It describes a practice of popular constitutional claims-making that can be used by socially conservative movements as well as by progressive ones. Given its content-neutral quality, it is important to recognize that this terrain is in play politically, so there is great value in naming it as a site of struggle, mapping its contours, and assessing its pros and cons as a tool for progressive organizing.

While constitutions set out many fundamental laws on the operation of democracy, they also establish fundamental rights, freedoms, and values, such as the *Charter*'s guarantee of the rights to life, liberty, and security of the person, as well as a right to equality and freedom from discrimination on prohibited grounds. Added to those guarantees are freedoms of speech, assembly, conscience, and religion and, importantly for workers, freedom of association.

In addition to these rights and freedoms that are expressly written in the *Charter*, courts also frequently reiterate that the *Charter* is intended to advance the unwritten "values and principles of a free and democratic society"[2] and that these *Charter* values should be used to assist in interpreting *Charter* rights and freedoms. For example, in the 2007 *B.C. Health Services* case[3] – in which the Court held that freedom of association protects a procedural right to collective bargaining – the Supreme Court identified the values of human dignity, liberty, respect for individual autonomy, and enhancement of democracy as *Charter* values. The Court held that one reason for extending constitutional protection to collective bargaining was because it promoted these very *Charter* values.

While fundamental rights and freedoms are set out by the *Charter*, they are nonetheless open to interpretation. Of particular interest to workers are the freedom of association and the right to equality. Both of these rights – which most directly engage notions of collective action and the redistribution of power – have been the subject of deep disagreement among the judiciary, and their legal meanings have changed repeatedly over the relatively short life of the *Charter*. Unwritten *Charter* values, because they are implied, are even more open to debate. As a result, there is room to argue both over what values should be identified as *Charter* values and over the meaning of those values.

Given the open-ended and unstable status of *Charter* values, they have become a location of struggle as competing groups endeavour to have their interpretation and vision legitimized as constitutionally significant. Because they are specifically about the principles of a free and democratic society, a debate about *Charter* values focuses attention directly on what, in substance, people want their lived experience of democracy to deliver. But who gets to decide? Who owns *Charter* values?

At one level, as a matter of formal law, the answer is obvious: the courts own *Charter* values, since their interpretation is authoritative. If the Supreme Court of Canada declares, as it did in 1987, that freedom of association does not protect collective bargaining, then governments are free to enact legislation that suspends or ends collective bargaining without having to worry about the validity of their laws. If the Court changes its mind, as it did in 2007, and decides that freedom of association does protect a limited right to collective bargaining, then governments have to think twice about whether legislation that interferes with that right will pass constitutional muster. And, if the Court changes its mind yet again, and proclaims that freedom of association protects only a limited right to good faith consultation, then governments may enjoy more power to attack collective bargaining rights.

Of course, no formal ruling necessarily alters working people's experiential understanding of the fundamental importance, urgency, and necessity of robust and meaningful rights to collective action in a free and democratic society, or their sense of betrayal when these rights are curtailed or denied. It is this tension between formal pronouncements and popular resonance/dissonance that creates the opportunity for democratic constitutional mobilization.

In a constitutional order, judges don't just expect their judgments to be obeyed; they also want them to be convincing, not just to lawyers, but also to Canadians generally. Their project is an imperial one in that, ideally, they would like the vision embodied in their judgments to colonize the minds of Canadians so that it is both authoritative and broadly accepted or hegemonic. That apparent goal, however, will never be completely successful. Although judges enjoy a great deal of societal prestige and their judgments will influence some of the people some of the time, we know that they are incapable of convincing all of the people all of the time. Popular, reflexive acceptance of all the law, including constitutional law as pronounced from the bench, is always incomplete in democratic, diverse, and class-divided societies. Thus, the judiciary's imperial project exists in tension with democratic claims that emerge from social movements and civil society groups that embrace a different normative vision and narrative of community and history from which they derive different understandings of what constitutional law is or should be.

Democratic constitutionalism lives in the gap between authoritative judgment by the courts and popular values, discourses, and narratives, and it is this space that we want to explore. What is the scope for democratic constitutionalism to influence judicial interpretations of the *Charter*, to mobilize trade union members and allies into action, and to reshape public discourse more generally?

We do not claim that the cultivation of democratic constitutionalism is necessarily the best way forward. It is, however, a tool worth examining. We begin this process by turning to some historical moments when democratic constitutionalism was central to movement discourse and mobilization.

The Rich History of Democratic Constitutionalism

English Radicals and the Constitutional Rights of Free-Born Englishman

There is a rich history of popular or democratic constitutionalism in England, the United States and, to a lesser extent, Canada, but it is not well known outside the scholarly community. In England, the period straddling the turn of the nineteenth century – after the Napoleonic wars and at the beginning of the Industrial Revolution – was a time of upheaval and uncertainty. The political state was built on a relatively narrow base of property holders who elected representatives to Parliament. What are now viewed as basic civil liberties, such as freedom of the press, freedom of assembly, and freedom to petition the government, were severely constrained. They were further restricted when, in the aftermath of the French Revolution, the government feared Jacobin conspiracies and popular uprisings.[4]

English radicals were meanwhile challenging the existing order by demanding universal male suffrage and recognition of civil liberties. They framed their demands in a "constitutional idiom," arguing that suffrage and civil liberties were the rights to which all free-born Englishmen were entitled under the British Constitution. While England did not have a written constitution at the time, there existed a very clear understanding of an unwritten one, constructed out of English history and drawing on key political and legal events, from the

Norman Conquest, *Magna Carta*, and *Habeas Corpus* to the *Bill of Rights* and the *Act of Settlement*. The meaning of that unwritten constitution, however, was deeply contested. Indeed, competing political groups invoked the language of constitutionalism to support very different political projects, and in so doing provided diverse interpretations of English constitutional history that, as one English historian aptly put it, "was all things to all Englishmen."[5] Moreover, the judiciary could not impose an authoritative interpretation of that unwritten constitution in its decisions because judges did not enjoy the power to review legislation and pronounce on its constitutionality.

Given its contested nature, why did English radicals wrap their claims in the mantle of English constitutionalism? Part of the answer was strategic. Jacobin practice and discourse were fiercely repressed in the 1790s, as were upsurges of plebeian radicalism at the end of the Napoleonic Wars and then again in the late 1830s. The strategic shift in emphasis to popular constitutionalist rhetoric and actions – such as petitioning and holding conventions – was in part a defensive reaction that aimed to protect a space for radical agitation. By framing claims in a constitutional idiom, radicals hoped to avoid further repressive state measures.

In addition, when radicals were arrested and tried for sedition or treason – charges that in their essence alleged advocacy or involvement in efforts to overthrow lawful authority, as distinct from an effort to reform it – popular constitutionalism offered a legal defence strategy. It provided the defendant an opportunity to win acquittal by convincing a jury that the rights to public assembly, petition, and universal suffrage were embedded in the ancient constitution, and that it was the authorities themselves who were acting illegitimately when they arrested people for publicly demanding those same rights.

Popular constitutionalism, however, was not just a defensive strategy; it was also a proactive one adopted because it resonated widely with "The People" – the (male) population that was excluded from the political state because they did not meet existing property qualifications. According to one historian, "Radicalism's leaders sensed that the constitutionalist idiom and repertoire of action endowed their movement with the sort of authority needed to mobilize the force of popular radicalism nationally, to create a mass insurgent movement."[6]

This perception was rooted in the understanding that the English constitution was a powerful national symbol or trope, perhaps in part because its meaning was so malleable that it permitted people of differing views to embrace it. But it was precisely because of its cultural

and political significance that the meaning of English constitutionalism was important to contest. Abandoning the ground of constitutionalism to one's enemies created the risk of allowing them to
occupy that space and use it as a base for launching damaging political, legal, and ideological attacks against one's cause. Another historian summarized the position succinctly:

> Constitutionalism allowed radicals to claim legitimacy for their
> demands and their actions, a legitimacy sanctioned by standards
> recognized nationwide; which was why their rivals could not allow
> them to monopolise this idiom, but had to contest their uses of it
> and reappropriate it in support of their own agendas, in order to
> defend their own grounds.[7]

The goal of radicals engaged in popular constitutionalism was not
just to influence juries or public opinion, but also to mobilize people
to participate in mass actions – public demonstrations, mass petitions,
or conventions – whose constitutionality was itself contested. One
engaged in popular constitutionalism by taking direct political action,
but for it to be successful, a large number of people had to be willing
to act, notwithstanding the risks associated with such activities.

Popular constitutionalism did not channel people away from
direct involvement in political activity, but instead demanded that
they act. The practice of democratic constitutionalism was in fact successful, as people were mobilized, political discourse was changed,
and eventually, the meaning of English constitutionalism was
advanced so that adult men were given the vote and basic civil rights
were recognized.

But here we must also acknowledge a key limitation of English
democratic constitutionalism. Because English radicals rooted their
claims in the narrative of the ancient British constitution, some
demands could not be made. For example, private property rights
could not be challenged and demands for social and economic equality did not resonate with this justificatory scheme. In particular,
women's rights did not fit comfortably into a discourse in which the
image of manly independence was so prominent.

This British example of popular constitutionalism occurred in the
context of a political order lacking a written constitution that the
judiciary had ultimate authority to interpret. But democratic constitutionalism still has space to operate in a world of written constitutions
like those of Canada and the United States.

For those concerned with labour rights, one of the most interesting studies of popular constitutionalism is James Gray Pope's "Labor's Constitution of Freedom." Pope is interested in what he calls a "constitutional insurgency," by which he means

> a social movement that: (1) rejects current constitutional doctrine, but rather than repudiating the Constitution altogether, draws on it for inspiration and justification; (2) unabashedly confronts official legal institutions with an outsider perspective that is either absent from or marginalized in official constitutional discourse; and (3) goes outside formally recognized channels of representative politics to exercise direct popular power, for example through extralegal assemblies, mass protests, strikes and boycotts.[8]

Pope begins his analysis by painting a picture of the labour relations scene that existed almost a century ago, a picture not too different from the contemporary one:

> In December 1919, the American Federation of Labor hosted a conference of unions . . . the delegates were in a gloomy mood . . . public opinion [was turning] against unionism. Sensing an opening, state and federal legislators had introduced scores of bills prohibiting or restricting strikes and mandating procedures for industrial dispute resolution. . . .
>
> In response, the conference delegates framed the issue of strikes, not as a question of economics or ethics, but as one of constitutional law. "Autocratic, political and corporate industrial and financial influences in our country have sought," they warned, "to infringe upon and limit the fundamental rights of the wage-earners guaranteed by the constitution of the United States." These rights were to be found . . . in the Thirteenth Amendment's . . . Involuntary Servitude Clause. The right to strike, proclaimed the conference statement, meant the difference between voluntary and involuntary servitude, between freedom and slavery.[9]

The Thirteenth Amendment, adopted in the aftermath of the American Civil War, outlawed slavery and involuntary servitude, thus providing a constitutional guarantee of free labour. But what constituted free labour? Did the fact that a worker had the freedom to quit make her free? The labour movement rejected that view, claiming labour was only effectively free when it could significantly influence the conditions of work. In order for that to occur, workers had to be able to act in combination, and they had to be free to use forms of collective action that made their combinations effective. Strikes, sympathy strikes, primary and secondary picketing, and boycotts were the most effective actions, but many were either illegal or highly restricted at the time.

Pope then focuses on the struggle of the Kansas mine workers against the *Kansas Industrial Court Act*, a statute passed in 1920 that prohibited strikes in industries with a public interest (including mining) and established a court to resolve disputes and set the terms of a contract. From the perspective of the miners, this law violated labour's constitution of freedom, and they mounted a campaign of resistance against what they called the Kansas slave law. They sought to demonstrate both to judges and politicians that workers would refuse to accept such a law, and thereby convince either the court to declare it unconstitutional and/or the legislature to repeal it. This could not be accomplished by hiring lawyers or making speeches, but rather required direct action by members and union leaders. The law was ignored and strikes were called following disputes over the interpretation and application of the collective agreement. Union leaders were jailed for contempt of court and members faced discharge. Although the workers were unsuccessful in having labour's constitution of freedom recognized, their vision sustained strong movement solidarity over a four-month period.

Bringing Forward Lessons from History

These historical examples of democratic constitutionalism are useful because they suggest some of the possibilities and limitations of pursuing it as a strategy. They also raise a number of questions with relevance to today's ongoing struggles, among them: What is the primary goal of democratic constitutionalism in Canada? If it is to influence judicial interpretations of the *Charter*, this approach may have strategic implications. Lawyers will necessarily become prominent actors and, in the process, may reinterpret a popular vision into one that conforms more to current judicial views in order to facilitate successful legal arguments. Alternatively, if democratic constitutionalism is primarily seen as a mobilization strategy that aims to increase participation and deepen commitment, then a different strategy and set of tactics grounded more in people's experience may be pursued.

In addition, what are the costs and benefits of pursuing democratic constitutionalism relative to other options? Do some claims get excluded or marginalized because they cannot be grounded in reasoning that may dovetail with a narrower interpretation of the constitution? Does an embrace of the constitution put one onto unfriendly terrain that favours individual rights over collective ones? Does it also have the effect, whether intended or not, of promoting judicial oversight when judges have rarely exhibited much sympathy for labour rights? Balanced against these concerns, however, is the potential cost of abandoning the constitutional terrain to groups seeking to use it to limit labour rights.

The *Charter* in the Canadian Cultural Imagination

As noted with the historical examples, whether democratic constitutionalism has potential traction in the popular discourse depends on the extent to which the constitution serves – or can serve – as a powerful national symbol. This precondition appears to exist in Canada despite the fact that the *Charter* remains a very young constitutional document, having only marked its thirtieth anniversary in 2012. Courts are still grappling with and recalibrating its principles in the formal constitutional narrative. As a result, it is not surprising that a counternarrative of Canadian democratic constitutionalism is also still in its developmental phases.

Nevertheless, in only three decades, the *Charter* has very quickly become a powerful symbol of Canadian identity and values. Numerous public surveys over the past two decades have found that the *Charter* is consistently identified as one of the most popular symbols of Canadian identity – often ranked second only to universal health care – and that levels of support for the *Charter* are consistently high in all regions of the country. That popularity persists despite the fact (or perhaps more precisely because of the fact) that attachment to the *Charter* is not paired with specific or in-depth knowledge of its content. Instead, the *Charter*'s role in the cultural imagination speaks to a strongly emotive, aspirational sense of Canadians' "best selves," as well as to generalized notions of justice, fairness, and the protection of fundamental rights.

At the same time that the *Charter* enjoys significant resonance with the general public, courts have yet to fully colonize its meaning. In particular, the unwritten *Charter* values remain largely unmapped territory. Their articulation, however, is an integral part of the constitutional project because at the same time that section 1 of the *Charter* guarantees the rights and freedoms written within it, it also states that they may be subject to "such reasonable limits prescribed by law as can be demonstrably justified in a free and democratic society."[10]

This necessarily calls into question the exact nature of the "underlying values and principles of a free and democratic society."[11] The Supreme Court has repeatedly adverted to an unwritten pool of values of a free and democratic society – which is broader than formal *Charter* rights – from which *Charter* rights are drawn and against which their breach must be justified. The vision of a just Canadian society marked by these values has potential to open the debate about constitutional meaning. While not purporting to provide a complete list, some of those values and principles that the Court has identified as "essential to a free and democratic society" include the following:

- the inherent dignity of the human person;
- commitment to social justice and equality;
- accommodation of a wide variety of beliefs;
- respect for cultural and group identity; and
- faith in social and political institutions that enhance the participation of individuals and groups in society.[12]

These values suggest a vision of society whose collective health is properly the interest of the *Charter*, honouring both individual and collective rights while also recognizing and tempering power differentials. As the Court has repeatedly stated, "the courts must be cautious to ensure that [the *Charter*] does not simply become an instrument of better situated individuals to roll back legislation which has as its object the improvement of the condition of less advantaged persons."[13]

Accordingly, the field tentatively marked by *Charter* values at the very least opens debate about democratic values that are supportive of a more progressive vision. It can also foster an alternative narrative in which specific struggles can be understood. What raises these democratic constitutionalism claims above mere politics is that the constitution provides the mandatory benchmark for measuring whether state conduct and laws that shape social relations have in fact delivered on the fundamental promise of a substantive democracy. In this way, *Charter* values may help preserve the space to shift public narratives and hold governments and employers to account, forcing them to answer whether their conduct complies with fundamental values focused not on narrow, short-term objectives, but instead on the collective health of a sustainable community.

Canada's Emerging Democratic Constitutionalism

Democratic constitutionalism can take many forms and possess a diverse range of goals from the immediate to the long-term. How a campaign of democratic constitutionalism may be shaped and how its shape may change through time will depend on who the audience is and what the objective is. For example, the audience for a specific campaign may be any one or a combination of a union's own members, other progressive organizations who could be potential allies, the general public, employers, courts, or politicians. At the same time, the broad purpose of a specific campaign could be about any one or a combination of the following: illuminating fundamental values that are at stake in a specific struggle, creating shared values where there is silence or revealing those values in a process of movement building, resisting the imposition of unrepresentative values, or changing the frame of public discussion.

Democratic constitutionalism can be as simple as reframing an important social issue so that a broader audience can understand it in a new light. For example, the "women's rights are human rights" campaign that emerged from organizing in the international human rights context shifted public discourse to the point that women's equality could be seen not as a special interest but as a core social value. It connected women's equality to the well-being of a community. Similarly, the campaign to recognize that "labour rights are human rights" invites a broader discourse on fundamental community values and common interests.

Democratic constitutionalism can also take more active transgressive or transformative shapes. While it is still early days, it has been invoked by recent social movements, sometimes in response to coercive state action. But even if it begins as a reactive or defensive campaign, democratic constitutionalism can enable a protest or social action to reach beyond the boundaries of its original participants to demand broader public engagement and state accountability. This was the case with both the 2010 protests against the G20 summit in Toronto and the Quebec student movement protests in 2012.

During the lead up to the G20 summit, labour and community groups actively asserted constitutional rights to protest in response to state efforts to circumscribe when and where demonstrations could occur. But the framing took on more urgency in the aftermath of the widespread, brutally excessive use of police force, as well as the kettling, mass arrests, and detention of over 1,100 protesters and bystanders.[14]

The Canadian Civil Liberties Association and the National Union of Public and General Employees asserted citizens' democratic rights to hold the police and government to constitutional standards by, among other efforts, organizing well-publicized public hearings on policing and governance at the G20 summit, and publishing a report both highlighting the breaches of constitutional rights and making recommendations for reform. These actions were explicitly framed in constitutional terms, declaring: "The constitutional rights our citizens value and enjoy are the cornerstone of Canadian democracy. They must never again be threatened by arbitrary and excessive policing and by the systemic failure of the government to protect them."[15] These responses sustained attention and mobilization on the issue long after the events transpired and, in addition to exerting pressure on the authorities to provide accountability, provided a strong alternative narrative that clearly signalled how the summit demonstrations and police violence should be understood and why the general public should care. While these were important activities, it is worth noting that the police repression came to dominate public discourse in the wake of the summit at the expense of other substantive issues, such as the G20's austerity programs.

Two years later, however, those very austerity measures again sparked a fire with the Quebec student strike against proposed tuition increases. The student protests were grounded in a vision of direct democracy and the public good, and a deep critique of the privatization and commodification of public services.[16] The movement secured much broader support after the provincial government enacted the draconian Bill 78, imposing restrictions on the right to public assembly, protest, and association. But rather than dampening down demonstration numbers, Bill 78 provoked weeks of widespread, defiant public protests by a broad array of community organizations and the general public. These democratic assertions of constitutional rights in the face of a repressive law helped sustain the student movement. By engaging a broader range of society with the issue, it also created the space for a wider discussion about the democratic vision and priorities at the heart of the student protest.

In other cases, movements have proactively and self-consciously framed themselves in constitutional terms. In 2012–13, the Ontario teachers' resistance to Bill 115 – which restricted rights to collective bargaining and the right to strike, while giving government the power to impose contracts – was proactively framed as a fight about democracy. The unions' campaigns were expressly framed in constitutional terms about the freedom of association and expression, and drew connections between Bill 115 and the interests and democratic rights of all Ontario workers. This created more space for public debate about the legislation, the government's actions, and the teachers' resistance. While this campaign used constitutional language to broaden alliances by highlighting the democratic interests at stake, it did not employ democratic constitutionalism to defy the law.

In this respect, the Bill 115 campaign differed from the 1996 Days of Action, during which Ontario labour and social movement organizations together asserted constitutional rights of expression, association, and assembly to support mass actions, protests, and political strikes in defiance of the law. These direct actions used tools of democratic constitutionalism to mobilize broad alliances of community groups against the austerity program implemented in the so-called Common Sense Revolution of Conservative premier Mike Harris. The subsequent 1997 Ontario teachers' protest similarly asserted fundamental constitutional rights of political expression and assembly, as teachers engaged in a ten-day province-wide political strike against provincial legislation that rammed through profound changes to the governance and funding of public education, collective bargaining, and the terms and conditions of teachers' work.

As these recent examples of popular action attest, different forms of democratic constitutional engagement, all to some degree shaped by *Charter* values, have the potential to provide a common language to highlight shared concerns. In turn, they can facilitate building alliances and can provide an alternative frame for public discourse. That potential remains tempered with the realization that the constitutional frame can become dominant, overshadowing other messages even as it may simultaneously open the space to begin conversations about alternatives.

Ultimately, *Charter* values do belong to the people. Whether or not labour and progressive movements choose to take ownership in shaping the meaning of *Charter* values, it is valuable to know that this strategic approach may prove one of the effective tools in the arsenal of democratic mobilizing for a just and democratic society.

Nine

Freedom of Association

The Right to Bargain Collectively and the Right to Organize

Paul J.J. Cavalluzzo and Adrienne Telford

WHEN THE *Canadian Charter of Rights and Freedoms* was adopted in 1982, listed among "fundamental freedoms" at section 2(d) was a phrase of particular importance to workers concerned about their rights to organize and to bargain collectively: *freedom of association.*[1] Given the prominent role of unions in Canada, such a right would seem a given, yet freedom of association has more often been interpreted by Canadian courts as an individual rather than a collective right. The scope of protection of workers' rights under section 2(d) of the *Charter* has developed in a somewhat ad hoc manner. In the early days, the courts gave section 2(d) a narrow and legalistic interpretation that focused on the individual. Trade unions and workers in Canada received little benefit from this interpretation. Unfortunately, the *Charter* provision was given a more robust interpretation by courts when it was used against unions in the context of a freedom *not* to associate.[2] In other instances, the Supreme Court of Canada has recognized that section 2(d) has a collective dimension under which group rights and interests are protected. The high-water mark for this more generous interpretation was the 2007 decision *B.C. Health Services,*[3] which held that section 2(d) protects a limited procedural right to collective bargaining.

In 2011, the Supreme Court decided the *Fraser* case[4] in the face of a concerted attack on *B.C. Health Services* by governments and intervening business interest groups. In a contentious debate between the justices on the legitimacy of *B.C. Health Services,* the majority of the Court upheld its earlier decision but "clarified" the reach of section 2(d) in the labour context. This so-called clarification has led to a number of lower court decisions that have produced a great deal of uncertainty in the law. An examination of the tensions underlying the history of Canadian judicial interpretation of workers' rights to organize and bargain collectively is crucial as the groundwork is laid for future Supreme Court decisions on just how fundamental freedom of association is to workers in Canada.

The Early Years

In the formative years of the *Charter,* the labour movement was neither methodical nor very co-ordinated in its approach to *Charter* litigation. At the time, unions employed the *Charter* to challenge laws that curtailed or restricted their activities. In the 1980s, unions challenged wage restraints on the basis that they violated section 2(d) by restricting workers' rights to collective bargaining. During the same period, unions also challenged back-to-work legislation and laws that restricted the right to strike of essential service workers.

These challenges were consolidated before the Supreme Court of Canada in what became known as the labour trilogy in 1987. Just five years after the enactment of the *Charter,* the Supreme Court was now faced with *Charter* claims engaging fundamental aspects of collective bargaining laws. But the litigation strategy raising these fundamental questions so early in the application of the *Charter* was questionable. Indeed, other progressive groups during this era were more methodical in selecting which cases should be litigated, adopting an incremental approach.

The Dickson/McIntyre Divide

The labour trilogy set the stage for a vigorous debate on the nature and scope of freedom of association in Canada.[5] The cases grew out of a history that saw numerous strikes in the 1970s and early 1980s by Alberta nurses and public servants, the provincial response to which was a ban on strikes by hospital workers, firefighters, and other public sector employees. One province over, Saskatchewan dairy workers were resisting back-to-work legislation, while at the federal level, the

Public Service Alliance of Canada was challenging the 1982 imposition of two-year wage restraints that limited increases to 6 per cent in the first year and 5 per cent in the second.

At the heart of these three cases were questions of whether section 2(d) protects the right to bargain collectively and the right to strike. The focus of the debate between Supreme Court Chief Justice Dickson and Justice McIntyre was whether freedom of association was solely an individual right or whether it also had a collective dimension. While both agreed that "freedom of association is the freedom to combine together for the pursuit of common purposes or the advancement of common causes,"[6] they quickly parted company on the scope of the protection afforded by section 2(d) of the *Charter*.

For the majority, Justice McIntyre took a narrow view based on the Western liberal conception of rights that places primacy on individual liberty and autonomy. Relying on American constitutional jurisprudence, Justice McIntyre asserted that freedom of association was an explicitly individual right, even though it may advance many group interests. Although that right cannot be exercised alone, the group or collective is "simply a device adopted by individuals to achieve a fuller realization of individual rights and aspirations."[7]

Relying on American doctrine, Justice McIntyre narrowly defined the scope of section 2(d)'s protection to include only three elements:

- the freedom to join with others in lawful, common pursuits, and to establish and maintain organizations and associations;
- the freedom to engage collectively in those activities which are constitutionally protected for each individual; and
- the freedom to pursue with others whatever action an individual can lawfully pursue as an individual.

Such a narrow conception of freedom of association essentially means that fundamental collective activities such as collective bargaining and strikes are not constitutionally protected. In Justice McIntyre's view, the courts have no labour relations expertise and are not politically accountable. Therefore, it was deemed far more prudent that such activities be regulated by legislatures.

Chief Justice Dickson's dissent, in contrast, allowed for a generous and purposive view of freedom of association. Grounding his contextual analysis in Canadian values and democratic traditions, Chief Justice Dickson distinguished the Canadian *Charter* from American doctrine on the basis that the former provides an fexplicit freedom of association in section 2(d). He also ocused fon the *Charter*'s balance of

the protection of fundamental freedoms with the larger societal interests in section 1 of the *Charter*, which "guarantees the rights and freedoms set out in it subject only to such reasonable limits prescribed by
law as can be demonstrably justified in a free and democratic society."

In Chief Justice Dickson's view, the derivative status of freedom of
association and the internal balancing at the rights definition stage
under American constitutional law rendered suspect reliance on the
doctrine in *Charter* jurisprudence.[8] Chief Justice Dickson thus rejected
the United States' narrow delineation of freedom of association wherein
the right entailed little more than a freedom to belong to or form an
association, or engage in those associational activities that related
specifically to one of the enumerated freedoms. Such an approach was
unduly restrictive and was not supported by the language of section 2,
which provided an explicit and independent guarantee of freedom of
association. Unlike the majority, he was not prepared to accept such a
"legalistic, ungenerous, indeed vapid" freedom.[9]

Chief Justice Dickson focused on the *Charter's* balance of the protection of fundamental freedoms with the larger societal interests in
section 1 of the *Charter*. In Chief Justice Dickson's view, section 2(d)
must be interpreted to give "effective protection to the interests to
which the constitutional guarantee is directed."[10] In other words, freedom of association recognizes the profoundly social nature of human
endeavours whereby acting with others is a primary condition of
community life, human progress, and civilized society. Moreover, the
chief justice's contextual analysis took into account the unequal distribution of power within society, noting that historically, freedom of
association has "enabled those who would otherwise be vulnerable
and ineffective to meet on more equal terms the power and strength
of those with whom their interests interact and, perhaps, conflict."[11]

Finally, Chief Justice Dickson recognized that confining freedom of
association to acts that can lawfully be performed by an individual is
far too restrictive. This freedom has a collective dimension for which
there is no analogy in individual action. In the labour context, his
purposive interpretation of the scope of section 2(d) protection
encompassed the right to bargain collectively and the right to strike.
In his view, these essential union activities advanced fundamental
Charter values such as human dignity, equality, and democracy. Moreover, the constitutional protection of these rights and freedoms was
consistent with international human rights law.

Unfortunately, Justice McIntyre's individualistic conception of
freedom of association carried in the labour trilogy and remained law

for the next two decades. From a labour relations perspective, this meant that section 2(d) only protected the right to form, join, and maintain a trade union. Essential labour activities such as collective bargaining and striking were left without the benefit of constitutional protection. However, Chief Justice Dickson's powerful dissent was revived in subsequent decisions, and it became the underlying analysis of section 2(d) jurisprudence twenty years later.

A Collective Breakthrough

The Dickson/McIntyre divide continues to be the backdrop to section 2(d) challenges in the labour context. Until 2001, the legalistic and individualistic view of freedom of association framed the judicial analysis. However, in *Dunmore,* a 2001 case concerning the exclusion of farm workers from collective bargaining laws, the Supreme Court of Canada set off in a new direction.[12] Significantly, the Court overcame a tenuous distinction drawn between rights and freedoms under the *Charter.* According to this doctrine, the fundamental freedoms under section 2 of the *Charter* guarantee freedom from state interference with respect to a protected activity, but do not go so far as to impose a positive obligation on government to facilitate that activity. However, in *Dunmore,* the Court found that in certain limited circumstances, section 2(d) of the *Charter* may require the state to take affirmative action to facilitate a meaningful freedom of association. In this particular instance, it required the government to extend protective legislation to vulnerable farm workers so that they could fully exercise their freedom to associate.

The Court also broadened the scope of section 2(d) protection to include associational activities with no individual analogue. The Court concluded that the collective is qualitatively distinct from the individual, and performs acts that could not be performed by an individual. For example, the making of collective representations to an employer is inconceivable on the individual level. Although the Court in *Dunmore* recognized that section 2(d) has a collective dimension, it maintained the prevailing labour trilogy interpretation that section 2(d) does not protect the right to bargain collectively.

An important breakthrough came in 2007, however, in *B.C. Health Services,* a case arising from a challenge to provincial legislation that invalidated provisions of existing collective agreements and prohibited future collective bargaining on a number of significant issues. This unilateral and arbitrary state action – the legislation was enacted without consulting the affected unions or their members – pushed the Supreme Court to review its jurisprudence dating back to the labour trilogy. In a stunning acknowledgement, the Court declared that "the grounds advanced in the earlier decisions for the exclusion of collective bargaining from the *Charter's* protection of freedom of association do not withstand principled scrutiny and should be rejected."[13] The Court found that a decontextualized approach focused on the individual ignored Canadian labour relations history, international law, and the fundamental *Charter* values of equality, human dignity, and democracy. The Court concluded that "historically, [collective bargaining] emerges as the most significant collective activity through which freedom of association is expressed in the labour context."[14]

Chief Justice Dickson's 1987 dissent came back to full life in *B.C. Health Services*. Ultimately, the Court now provided for a limited procedural right to bargain collectively under section 2(d). However, it guarantees neither a particular substantive outcome nor access to a particular model of labour relations or bargaining method. Rather, it protects both the ability of workers to engage in associational activities, and their capacity to act in common to achieve workplace goals. Where a government measure substantially interferes with the collective bargaining process insofar as it affects a matter important to the bargaining process – and it does so in a way that undermines the duty of good faith negotiation – the government will have infringed section 2(d) of the *Charter*.

Attempted Revival of the Debate – *Fraser*

In 2011, the Supreme Court returned to the same debate over individual versus collective association rights that it had wrestled with in the labour trilogy. Like *Dunmore*, the *Fraser* case concerned the exclusion of farm workers from collective bargaining laws. In response to *Dunmore*, the Ontario legislature had passed a separate law, the *Agricultural Employees Protection Act* (AEPA). It provided limited rights to farm workers, far below those afforded under the *Labour Relations Act*. Since the AEPA did not provide the right to bargain collectively, the workers challenged the law on the basis of the *B.C. Health Services* decision. In an extraordinarily divided court, the majority was put on the defensive by Justice Rothstein's attack on *B.C. Health Services*. He disagreed with the majority ruling in that seminal case that section 2(d) protects the right to bargain collectively. In a bid to overrule *B.C. Health Services*, Justice Rothstein attempted to revive the Dickson/McIntyre debate by arguing that section 2(d) protects individual interests, but does not offer constitutional protection to such activities as collective bargaining or the other collective rights granted by the U.S. Wagner Act model of labour legislation.[15]

In response to Justice Rothstein's attack, the majority judgment in *Fraser* – written by Chief Justice McLachlin and Justice LeBel (both of whom co-authored *B.C. Health Services*) – stated clearly that the Court was upholding *B.C. Health Services*. However, the majority framed the ultimate issue in narrow terms by asking whether the impugned law or state action has the effect of making it impossible to act collectively to achieve workplace goals. Applying this standard, the Court determined that it was premature to conclude that the impugned legislation offered insufficient protections for section 2(d) rights. It came to this conclusion despite clear evidence that the agricultural workers had thus far been unable to meaningfully exercise their collective bargaining rights under the impugned legislation. Moreover, at the time of writing, not one agricultural business in Ontario has become subject to any good faith collective bargaining process, let alone a collective agreement under the AEPA – a startling outcome for purported "collective bargaining" legislation.

As a result, those seeking to uphold labour rights to organize and collectively bargain are faced with a re-emergence of the Dickson/McIntyre divide and a possible retreat from the generous and purposive analysis of freedom of association put forward by Chief Justice Dickson in the labour trilogy and adopted by the Court in *B.C. Health Services*. As it stands, section 2(d) in the labour relations context currently guarantees a meaningful process of engagement that permits employee associations to make representations that employers must consider and discuss in good faith. Whether Justice McIntyre's narrow conception of freedom of association will gain currency with future members of the Court is difficult to predict. In the meantime, workers and their allies should rely upon the majority's clear statement in *Fraser* that upheld the decision in *B.C. Health Services*: section 2(d) protects the right to a process of collective bargaining.

Post-*Fraser*

In the aftermath of *Fraser*, there have been a number of section 2(d) cases in the labour context. Two of those are 2012 decisions of the Ontario Court of Appeal that deal with the scope of section 2(d) protection for the right to bargain collectively.

In *Mounted Police Association of Ontario*, three independent associations of RCMP members challenged the Mounties' "labour relations" scheme under section 2(d) of the *Charter*.[16] The RCMP are expressly excluded from the application of the federal public sector collective bargaining law, saddled instead with a separate employee relations framework established by federal regulations "to provide for representation of the interests of all members with respect to staff relations matters." The internal mechanism, called the Staff Relations Representative Program (SRRP), is a body recognized by the RCMP both to present proposals and to be consulted in a meaningful and timely manner by the RCMP on human resources initiatives. Final decision-making authority rests with management. Meanwhile, the Treasury Board has ultimate authority on the issues of pay and benefits, which are decided after reviewing submissions from the RCMP Pay Council. That body is composed of two employees, two management representatives, and an impartial chair who solicits the views and input from the RCMP membership.

Two key questions were posed by the associations' *Charter* challenges. The first related to the refusal of the RCMP to recognize the three associations: Does the protection of collective bargaining under section 2(d) guarantee workers the right to be represented by an association of their own choosing? Secondly, does the right to collective bargaining under section 2(d) require that the workers' representative association be structurally independent of management?

In a conservative and legalistic decision, the Ontario Court of Appeal dismissed the constitutional challenges by affording *Fraser* a very restrictive interpretation. Indeed, it seized upon a statement in *Fraser* suggesting that, in order to establish a breach of section 2(d), the threshold of state action must make it impossible to act collectively or achieve collective goals. The court also relied on the Supreme Court's holding that section 2(d) protects the right to collective bargaining in a "derivative sense." The Court of Appeal interpreted this to mean that "a positive obligation to engage in good faith collective bargaining will only be imposed on an employer when it is effectively impossible to achieve workplace goals."[17]

In applying this analysis to the RCMP, the Court of Appeal found that there was no violation of section 2(d) because, unlike the plight of farm workers in *Dunmore*, RCMP members have been able to form voluntary associations, as evidenced by the three applicants before the court. In addition, the court pointed to the SRRP as a mechanism whereby RCMP members could act collectively to achieve workplace goals. Although the RCMP scheme lacks the attributes of the American Wagner Act model, the Supreme Court was clear in *B.C. Health Services* and *Fraser* that it was not constitutionalizing that U.S. regime. Finally, the court relied upon the existence of an independent fund that could finance legal representation to RCMP members in employment and other matters. Because the RCMP members had not established that it was effectively impossible to achieve collective workplace goals – the court relied on these three pre-existing outlets in its reasoning – it was concluded that the applicants could not claim that the derivative right to collective bargaining had been breached.

In *Association of Justice Counsel*, the Ontario Court of Appeal again provided a conservative and legalistic reading of *Fraser*.[18] This case arose from a challenge by federal government lawyers to the *Expenditure Restraint Act*, which limited wage increases for a five-year period. The Association of Justice Counsel argued that the wage restraint law violated section 2(d) by rendering collective bargaining on salary "useless" during the period of the legislation.

On the facts before the court, the union and employer had engaged in a lengthy process of collective bargaining over a two-year period prior to the introduction of legislated wage controls. The court reiterated *Fraser*'s position that section 2(d) guarantees a process, not a result. Although the government took a tough position in bargaining, the union failed to establish that it was denied the opportunity to present the wage demands of its members, or that the government failed to consider these demands in good faith. As stated in *Fraser*, section 2(d) does not require that the process of collective bargaining yield a collective agreement. Moreover, the fact that the union had referred the issue of wages to arbitration and that this issue was now predetermined by the wage restraint law, did not amount to a breach of section 2(d) because *Fraser* held that section 2(d) does not guarantee a dispute settlement mechanism for a bargaining impasse. The court concluded by stating that "the validity of the [law] must be assessed on the basis of whether, at the time it was enacted, the parties had had the opportunity for a meaningful process of collective bargaining."[19]

The Court of Appeal arrived at its finding by applying what it called the "effectively impossible" test, ruling that "the substantive content of s. 2(d) must be the same whether raised as a sword to claim the right to an effective legislative regime to protect freedom of association or used as a shield to defend against legislation that impinges upon existing statutory protections."[20] Examples of the sword (positive rights) would be the *Mounted Police Association of Ontario* case and *Fraser*. Examples of the shield (negative rights) would be *Association of Justice Counsel* and *B.C. Health Services*. Despite the Supreme Court's rejection of the positive-negative rights distinction in *Dunmore* and *Fraser*, it lives on in the lower courts and in the dissent in *Fraser*. This positivist doctrine is clearly not quite dead yet.

Going forward, the post-*Fraser* legal landscape of section 2(d) in the labour context is uncertain. Although *Fraser* "clarified" the reach of *B.C. Health Services*, it would appear that the Ontario Court of Appeal is retrenching the reach of section 2(d) to the pre–*B.C. Health Services* era. An "effective impossibility" test or a derivative right analysis brings us back to the days when section 2(d) only protected the right to form, join, and maintain a trade union. As Chief Justice Dickson said in the labour trilogy, such an interpretation renders freedom of association a "legalistic, ungenerous, indeed vapid" freedom. Upon its next opportunity, the Supreme Court of Canada must render an interpretation ensuring that freedom of association is meaningful in the workplace. After all, the *Charter* explicitly recognizes that this freedom is fundamental in Canadian society.

At the time of writing, of all of the fundamental freedoms found in section 2 of the *Charter* – which include freedom of conscience, religion, thought, belief, opinion, and expression, as well as peaceful assembly – only freedom of association is qualified by such restrictive thresholds as "substantial interference" or "effective impossibility." Under the *Charter*, such qualifications on a fundamental freedom are to be considered and balanced at the section 1 stage of justification, on the basis of clear and convincing evidence. All of the freedoms guaranteed under section 2 of the *Charter* are fundamental, and the challenge ahead entails a struggle to guarantee that the courts do not prioritize certain freedoms over others. Like the other fundamental freedoms, freedom of association is entitled to a broad, generous, and purposive interpretation. It is not for the courts to place limits on the scope of this freedom as it is exercised in the workplace. Such restrictions on freedom of association at the threshold stage of section 2(d) defy the will of the drafters of the *Charter* and deprive workers of the full protection of a fundamental freedom that was constitutionally entrenched for their benefit. After all, the *Charter* belongs to the people. It was never intended to be stifled by the legalistic and positivist concerns or philosophical inclinations of the judiciary.

Ten

Constitutional Protection for the Right to Strike

The Role of the Courts

Steven Barrett and Benjamin Oliphant

Where Are We Now?

IN A BREAKTHROUGH 2007 DECISION, the Supreme Court of Canada held in *B.C. Health Services* that constitutional protection of freedom of association – under section 2(d) of the *Canadian Charter of Rights and Freedoms* – must extend to the process of collective bargaining.[1] In the specific context of that case, the Court found that overriding important terms in freely negotiated agreements and/or prohibiting employers and unions from collectively bargaining over important terms in future constituted a "substantial interference" with the newly discovered right to "meaningful collective bargaining."[2] That decision effectively overruled twenty years of precedent[3] which, as applied, had effectively rendered labour relations "a judicial 'no go' zone" with respect to *Charter* protection.[4]

In the 2011 *Fraser* decision,[5] however, the Court appeared to impose restrictions on the scope of its *B.C. Health Services* decision.[6] While the majority reaffirmed that section 2(d) of the *Charter* protects a "meaningful process of consultation and discussion,"[7] including a derivative right to some form of "good faith" collective bargaining,[8] it ruled that the deliberate exclusion of agricultural workers from collective bargaining legislation applicable to most other employees did not infringe section 2(d). There was not, as one reading of *B.C. Health Services* might have suggested,[9] a positive constitutional obligation on the state to afford to vulnerable agricultural workers the same degree of legislative collective bargaining protection – including majoritarian exclusivity and a dispute resolution mechanism for breaking collective bargaining impasses – available to most other employees.[10] Rather, the constitutional right of agricultural workers to a meaningful process of collective bargaining appears to require only legislative protection for some process of "good faith" discussion, dialogue, exchanges, or bargaining.[11] In what has been called "a triumph of imaginative statutory interpretation,"[12] the Court found that the applicable legislation did, in fact, guarantee a process of meaningful discussion in good faith,[13] which was sufficient legislative protection to fulfil the constitutional right to collective bargaining affirmed by *B.C. Health Services*. As such, freedom of association was not infringed by the failure of the government to afford further legislative protection.

As a result, *Fraser* provides little support for the proposition that section 2(d) affirmatively requires legislatures to enact a protective statutory framework for strike action. However, nothing in the judgment can be construed as licence for legislatures to directly interfere with the exercise of the freedom to withdraw services through strike activity.[14] *Fraser* was a protect case: it focused on what positive obligations section 2(d) imposes on legislatures in order to make freedom of association sufficiently meaningful to pass constitutional muster.[15] It does not address the scope of the legislature's obligation to respect the "negative" freedom – that is, to refrain from acting in such a way as to prohibit or otherwise restrict the exercise of constitutionally protected associational activities (for example, through back-to-work orders).

In our view, the freedom to strike is an associational activity falling within the section 2(d) guarantee on any plausible conception of freedom of association offered by the courts to date. Below, we address the three principal interpretations of freedom of association offered by various justices of the Supreme Court of Canada, and show how each entails at least some protection for strike action. Thus, regardless of what formulation ultimately is settled upon, the real debate should centre on what reasonable limitations may be placed on that freedom under section 1 of the *Charter*.

Various Methods of Reaching the Freedom to Strike

Chief Justice Dickson: Strike Activity Inherent in Freedom of Association

One method of demonstrating section 2(d) protection for strike action is found in Chief Justice Dickson's influential dissent in the *Alberta Reference* case. In finding that strike action falls under the rubric of freedom of association, he relied on a purposive approach to the interpretation of section 2(d) that was heavily influenced by international and comparative norms.

Drawing from seminal cases like *Big M Drug Mart*, Chief Justice Dickson's analysis began by emphasizing that the meaning of *Charter* guarantees must be ascertained and understood "in the light of the interest it was meant to protect."[16] To the chief justice, the overriding purpose of freedom of association is "to recognize the profoundly social nature of human endeavours and to protect the individual from state-enforced isolation in the pursuit of his or her ends."[17] From this foundation, he reasoned that in light of the critical importance of work to human dignity and self-respect,[18] and the need for protection of the employees' interest in the collective bargaining context, section 2(d) must afford "concomitant protection of their freedom to withdraw collectively their services."[19]

Chief Justice Dickson determined (rightly, in our view) that any definition of freedom of association must go beyond the constitutive approach[20] – the bare freedom to *join* and *be in* an association. However, he did not clearly delimit how much further the guarantee should reach,[21] and in what other circumstances it should be found to offer protection. Rather, the chief justice inferred directly from the importance of strike action to workers – particularly given the crucial role of associations in circumstances "where the individual is liable to be prejudiced by the actions of some larger and more powerful entity"[22] – that such activities fell within the intended scope of the guarantee. Chief Justice Dickson effectively found that whatever other interests section 2(d) protects, the right to strike must be one of them.[23]

In coming to this conclusion, he relied heavily on international norms in finding that strike action was protected by section 2(d). According to the chief justice, the "*Charter* conforms to the spirit of this contemporary international human rights movement, and it incorporates many of the policies and prescriptions of the various international documents pertaining to human rights"; as such, international sources serve as "an important indicia of the meaning" of the *Charter*.[24] On this theory, there may be no pressing need to clearly or exhaustively define the standard of breach. Looking to international law and practice for inspiration and confirmation, and the underlying nature of protecting freedom of association, one can divine whether the activity in question fits within the provision's purpose.[25]

In undertaking his survey, the chief justice noted that the UN International Covenant on Economic, Social and Cultural Rights,[26] the UN International Covenant on Civil and Political Rights,[27] and Convention 87 of the International Labour Organization (ILO)[28] – to all of which Canada is a signatory – protect some conception of the freedom to strike, either explicitly or in their application. According to the ILO, the right to strike is "an intrinsic corollary to the right to organize protected by Convention No. 87"[29] as it is a vital means through which workers and their organizations may promote and defend their interests.[30] Chief Justice Dickson determined that the most salient feature of these international human rights documents "is the close relationship in each of them between the concept of freedom of association and the organization and activities of labour unions."[31] On this approach, international law and norms offer compelling support for the proposition that the freedom to strike simply inheres in, or is a necessary incident to, the concept of freedom of association as enshrined in the *Charter*.[32]

The expanding international consensus on the importance of constitutional protection for strike action since Chief Justice Dickson's dissent in the so-called labour trilogy of 1987,[33] along with academic literature characterizing labour rights – such as the right to strike – as fundamental human rights,[34] would presumably lend further support to finding protection for strike action under section 2(d) on this approach.[35] Notably, Chief Justice Dickson's approach also formed the backbone of the revamped approach to section 2(d) in *Dunmore*,[36] and both *B.C. Health Services* and *Fraser* professed consistency with *Dunmore* and focused on the importance of international human rights in defining the content of *Charter* guarantees.[37]

Another approach to deriving a right to strike from section 2(d) starts from the proposition that both *B.C. Health Services* and *Fraser* extend some degree of protection to a meaningful process of collective bargaining (although, as noted, it is not entirely clear what this entitlement amounts to). On this approach, the question is whether such a constitutional right to collective bargaining can exist – in any meaningful fashion – without a concomitant protection for the freedom to strike.

We do not think one is possible without the other. Simply put, the opportunity for collective action (or an alternative dispute resolution mechanism) is a necessary corollary to any meaningful conception of collective bargaining.[38] It is an "indispensable condition to the existence of collective bargaining,"[39] as the process of collective bargaining so conceived is only feasible if the parties have a means of compelling each other to resolve impasses.[40] Providing a constitutional right to meaningful collective bargaining without the opportunity for collective action would, in the colourful words of the late professor Geoffrey England, be "illogical and a sham."[41]

The indispensability of strike action to a meaningful process of collective bargaining has long been recognized in the literature[42] and jurisprudence,[43] and is undeniably central in the history and practice of Canadian unions, labour law, and collective bargaining. The importance of the freedom to strike is immense in both the historical and current collective bargaining framework. As explained by Justice Galligan in *Broadway Manor Nursing Home*, an early *Charter* case handed down before the labour trilogy:

> Freedom of association contains a sanction that can convince an employer to recognize the workers' representatives and bargain effectively with them. That sanction is the freedom to strike. . . . If that sanction is removed the freedom is valueless because there is no effective means to force an employer to recognize the workers' representatives and bargain with them. When that happens the raison d'être for workers to organize themselves into a union is gone. Thus I think that the removal of the freedom to strike renders the freedom to organize a hollow thing.[44]

Indeed, protection for the freedom to strike in international law is largely based on the reasoning that there can be no meaningful collective bargaining without the opportunity for strike action.[45] In view of the Court's recent emphasis on the constitutional right to a meaningful process of collective bargaining, it is difficult to see how the need to preserve the freedom of workers to withdraw their services could now be denied.[46] Paul Weiler said it well:

> If we cannot accept the cold-blooded logic of collective bargaining, let us be candid about what we are doing. If we tell a school union that in order to secure concessions from the school board they can go on strike, as long as they do not interrupt the delivery of education – or we tell other government unions that they can strike but they cannot disturb the welfare of the public – then we are really telling these unions that they will not have an effective lever with which to budge a recalcitrant government employer from the bargaining position to which it has committed itself. We do leave the public employees with the right to unionize, to try to persuade their employer to improve their contract offers – with the right to collective "begging" as some unionists derisively put it – but we do not give them collective bargaining in the true sense of the word.[47]

Indeed, one lower court has already endorsed the view that the Court's recent explication of freedom of association must include the right to strike, and largely on the reasoning just described. *Saskatchewan* v. *Saskatchewan Federation of Labour* involved a challenge to provincial legislation allowing employers to unilaterally designate certain workers as essential and thereby preclude them from engaging in strike action.[48] Justice Ball recognized that "devoid of the right to strike, a constitutionalized right to bargain collectively is meaningless."[49] Taking the *B.C. Health Services* and *Fraser* "right to bargain collectively" at face value, Justice Ball determined that the right to strike is an essential element of any such right, for the reasons outlined above.[50] Thus, if the Supreme Court is protecting what it repeatedly said it was protecting[51] – a constitutional right to a *meaningful* process of collective bargaining – such a right would necessarily include some protection for strike action.[52]

Rothstein/McIntyre Approach

In his minority judgment in *Fraser*, Justice Rothstein (Justice Charron concurring) sought to reverse the holding in *B.C. Health* that section 2(d) imposes a "right" to collectively bargain, insofar as it entails positive obligations on the state to impose on employers a duty to bargain in good faith. However, even Justice Rothstein recognized that section 2(d) protects the freedom of workers to come together, organize, and attempt to bargain collectively with their employer on terms and conditions of employment.[53] This conclusion flows necessarily from his adoption of the approach championed by Justice McIntyre in the labour trilogy – that section 2(d) protects not only the mere freedom to join an association, but the attendant freedom to do together in association what one can lawfully do alone.[54] Thus, because individuals are generally free to bargain over terms of employment, that freedom must be extended to associations as well, subject as always to a section 1, or reasonable limits, justification.[55]

On this reasoning, it also follows that restrictions on the freedom of workers to collectively withdraw their services would violate section 2(d). This is because individuals are not prohibited by law from withdrawing their services in order to negotiate better contractual terms.[56]

In the labour trilogy, the parallel liberty approach was endorsed by both Chief Justice Dickson and Justice McIntyre (i.e., if a freedom is possessed by individuals, then it should be guaranteed for a group of individuals acting in concert). However, neither found strike action was protected on this basis, since both justices agreed that strikes were qualitatively as opposed to just quantitatively different from an individual withdrawal of services. This premise led them to starkly different conclusions. To the chief justice, the failure of the parallel liberty approach to protect strike action demonstrated its insufficiency as an exhaustive indicium for a section 2(d) violation, leading him to further adopt the approach discussed above.[57] By contrast, Justice McIntyre found that the qualitative difference between strike action and an individual withdrawal demonstrated that strike action did not fall within the ambit of section 2(d) protection at all.

Justice McIntyre reasoned that because it is not "lawful" for an individual employee to cease work during the period of his contract, there can be "no analogy whatever between the cessation of work by a single employee and a strike conducted in accordance with modern labour legislation."[58] This conclusion is highly questionable,[59] since it is simply not the case that it is unlawful for an individual employee to quit his or her job, much less to refuse to work without a contract in place. As David Beatty and Steve Kennett have argued:

> It is not that the workers in [the trilogy] were attempting to secure
> the freedom to do collectively what the law rendered unlawful if
> they tried to act in this way on their own. Just the opposite. They
> wanted the laws under review, which rendered their collective deci-
> sion to withhold their services unlawful, to match the [common]

law which permitted them to refuse work when they acted on their own.[60]

Moreover, as Professor Dianne Pothier has explained, the qualitative-quantitative distinction is not helpful in the context of the parallel liberty approach adopted by Justice McIntyre (and Justice Rothstein). This is because

> to accept it undermines the real point of Justice McIntyre's third proposition in drawing a parallel between individual and collective activities. In large measure, it is precisely because collective action is qualitatively different from individual activity that people choose to engage in collective action; it is often the collective exercise which turns ineffective action into effective action. . . . To say that activities lawful for the individual are constitutionally protected for the group only in cases of quantitative, but not qualitative difference, undercuts the point of drawing an analogy between individual and group activity.[61]

The fact that strike action is qualitatively different is, we agree, neither normatively significant nor analytically useful in the context of section 2(d). Indeed, as Justice Rothstein recognized, many activities become qualitatively different (at least in terms of their effect) when done in concert, but that does not negate the fact that the qualitatively different effect is being produced by members of a group undertaking activity that is lawful for individuals.[62]

We would submit that on the parallel freedom approach endorsed by Justice Rothstein, then, the freedom to strike is protected under section 2(d), and may ultimately be the foundational labour freedom in the workplace context. While Justice Rothstein objected to giving "individuals who are members of specific groups . . . greater constitutional rights than those who are not"[63] – such as rights to a meaningful process of collective bargaining, including a duty on the employer to bargain – applying the parallel liberty approach rectifies the converse deficiency. It serves to permit union members the same freedom to withdraw their services that all other individuals take for granted. It would also prohibit the state from unjustifiably interfering with the individual freedom simply because the individual chose to exercise that freedom in concert with others, which, on this view, is precisely the mischief section 2(d) is aimed at preventing.

A Constitutionally Protected Right?

While the jurisprudence on section 2(d) has been in a state of flux since the labour trilogy was supplanted in *Dunmore* and reversed in *B.C. Health Services*, we can see that under each of the various approaches to freedom of association discussed above, there is strong support for protection of the freedom to strike under the *Charter*.[64] Chief Justice Dickson's approach – subsequently endorsed in *Dunmore* – necessarily involves protection for collective action, drawing heavily as it does from international freedom of association norms. On this conception, whatever else freedom of association means, it means that workers must not be prohibited from withdrawing their services, absent a compelling justification under section 1 of the *Charter*. Likewise, whatever the precise content of the constitutional right to a meaningful process of collective bargaining – as established in *B.C. Health Services* and *Fraser* – it must entail protection for striking, given its centrality to the effective operation of any system of meaningful collective bargaining. Finally, the parallel liberty approach – endorsed most recently by Justice Rothstein in *Fraser* – likewise requires strike protection, as individuals are free to withdraw their labour. Ultimately, while the various conceptions will differ on the margins, we believe that on any reasonable or principled approach to section 2(d) offered by the Supreme Court to date, prohibiting workers from engaging in strike action at the conclusion of a collective agreement constitutes a violation of section 2(d), and requires justification under section 1.

Of course, there is no guarantee that the Supreme Court will share our opinion that section 2(d) must include some protection for the freedom to strike, despite the arguments advanced above. Indeed, we may have reason to be insecure. Harry Arthurs, perhaps Canada's most respected labour law scholar, is famously pessimistic about the role of the *Charter* in protecting workers' rights. After the labour trilogy, he warned that Anglo-Canadian courts have been dealing with individual and collective labour law and workers' rights for at least two hundred years, yet have never – and, he bravely predicted, would never – create a right that may be effectively asserted by or on behalf of working people.[65] His point was in part that workers cannot rely on courts – or for that matter the law or the state – to advance their interests, but only on their own collective strength, organization, mobilization, and militancy.

Fast forward to 2007, and the Supreme Court's ground-breaking

---

decision in B.C. *Health Services*. While the Court emphasized the importance of unions and collective bargaining in promoting democracy, worker autonomy, and dignity in the workplace,[66] and declared an end to the "no go" zone mentality that pervaded the labour trilogy, the real test of the Court's commitment to finding meaningful protection for Canadian workers' freedom of association will be when it is called on to decide whether the freedom to strike is constitutionally protected. As we have attempted to demonstrate, applying any of the credible theories of freedom of association that have been asserted over the life of the *Charter* would require governments and legislatures to respect the freedom to strike, whatever further obligations may be on the state to erect a framework to protect that freedom from the actions of governments or third parties. When the issue eventually reaches the top court – and we have no doubt that it will at some point – the Supreme Court's disposition will go some ways towards either rejecting, or confirming, Arthurs's *Charter*-nihilism.

Recent Developments

Recently, Justice Ball's decision in *Saskatchewan Federation of Labour*, affirming the right to strike, was overturned.[67] In a nutshell, the Saskatchewan Court of Appeal found that because the Supreme Court had expressly decided in the labour trilogy that the right to strike was not protected under section 2(d), the doctrine of *stare decisis* (binding precedent) operated to bind lower courts, notwithstanding subsequent Supreme Court jurisprudence.

Of course, lower courts should not blithely abandon the precedents of superior courts. However, in our view, the court was not being asked, as the Court of Appeal characterized the case, to "depart from a Supreme Court precedent on the basis that the Supreme Court would overrule it if invited to do so."[68] Rather, the court was being asked to apply to the case at hand a *new* Supreme Court precedent, which has unearthed any precedential stability in the context of section 2(d). If the Supreme Court has "shifted the approach to s. 2(d),"[69] which Justice Richards accepts, the task of the courts is to identify whether this shift in the meaning of the constitution affects past precedents, and how. Indeed, Justice Richards acknowledged that there were "uncertainties as to how, on any future appeal, the Supreme Court might choose to characterize the right to strike for purposes of a s. 2(d) analysis."[70] With respect, a lower court can hardly be bound if the precedents they feel bound by are themselves

Constitutional Protection of Labour Rights

unclear. The fact that the Supreme Court may subsequently agree or disagree with the lower court's assessment of the state of a law does not absolve the latter from fulfilling its judicial role.

Indeed, subsequent decisions of the Supreme Court have expressly rejected the reasons provided in the labour trilogy,[71] the very reasons used to justify the finding that section 2(d) did not protect strike action. In *Dunmore*, the Court recognized a "collective dimension" to section 2(d) beyond that established in the labour trilogy, on the basis that "to limit s. 2(d) to activities that are performable by individuals would. . . . render futile these fundamental [collective] initiatives."[72] In *B.C. Health Services*, the Court further confirmed that the doctrinal approach endorsed in the labour trilogy was no longer an appropriate definition of section 2(d), as the "reasons evoked in the past for holding that the guarantee of freedom of association does not extend to collective bargaining can no longer stand."[73] Those reasons, it must be recalled, were provided in the *Alberta Reference* case, where the specific issue was whether the right to strike was protected under section 2(d). On this view, *B.C. Health Services* pulled the rug out beneath the feet of the Court's holding in the 1987 labour trilogy.[74] In our view, the Court of Appeal should have applied the entire body of the law, including that laid down by the Supreme Court *following* the labour trilogy, in determining whether a freedom to strike was covered by section 2(d). In this sense, it could be argued that far from being an affirmation of *stare decisis*, the decision undermined it.

It is also worth noting that while the Court of Appeal felt itself bound by the labour trilogy, it did recognize that there are at least two approaches upon which the freedom to strike could be found to fall within the constitutional protection for freedom of association, based on the Supreme Court's more recent decisions. These approaches closely map those outlined above:

> First, strike activity might be seen as being, in effect, an aspect or a dimension of collective bargaining and, more particularly, as being a mechanism for giving employees the economic muscle *necessary to make collective bargaining meaningful*. . . . [75]
>
> Second, and on the other hand, the right to strike might be seen as conceptually independent of collective bargaining and, as a result, seen as something which must be analysed on its own terms. . . . [on this approach] strike activity is seen simply as the coordinated withdrawal of labour by employees for the purpose of obliging an employer to make concessions with respect to matters of workplace concern.[76]

We recognize that, with respect to the first approach (which roughly mirrors the approach outlined earlier in this chapter under Derivative of a *B.C. Health Services/Fraser* Right), the Saskatchewan Court of Appeal suggested that *Fraser* leaves open the possibility that all section 2(d) requires in order to make collective bargaining meaningful for workers is to have their collective representations considered in good faith.[77]

With respect, however, it is naive (and contrary to the real-life experience of anyone involved in collective bargaining on either the union or employer side) to suggest that merely requiring an employer to consider employee representations in good faith is sufficient to permit workers to exercise a constitutional right to meaningful collective bargaining. Such an interpretation would risk reverting to the "'no go' zone" black hole that was ostensibly abandoned in *B.C. Health Services*. The Court of Appeal may turn out to be correct about the Supreme Court's narrow conception of collective bargaining; however, we would submit that if it is, the notion that there is a constitutional right to meaningful collective bargaining must itself be abandoned.

Moreover, the Court in *Fraser* was dealing with the scope of the legislator's affirmative obligation to extend statutory protections to a process of collective bargaining. The Court was not commenting on the scope of section 2(d) when invoked as freedom *from* government or legislative interference.[78] Thus, while the Court in *Fraser* may have limited the affirmative obligation to ensure a process of good faith bargaining, it does not follow that the government can therefore proceed to interfere with all other collective activities not captured in the narrow range of positive protections it must actively provide.

With respect to the second approach floated (conceiving of strike activity as an independent component of freedom of association, which is compatible with the approaches outlined under Chief Justice Dickson and Rothstein/McIntyre Approach above), the Court of Appeal raised the concern that the right to strike is so bound up with other statutory features of the Canadian labour relations regime that it cannot be regarded as a fundamental freedom.[79] Thus, on the basis of the Supreme Court's caution in *Fraser* that section 2(d) "does not contemplate any particular sort of labour relations regime," constitutional protection was deemed to be an uncertain proposition.[80]

However, it should be noted that this very argument has already been explicitly rejected by the Supreme Court of Canada in the *B.C. Health Services* decision.[81] While the right to strike may also be a feature of modern labour relations legislation, this does not mean that the freedom to strike cannot obtain separate constitutional status as a fundamental freedom.

Secondly, the Court of Appeal's concerns seem to be influenced by an overly broad conception of the legal issues at play. In particular, Justice Richards stated:

> Speaking practically, SFL and the unions do not wish to return to a world where employees can withdraw their labour in concert, but where employers are not obliged to recognize unions, where union representation is based on something other than exclusive majoritarianism, where employers are not required to bargain, or to bargain in good faith, where employees who participate in strikes can be dismissed for breach of their employment contracts and so forth.

Whether or not this is what unions desire, it was simply not the question before the Court of Appeal. The challenge was to legislation that granted government employers the power to unilaterally determine that certain workers were essential, and thereby prohibit those employees – by the operation of legislation – from withdrawing their services. In other words, the unions challenged that aspect of the legislation that limited the freedom to strike, whether or not other statutory rights have been put in place to protect that freedom, and whether or not the government is under a constitutional obligation to enact such protections. It was the latter question that the Supreme Court addressed in *Fraser*, regarding what (if any) affirmative obligations should be placed on governments in order to protect the exercise of freedom of association from third parties. Again, however, *Fraser* did not address the scope and content of the state's constitutional obligation to *respect* (i.e., not prohibit or limit) the exercise of freedom of association.

At this stage, the most that can be said of the Saskatchewan Court of Appeal's decision is that it has shuffled the issue off to the Supreme Court of Canada, which, sooner or later, and perhaps sooner, will have to decide the issue without the luxury of deferring the issue to a higher court. Should the Court apply any of the doctrinal approaches set out in this chapter, it will have compelling reasons for finding that section 2(d) extends protection to strike activity.

Eleven

Working towards Equality

Putting Vision into Practice

Fay Faraday

EQUALITY IN CANADA REMAINS very much a work in progress. While a generation of equality litigation under the *Canadian Charter of Rights and Freedoms* has established a strong foundation from which to advocate – and there have been significant, profoundly transformative legal victories, particularly in the areas of LGBTQ and disability rights – a gap persists between constitutional promise and achievement. Indeed, equality-seeking communities, labour, and social movements continue to face strong resistance to the judicial recognition of their legal claims for equality under the *Charter*. Litigating in this area is challenging at the best of times, and the challenge is even greater in an age of neoliberalism, manufactured insecurity, and the cynical politics of austerity. Those fighting for equality know that progress comes in cycles, and so an approach that considers the long haul is necessary given the current array of challenges.

Why Is Equality So Hard?

The Supreme Court of Canada has declared that while equality is one of Canadians' most cherished rights, it is "perhaps the *Charter*'s most

---

163

conceptually difficult provision." On the one hand, the "quest for equality expresses some of humanity's highest ideals and aspirations"; yet on the other, "the difficulty lies in giving real effect to equality." The challenge is "to transform these ideals and aspirations into practice in a manner which is meaningful for Canadians."[1]

While there are conceptual difficulties in analyzing equality, the deeper problem comes from a rarely acknowledged failure in mainstream legal discourse to name the elephant in the room: power. What makes equality so challenging is that it is an inherently redistributive right. As I have written elsewhere:

> [Equality] calls into scrutiny the quality of the relationships we forge with others in society. It questions the justice of the distribution of rights, privileges, burdens, power, and material resources in society and the basis for that distribution. It requires us to articulate and critically examine previously unspoken assumptions and norms and how these norms are embedded in the laws that structure our relationships. Most significantly, it requires us to transform those legal structures to secure substantive equality.[2]

As a result, as Sheila McIntyre puts it, "when equality claims are really substantive, they should challenge privileged understandings of the world and privileged players' understandings of themselves."[3]

Yet, it is only in rare cases that courts identify or analyze the power dynamic that drives inequality, preferring to gloss over or ignore who benefits from an existing arrangement, and at whose cost. Legal discourse rarely analyzes the mechanisms by which certain groups of people are constructed on the margins of society. A reluctance to engage with these issues, however, implicitly suggests that current legal and social arrangements are neutral or natural, thereby erasing their discriminatory impacts and reinforcing the notion that discrimination is aberrant rather than endemic. The challenge for advocates is to repeatedly name the power dynamics and insist that they be part of the analysis. Without discussing power, it is difficult to describe what discrimination is, or how and why particular social, economic, and political relationships are harmful. This difficulty is reflected in a jurisprudence that has at many points talked around the notions of discrimination and equality while struggling to pin them down.

Proving Discrimination: The Constantly Moving Target

Section 15 of the *Charter* guarantees the right to equality in the following terms:

> 15. (1) Every individual is equal before and under the law and has the right to the equal protection and equal benefit of the law without discrimination and, in particular, without discrimination based on race, national or ethnic origin, colour, religion, sex, age or mental or physical disability.
>
> (2) Subsection (1) does not preclude any law, program or activity that has as its object the amelioration of conditions of disadvantaged individuals or groups including those that are disadvantaged because of race, national or ethnic origin, colour, religion, sex, age or mental or physical disability.

From the outset, the Supreme Court has stressed that "the section 15(1) guarantee is the broadest of all guarantees. It applies to and supports all other rights guaranteed by the *Charter*."[4] But, more than for any other *Charter* right, the Court has exhibited particular difficulty in articulating a legal test for proving discrimination.

In the short quarter-century since its first *Charter* equality case in 1989 – *Andrews* v. *Law Society of British Columbia* – the Court has made at least seven significant changes to the legal test, including a four-year period during which there was no majority position whatsoever on the legal test.[5] That was followed by fourteen years during which three core equality concepts were adopted by a unanimous or majority court, only to be explicitly rejected in very short order,[6] and then situated in a new relationship that was articulated between sections 15(1) and 15(2) of the *Charter*.[7] As can be expected, this lack of clarity makes it tremendously difficult to enforce rights and apply the law. Equally troubling, this confusion also undermines the development of a meaningful social discourse about and commitment to equality, colouring efforts to both organize communities and engage people politically.

This winding legal road, however, should not distract from the fact that strong bedrock principles in support of equality have been established and endure to this day. In particular, these principles include the following:

- Section 15 of the *Charter* has strong remedial purposes that are about promoting the objective of a more equal society. These purposes are

i. to rectify and prevent discrimination against groups suffering social, political, and legal disadvantage in society;

ii. to ameliorate the conditions of disadvantaged persons; and

iii. to promote a society in which all are secure in the knowledge that they are recognized at law as human beings equally deserving of concern, respect and consideration.

- Discrimination is often systemic. This means that the problem of discrimination is not primarily one of discrete intentional direct acts of discrimination (although those still arise). Instead, discrimination is a product of the way institutions, systems, practices, and norms have developed over time to reflect, replicate, and serve the interests and experiences of dominant groups in society. As a result, these facially neutral systems have adverse impacts on those who do not conform to those dominant norms.

- The goal of the *Charter* is to protect substantive equality. It aims to ensure that people are subject, as far as possible, to equal benefits and burdens of the law. This approach rejects a narrow, formal approach to equality because "treating likes alike" fails to accommodate the real differences between people and perpetuates dominant norms that exclude many. Substantive equality recognizes that sometimes different treatment is necessary to secure equality and eliminate discrimination.

- In formulating law and policy, government has a duty to take into account how those laws and policies will affect groups of people who are already disadvantaged and ensure that they do not perpetuate or exacerbate their disadvantage.

- Section 15 is concerned with effects of laws and policies and it examines those effects from the perspective of the claimant. When assessing if there is discrimination, the *Charter* is concerned with "the law's real impact on the claimants and members of the group to which they belong." It looks at that real impact in the full context in which it operates, "taking full account of social, political, economic and historical factors concerning the group."[8]

- The right to equality protects against discrimination on the nine grounds enumerated in section 15(1), an open-ended list of analogous grounds, and on the basis of intersecting combinations of enumerated and/or analogous grounds. In this way, the *Charter* ensures that section 15's protection can continue to evolve and be responsive to the multitude of ways in which discrimination actually occurs. The Court will recognize new analogous grounds where doing so "would serve to advance the fundamental purpose of s.

15(1)."[9] In undertaking this analysis, the Court looks at a wide matrix of considerations, no single element of which is determinative, including the nature and situation of the group at issue; the social, political, and legal history of Canadian society's treatment of the group; whether the characteristic at issue is one that cannot be changed, can only be changed with difficulty, or one that the government has no legitimate interest in expecting a person to change; and whether the group is lacking in political power, vulnerable to having its interests overlooked, or vulnerable to becoming a disadvantaged group.

At the end of the day, the legal principles are not the barrier to achieving equality. All the legal principles needed to mount a strong defence of equality rights already exist. So why does equality remain so elusive?

Revealing Discrimination

The real challenge to equality advocacy lies in getting courts to see and understand experiences of discrimination from the perspective of those whose rights are violated. The lived experiences of profound social and economic exclusion that are daily fare for many equality-seeking groups are alien to the life experiences of many judges. As a result, experiences that for equality-seeking groups resonate with clear and palpable discrimination are not immediately recognized as such by others. In making an argument about discrimination, one is not only dealing with the law, but also with decision makers' capacity to relate to life experiences different from their own. In addition, to the degree that equality is a highly cherished constitutional value, the label of discrimination carries a correspondingly deep stigma. In combination, these dynamics operate at an individual level to create in those who enjoy relative privilege a certain level of resistance to seeing and acknowledging discrimination.

As a result, equality advocates must be very explicit about all the dynamics at play when they allege discrimination because it cannot be assumed that decision makers will understand the significance of the issue without assistance. While the law is important, the facts are even more crucial, as is having the right evidence:

> While courts may, in theory, take judicial notice of whether discrimination exists, the perspectives and experiences of marginalized groups are typically not reflected in mainstream assumptions and

"logical reasoning" about how the world works. Expert and experiential evidence is needed to shift the legal gaze onto the uncomfortable truths about the real experiences of those who are "vulnerable to having their interests overlooked and their rights to equal concern and respect violated."[10]

Evidence is tremendously important to establish the context in which one can understand the claimant's perspective, identify what has happened, and determine both what the precise effects are and why they are experienced as discriminatory. This evidentiary challenge is particularly great when dealing with systemic discrimination because it becomes necessary to map out the elements of the system and explain how they interact to produce discrimination.

The case of low-wage migrant workers in Canada is instructive.[11] One can say that migrant workers experience discrimination in employment because they are a "vulnerable group," focusing on characteristics such as their precarious immigration status and race. However, identification of those grounds is only the beginning, and does not touch the ways in which government policies and laws actively construct migrant workers as a group on the margins. Nor does it explain why laws of general application fail to protect their needs and circumstances. No worker is inherently vulnerable; they are made vulnerable both by laws that facilitate relationships of inequality and laws that fail to address exploitation. It is necessary to name both how that inequality is constructed and who benefits from it.

When one maps out the relevant system undermining migrant workers' equality, it consists of all the ways in which

- laws fail to protect migrant workers against exploitative recruitment practices;
- immigration policies create unfree work relations by tying migrant workers' work permits and often also their housing to a single employer;
- administrative policies fail to build in practices to inform migrant workers of their rights and how to enforce them;
- employment standards laws depend on migrant workers coming forward to file complaints rather than proactive investigation by responsible agencies; and
- immigration laws and policies exclude low-wage migrant workers from routes to permanent residency and mandate repatriation after a defined period.

Within this context, migrant workers very predictably face almost insurmountable barriers to enforcing their rights to decent work. While migrant workers' poverty, race, language barriers, and precarious immigration status explain why they can be targeted for marginalization, it is the legal architecture that builds upon and amplifies their distance from dominant norms that leaves them open to exploitation. Outlining that elaborate architecture and relating it to the lived experience of a worker toiling under that system illuminates how discrimination operates and why particular legal moments may be experienced as discriminatory.[12]

Many of the problems that labour and progressive social movements now face are problems of systemic discrimination. While the concept of systemic discrimination has been around for several decades, its significance and implications for labour and progressive social movements – and the potential for systemic remedies – have not yet been fully confronted in law.

Organizing for Equality

Equality builds slowly. Because substantive equality is deeply challenging to established privilege, progress is met with resistance. It must be remembered, though, that section 15 of the *Charter* has been in effect for less than thirty years,[13] which in constitutional terms is still early days. Indeed, those activists who strongly and effectively advocated for amendments to language in the early drafts of the *Charter* are still actively engaged in advocating for its interpretation and enforcement, driven by the vision that informed its adoption.

One of those advocates is Bruce Porter, whose reflections on the twentieth anniversary of section 15 detail the collective vision that forged what is now section 15(1).[14] When the *Charter* was being drafted, a wide range of progressive social movements – feminist organizations, Aboriginal women's groups, disability rights activists, groups representing racialized communities, and organizations advocating for gay and lesbian rights – were all actively engaged in lobbying for changes to the proposed language of section 15. Painfully aware of the narrow and restrictive interpretation of equality under the *Bill of Rights*, they wanted to ensure that the language of the *Charter* protected a robust and meaningful vision of equality that would reach and improve the daily lives of people across Canada.

After a draft of the *Charter* was tabled, the Special Joint Committee on the Constitution held four months of hearings, during which it received hundreds of oral submissions and about a thousand written submissions. These interventions resulted in truly profound changes to the language of section 15(1), reorienting it in the direction of equality rights protection (rather than a more limited vision of anti-discrimination), and extending its protection to equality before *and under* the law, and to equal protection *and equal benefit* of the law. It also added protection for those with mental and physical disabilities and added the open-ended language that supports the extension of protection to analogous grounds. Underlying this massive push for change was a vision of equality as "a substantive social right," one that was legally enforceable and drew on the values of social and economic rights then developing in international human rights law, including positive governmental obligations and responsibility to address socio-economic disadvantage.[15]

In looking back at its drafting, Porter reflects on "expectations of equality" and observes:

> It is helpful to remember, however, that the word "expect" in English has two different meanings. One meaning refers to the prediction of a probable outcome of something entirely beyond our control. . . . Another meaning, however, is perhaps closer to the original meaning of the word, whose etymology, in Latin, means "to await" or "to look forward to"; it refers not to a predicted outcome, but to what is more subjectively considered or anticipated as an entitlement. So we say: "We expect government officials to act with honesty and integrity" or "We expect participants to be punctual". These statements are not predictions of probable outcomes but moral imperatives. They are forcefully stated not out of naïve optimism, but rather, in an effort to produce appropriate outcomes. The expectations may remain valid, even if they are not realized.[16]

While Canada is currently in a period of slow progress towards equality, this does not mean that expectations of the *Charter* guarantee for equality are misplaced. Our expectations remain valid. But those rights will never be won in a courtroom alone. A legal campaign for equality will only succeed in conjunction with robust, collective community action and mobilization by a broad community of allies whose shared vision opens the space necessary to grow real experiences of equality.

Twelve

The Power of Collective Bargaining

International Rights in a Neoliberal Age

John Hendy

Neoliberalism: The British Experience

THE ECONOMIC CRASH OF 2008 and the destructive policies of austerity unleashed since are, without doubt, outcomes of neoliberalism.[1] This ideology – which gives a central role to industrial relations and to how the labour market is to be structured (or, rather, unstructured) – regards trade unions and collective bargaining as impediments to a free labour market.

This is not an entirely new point of view, of course; a similar view dominated the British courts and legislature from the eighteenth century onwards. But neoliberalism in its modern form was born in 1948, with the aim of rolling back the vaguely egalitarian, state-dominated, postwar economic settlement taking hold across Western Europe and North America. Instead, its advocates called for a return to the "free market," and to inequality on a massive scale.[2] In this enterprise, neoliberalism has been astonishingly successful. It has become the dominant ideology across most of the globe, and remains dominant even after the 2008 crash and subsequent slump.

Neoliberalism's defects are masked by the propaganda that there is, in the words of Margaret Thatcher, "no alternative." Meanwhile, its champions have taken advantage of the crisis they created to further push privatization, deregulation, and attacks on trade unionism in the name of "austerity" (an austerity, of course, that affects only the 99 per cent and not the rich).

But nothing can hide the inherent contradictions of neoliberalism. The system requires rich consumers, but it seeks cheap labour. As it drives down labour costs by slashing wages and benefits,[3] it simultaneously reduces demand and consumption. This has the further effect of depriving the government of the tax revenue that is necessary to reduce state deficits (although state deficit reduction is ostensibly the prime purpose of austerity).

Inequality is an inevitable outcome of neoliberalism, and Britain has experienced a rapidly growing rich-poor gap since the 1970s (the U.K.'s most equal decade). But making the rich richer does not make up for the reduction of demand that results from making the poor poorer. Despite ostentatious consumption by many of the rich, the well-heeled save as well as spend, whereas the poor spend everything in order to survive.

It's no secret that inequality comes with a huge cost, even for those whose income has so disproportionately increased. Richard Wilkinson and Kate Pickett illustrate that by any scientific measure, even the rich suffer in a more unequal society.[4] Growth in inequality and poverty are associated with increases in crime, drug abuse, anti-social behaviour, mental illness, and hopelessness. Disparity in wealth is mirrored by disparity in health and life expectancy. This ever-deepening spiral creates both human misery and huge burdens on the state.

A central tenet of neoliberalism is that trade unions and collective bargaining must be destroyed or rendered toothless, because they interfere with the operation of a free market in labour. Yet Austrian neoliberal economist Friedrich Hayek's claim that free trade unions create unemployment, inequality, and poverty[5] is conclusively refuted by the historical record, which shows that these social ills have grown with the increasingly tight legal restrictions on British trade union freedom. In fact, ironically, it was the removal of restrictions on the freedoms of capital that triggered the current crisis by permitting the creation of mountains of toxic debt and unsustainable derivatives.

Over the past three decades, unions in the United Kingdom have been so bound up with legal impediments to the freedom to organize industrial action that they have been unable to protect the living conditions of working-class people from the policies of neoliberal governments. While the recent death of Margaret Thatcher stirred debate on the deleterious effects of her policies, the present Conservative – Liberal Democratic coalition government is probably the most reactionary Britain has seen in two hundred years.

International Trade Union Rights

The tension between neoliberalism and fundamental labour rights has always been obvious. But it has recently become particularly evident in the realm of international labour law.[6] The tension is seen in the austerity measures imposed by the so-called European Union troika (the European Commission, the European Central Bank, and the International Monetary Fund) on the weaker EU states, and also in the undermining of sectoral collective bargaining in Romania, Greece, Ireland, and Spain. The fight is also being waged at the International Labour Organization (ILO), where in 2012 the employers' group walked out of an important committee to protest the ILO's recognition over the past half century of the right to strike.[7]

Given the dominance of neoliberalism, it might be surprising to some that international labour law ever protected – and in fact, still protects – the right to strike and the right to collective bargaining. Yet it does, and these instruments still have some utility.

The international rights are well known: the ILO's *Convention 98* of 1949 requires the promotion of collective bargaining by member states. Article 8(1)(d) of the *International Covenant on Economic, Social and Cultural Rights* and ILO *Convention 87* of 1948 (as interpreted by the Committee of Experts and the Committee on Freedom of Association since 1952) protect the right to strike.

The European Union (twenty-seven member states of what used to be called, tellingly, the "common market") declares the rights both to strike and to collective bargaining in Article 28 of the *EU Charter of Fundamental Rights* (which came into force December 7, 2000, and now has "the same legal value as the Treaties" via Article 6 of the *Treaty on the Functioning of European Union*).[8] The other Europe – the forty-seven contracting states of the Council of Europe – protects the rights to strike and to collective bargaining by Article 6 of the *European Social Charter* of 1961 (revised in 1996). Article 11 of its *European Convention on Human Rights and Fundamental Freedoms* protects freedom of assembly, freedom of association and, in particular, the right "to join trade unions for the protection of [one's] interests." A series of European Court of Human Rights (ECtHR) decisions has held that these latter words contain a right to strike,[9] and since the landmark case of *Demir and Baykara* v. *Turkey*,[10] the Grand Chamber of the ECtHR has established the right to bargain collectively:

> . . . the right to bargain collectively with the employer has, in principle, become one of the essential elements of the "right to form and to join trade unions for the protection of [one's] interests" set forth in Article 11 of the Convention . . . [11]

While the ECtHR did not define the nature of the collective bargaining that it protected, it is clear that it goes beyond mere consultation.[12]

Where Did These Rights Come From?

In times like these, it is difficult to imagine how trade union rights became hallmarks of international human rights law. Clearly, a rising labour movement and socialist European governments following the Second World War were powerful drivers. Pressure from left-wing resistance leaders in postwar governments and from the progressive working-class populations who elected them, coupled with efforts to choke off any interest in communism, played a part. But it was the success of industry-wide collective bargaining as a means of economic recovery from the Great Depression of the 1930s in Europe, North America, and Australia that set the stage for constitutionalizing collective bargaining, in particular, in international law.

Mexico embedded the right to strike in its constitution in 1918. The right to collective bargaining has almost as long a legislative history: Article 159 of the German *Weimar Constitution* of 1919 protected the right to form unions and to improve conditions at work, declaring "all agreements and measures limiting this right are illegal." Article 165 provided:

> Workers and employees are called upon to participate, on an equal footing and in cooperation with the employers, in the regulation of wages and working conditions as well as in the economic development of productive forces. The organizations formed by both sides and their mutual agreements are recognized. Workers and employees are granted, in order to represent their social and economic

interests, legal representations in Enterprise Workers' Councils as well as in District Workers' Councils, organized for the various economic areas, and in a Reich Workers' Council . . .

Perhaps surprisingly, in the light of recent history, the United States was also an early leader. Its *Railway Labor Act* (1926) required railway companies to bargain collectively,[13] and the *National Labor Relations Act* of 1935 (a product of the Great Depression), stated in its still extant preamble:

> The inequality of bargaining power between employees who do not possess full freedom of association or actual liberty of contract and employers who are organized in the corporate or other forms of ownership association substantially burdens and affects the flow of commerce, and tends to aggravate recurrent business depressions, by depressing wage rates and the purchasing power of wage earners in industry and by preventing the stabilization of competitive wage rates and working conditions within and between industries.

The scheme of the *National Labor Relations Act* (known as the Wagner model) was also adapted in Canada after the Second World War.[14]

In June 1936, France's Popular Front government provided for the rights both to strike and to bargain collectively (as well as the forty-hour workweek and paid holidays) in the Matignon Accords, which settled the general strike of that year.

In the United Kingdom, meanwhile, sectoral collective bargaining had been state policy since the First World War. In 1916, the wartime government asked J.H. Whitley, a former Speaker of the House of Commons, to chair a committee established to "make and consider suggestions for securing a permanent improvement in the relations between employers and workmen."[15] The committee produced five reports on industrial relations issues, with the first recommending that the government should "without delay propose to the various associations of employers and employed the formation of Joint Standing Industrial Councils [JICs] in each industry."[16] The final report of the committee stated that "taking our first and final reports together, they constitute a scheme designed to cover all the chief industries of the country and to equip each of them with a representative joint body capable of dealing with matters affecting the welfare of the industry in which employers and employed are concerned."[17] This led to the creation of seventy-three JICs (though this number was subsequently reduced).

Notably, there was no suggestion that legal intervention was required to set up the JICs, but the system of sectoral collective bargaining was buttressed by other measures. For example, government contractors and subcontractors were required to abide by the relevant JIC agreements under the Fair Wages Resolutions.[18] In industries where unions did not have sufficient strength to form the employee side of a JIC, the *Trade Boards Acts* of 1909 and 1918 and the *Wages Council Act* of 1945 required the creation of tripartite boards (employers' representatives, workers' representatives, and independent members appointed by the relevant minister) to set terms and conditions of employment in the sector.

Most important was government support for collective bargaining (and to a lesser extent for the right to strike), especially during the Great Depression. The Ministry of Labour's Annual Report for 1934 said:

> It has been the policy of the Department to take every opportunity of stimulating the establishment of joint voluntary machinery or of strengthening that already in existence.[19]

During the Second World War, the collective bargaining system was heavily relied upon to enhance Britain's war effort. Order 1305 was a compulsory measure that provided the legal machinery to extend collective agreements to non-parties in an effort to prevent undercutting.

In fact, collective bargaining was the policy of all U.K. governments for almost seventy-five years until Thatcher's 1979 election. Since then, in the cause of neoliberalism, the attack on collective bargaining and on the right to strike has been remorseless. Deliberate government policy has dismantled every prop to collective bargaining and waged a ceaseless media war on it.

In particular, the removal of trade union freedom to take industrial action, except under the most restrictive conditions, has prevented unions from maintaining sectoral collective bargaining machinery. As a result, collective bargaining coverage in the United Kingdom has fallen from 82 per cent in 1979 (around the western European average even today) to a mere 23 per cent in 2011,[20] while union membership has been halved, from 12.25 million members in 1979 to 6.2 million in 2012.

The Importance of Basic Trade Union Rights

Union density and collective bargaining coverage are related measures, but they not synonymous.[21] It is the latter that is most crucial to improving conditions for working-class people. Ironically, sometimes even trade unions need to be reminded of the importance of collective bargaining, which, of course, must be buttressed by the right to strike. Without this right, collective bargaining is no more than collective begging.

Collective bargaining not only prevents undercutting by competitors seeking to reduce labour costs, but it also encourages competition by investment in research and development. Collective bargaining is also good for productivity.[22] Employers need to recognize that reducing labour costs may present a short-term advantage for the undercutter, but it results in a reduction in consumption and demand. This reduction, in turn, diminishes sales of goods and services, reduces the amount of taxes collected, decreases government investment and support, and ultimately damages the economy.

Historical statistics show that a decline in collective bargaining coverage is mirrored by growth in inequality, and vice versa. It is no coincidence that the strong and efficient economies of Germany, Sweden, Norway, and Denmark have extensive sectoral collective bargaining coverage underpinned by strong trade union rights. A growing literature illustrates that collective bargaining is a solution to the problem of inequality.[23] As research for the ILO has found:

> . . . income distribution is not primarily determined by technological progress, but rather depends on social institutions and on the structure of the financial system. Strengthening the welfare state, in particular changing union legislation to foster collective bargaining and financial regulation could help increase the wage share with little if any costs in terms of economic efficiency.[24]

Of course, there are other reasons why collective bargaining is a good thing. It is a means of achieving justice at the workplace between the conflicting interests of the employer and the workers. Without collective bargaining, that conflict of interest would merely reflect the inherent imbalance in power between the worker and the employer.

Even where collective bargaining is insufficient to negate the inherent inequality of bargaining power, it still provides the means by which workers can be heard by those who make decisions. Collective bargaining is usually the only satisfactory way of achieving any degree of democracy at work; without it, workers have no voice in the conditions of their working lives, and remain at the mercy of management dictates.

Governments that do not promote collective bargaining as a human right are defying international law. Unions have limited – but still valuable – tools at their disposal, and they need to put the fight to restore sector-wide collective bargaining at the top of their agendas. They need to act globally as well as locally, and carefully consider using the principles of international labour law where they can be applied to appropriate cases. Unions also need to support organizations that campaign for other human rights – the forces of neoliberalism are intent on neutering them, too. As history has shown, it is the power of collective organization, and not lawyers and judges, that ultimately secures and maintains fundamental rights.

Notes

Introduction

1 Bruce Campbell, "Rising Inequality, Declining Democracy," Canadian Centre for Policy Alternatives, December 2011, www.policyalternatives.ca.

2 Dave Coles, "Close the Gap: Time for Canada to Limit CEO-Worker Pay Differentials," *Rabble.ca*, May 29, 2013, http://rabble.ca/blogs.

3 Tavia Grant, "Canadians Believe Income Inequality Getting Worse," *The Globe and Mail*, May 27, 2013.

4 Andrew Coyne, "The Myth of Income Inequality: Since the Bleak 90s, Things Have Actually Gotten Better," *The National Post*, September 2, 2013.

5 Terence Corcoran: "Beware of Bogus Union Claims That Wage Hikes Will Bring Growth," *The National Post*, September 2, 2013.

6 Lawrence Mishel and Matthew Walters, "How Unions Help All Workers," Economic Policy Institute, August 26, 2003, www.epi.org.

7 A. Jackson, *Work and Labour in Canada* (Toronto: Canadian Scholars' Press Inc., 2005).

8 Mishel and Walters, "How Unions Help All Workers."

9 Toke Aidt and Zafiris Tzannatos, *Unions and Collective Bargaining Economic Effects in a Global Environment* (Washington, D.C.: The World Bank, 2003).

10 Alex Bryson, Rafael Gomez, Tobias Kretschmer, and Paul Willman, *Union Workplace Voice and Civic Engagement*, Discussion Paper No. 394 (London: National Institute of Economic and Social Research, 2012).

11 Nick Bunker and David Madland, *Unions Make Democracy Work for the Middle Class* (Washington, D.C.: Center for American Progress Action Fund, 2012).

12 International Institute for Labour Studies, *World of Work Report 2008: Income Inequalities in the Age of Financial Globalization* (Geneva: International Labour Organization, 2008).

One: Why Unions Matter

1 Richard Wilkinson and Kate Pickett, *The Spirit Level: Why Equality Is Better for Everyone* (London: Penguin, 2010).

2 Conference Board of Canada, "How Canada Performs: A Report Card on Canada," January 2013, www.conferenceboard.ca.

3 The term "Great Compression" was coined by Claudia Dale Goldin and Robert A. Margo, "The Great Compression: The Wage Structure in the United States at Mid-Century," *Quarterly Journal of Economics* 107,1 (1992), 1–34.

4 Andrew Jackson, *Work and Labour in Canada* (Toronto: Canadian Scholars' Press Inc., 2005).

5 Michael Lynk, "Labour Law and the New Inequality," *University of New Brunswick Law Journal* 59 (2009), 14–40.

6 Ibid., 35.

7 Toke Aidt and Zafiris Tzannatos, *Unions and Collective Bargaining: Economic Effects in a Global Environment* (Washington, D.C.: The World Bank, 2002).

8 Andrew Berg and Jonathan Ostry, *Inequality and Unsustainable Growth: Two Sides of the Same Coin?* (Washington, D.C.: International Monetary Fund Research Department, 2011).

9 Selected research papers that discuss the important link between union density and reduction in income inequality: Derek Fudge, "Labour Rights: A Democratic Counterweight to Growing Income Inequality in Canada," in *Constitutional Labour Rights in Canada: Farm Workers and the Fraser Case*, ed. Fay Faraday, Judy Fudge, and Eric Tucker (Toronto: Irwin Law Books, 2012), 234–60; Lawrence Mishel, "Unions, Inequality, and Faltering Middle-Class Wages," Issue Brief #342 (Washington, D.C.: Economic Policy Institute, 2012); Jake Rosenfeld and Bruce Western, "Unions, Norms, and the Rise in U.S. Wage Inequality," *American Sociological Review* 76,4 (2011), 513–37; Arthur S. Alderson, Stephanie Moller, and François Nielsen, "Changing Patterns of Income Inequality in U.S. Counties, 1970–2001," *American Journal of Sociology* 114,4 (2009) 1037–1101; Daniele Checchi and Jelle Visser, *Inequality and the Labour Market: Unions*, Oxford Handbook on Economic Inequality (Oxford: Oxford University Press, 2009), 230–56; John Godard, "Do Labor Laws Matter? The Density Decline and Convergence Thesis Revisited," *Industrial Relations: A Journal of Economy and Society* 42,3 (2003), 458–92.

10 International Institute for Labour Studies, *World of Work Report 2008: Income Inequalities in the Age of Financial Globalization* (Geneva: International Labour Office, 2008), 83–4.

11 Fudge, "Labour Rights."

12 Nicole Fortin, David A. Green, Thomas Lemieux, Kevin Milligan, and W. Craig Riddell, "Canadian Inequality: Recent Developments and Policy Options," *Canadian Public Policy* 38,2 (2012), 121–45.

13 Jacob S. Hacker and Paul Pierson, "Winner-Take-All Politics: Public Policy, Political Organization, and the Precipitous Rise of Top Incomes in the United States," *Politics & Society* 38,2 (2010), 152–204.

14 Paul Krugman, *The Conscience of a Liberal* (New York: W.W. Norton & Company Inc., 2007), 125.

15 Rachel Mendelson, "Richard Wilkinson in Canada: Income Inequality Guru's Ideas Gaining Traction in Halls of Power," *The Huffington Post Canada*, May 5, 2012, www.huffingtonpost.ca.

16 Armine Yalnizyan, "Welcome to Canada's Wageless Recovery," Canadian Centre for Policy Alternatives, November 2, 2012, www.behindthenumbers.ca.

17 Richard Smith, "Editor's Choice: The Big Idea," *British Medical Journal* 312,7037, quoted in Wilkinson and Pickett, *The Spirit Level*, 81n82.

18 Wilkinson and Pickett, *The Spirit Level*; *World of Work Report 2008*, n13; and *World Development Report 2006: Equity and Development* (Washington, DC: The World Bank, 2007), n11.

19 Lynk, "Labour Law and the New Inequality."

20 Krugman, *The Conscience of a Liberal*, 51.

21 Armine Yalnizyan, *The Rise of Canada's Richest 1%* (Ottawa: Canadian Centre for Policy Alternatives, 2010).

22 Raghuram Govinda Rajan, *Fault Lines: How Hidden Fractures Still Threaten the World Economy* (Princeton: Princeton University Press, 2010).

23 Romain Rancière and Michael Kumhof, *Inequality, Leverage and Crises* (Washington, D.C.: International Monetary Fund Working Papers, WP/10/268, 2010).

24 Lynk, "Labour Law and the New Inequality."

25 Krugman, *The Conscience of a Liberal*, 2.

26 Raymond Lonergan, "A Steadfast Friend of Labor," in *Mr. Justice Brandeis, Great American: Press Opinion and Public Appraisal*, ed. Irving Dilliard (St.Louis: The Modern Day Press, 1941), 42.

27 Organisation for Economic Co-operation and Development, *Divided We Stand: Why Inequality Keeps Rising* (Brussells: OECD Publishing, 2011), 3.

28 Ibid., 22.

29 Joseph Stiglitz, "Inequality Is Holding Back the Recovery," *New York Times* online commentary, January 19, 2013, http://opinionator.blogs.nytimes.com.

30 OECD, *Divided We Stand*, 22.

31 Joseph Stiglitz, *The Price of Inequality: How Today's Divided Society Endangers Our Future* (New York: W.W. Norton & Company, 2012).

32 Evan Capeluck and Andrew Sharpe, *The Impact of Redistribution on Income Inequality in Canada and the Provinces, 1981–2010* (Ottawa: The Centre for the Study of Living Standards, 2012).

33 Krugman, *The Conscience of a Liberal*, 134.

34 Paul Krugman blog, "Introducing This Blog," September 18, 2007, www.krugman.blogs.nytimes.com.

35 Bruce Campbell and Armine Yalnizyan, "Why Unions Matter" blog post, Canadian Centre for Policy Alternatives, www.behindthenumbers.ca.

36 Craig Alexander and Francis Fong, *Income and Income Inequality: A Tale of Two Countries* (Toronto: TD Economics, 2012).

37 Mishel, "Unions, Inequality, and Faltering Middle-Class Wages"; Checchi and Visser, *Inequality and the Labour Market*.

38 OECD, *Divided We Stand*.

39 David Card, Thomas Lemieux, and W. Craig Riddell, "Unions and Wage Inequality," *Journal of Labor Research* 25,4 (2004), 519–59.

40 *World of Work Report 2008*.

41 Robert Fox, "Wealth and Income Extremes Hurt Us All," Straight Goods News, January 23, 2013, http://sgnews.ca.

42 Alexandra Mitukiewicz and John Schmitt, "Politics Matter: Changes in Unionisation Rates in Rich Countries, 1960–2010," *Industrial Relations Journal* 43,3 (2012), 260–80.

43 Fudge, "Labour Rights." The data on regressive labour laws in Canada is regularly updated on www.labourrights.ca.

44 Susan Johnson, "Card Check or Mandatory Representation Vote? How the Type of Union Recognition Procedure Affects Union Certification Success," *The Economic Journal* 112,479 (2002), 344–61.

45 W. Craig Riddell, "Union Suppression and Certification Success," *Canadian Journal of Economics* 34,2 (2001), 396–410.

46 Among the many affected: Elementary Teachers Federation of Ontario (ETFO) has 76,000 members; Ontario Secondary School Teachers Federation (OSSTF) has 60,000 members; Canadian Union of Public Employees (CUPE) represents 55,000 education workers, including custodians, secretaries, educational assistants, and library staff; Ontario Public Service Employees Union (OPSEU) represents 2,000 education workers.

47 Kris Warner, *Protecting Fundamental Labor Rights: Lessons from Canada for the United States* (Washington, D.C.: Center for Economic and Policy Research [CEPR], 2012).

48 Ibid., 1.

49 Ibid., 20.

50 Ibid., 12.

51 King was speaking on right-to-work laws in 1961. Southern Labor Institute, "Now Is the Time. Dr. Martin Luther King Jr. on Labor in the South: The Case for a Coalition,"

booklet prepared under the auspices of the Labor Subcommittee of the King Holiday Commission, designed by the AFT and printed by AFSCME, January 1986.

52 Elise Gould and Heidi Shierholz, *The Compensation Penalty of "Right-to-Work" Laws* (Washington, D.C.: Economic Policy Institute: Issue Brief #299, 2011).

53 Christopher Schenk, *Unions in a Democratic Society* (Ottawa: Canadian Centre for Policy Alternatives, 2012).

54 Ibid.

55 Andrew Jackson, "Labour Law and Jobs: A Tale of Two Provinces," August 9, 2012, www.progressive-economics.ca.

56 Garry Sran and Jim Stanford, "Further Tests of the Link Between Unionization, Unemployment, and Employment: Findings from Canadian National and Provincial Data," *Just Labour: A Canadian Journal of Work and Society* 15 (2009), 29–77.

57 Osmond Kessler Fraenkel, ed., *The Curse of Bigness: Miscellaneous Papers of Louis D. Brandeis* (New York: Viking Press, 1965), 43.

58 Tony Fang and Anil Verma, *Workplace Innovation and Union Status: Synergy or Strife?* Proceedings of the 55th Annual Meeting, Industrial Relations Research Association (Ithaca, New York: 2003), 189–98.

59 Jackson, "Labour Law and Jobs."

60 Paul Beaudry, David A. Green, and Benjamin Sand, "Does Industrial Composition Matter for Wages? A Test of Search and Bargaining Theory," *Econometrica* 80,3 (2012), 1063–1104.

61 Hacker and Pierson, "Winner Take-All Politics."

62 John Kenneth Galbraith, *Created Unequal: The Crisis in American Pay* (New York: Free Press, 1998), 265.

63 Alex Bryson, Rafael Gomez, Tobias, Kretschmer, and Paul Willman, *Union Workplace Voice and Civic Engagement* (London: National Institute of Economic and Social Research, Discussion Paper No. 394, 2012).

64 Nick Bunker and David Madland, *Unions Make Democracy Work for the Middle Class* (Washington, D.C.: Center for American Progress Action Fund, 2012).

65 Ibid.

66 William Dean Howells, "Equality as the Basis of Good Society," *The Century Magazine* (November 1895), 63–67, www.unz.org.

Two: Income Inequality in Canada

1 Organisation for Economic Co-operation and Development, OECD.StateExtracts, http://stats.oecd.org.

2 Richard Wilkinson and Kate Pickett, *The Spirit Level: Why Equality Is Better for Everyone* (London: Penguin, 2010).

3 Andrew Heisz, *Income Inequality and Redistribution in Canada, 1976 to 2004*, Catalogue no. 11F0019MIE – No. 298 (Ottawa: Statistics Canada, 2007); Conference Board of Canada, Conference Board of Canada, "Canadian Income Inequality: Is Canada Becoming More Unequal?" www.conferenceboard.ca.

4 Shauna MacKinnon, "National Housing Day: Still Waiting for a Plan" (Ottawa: Canadian Centre for Policy Alternatives, November 21, 20120), www.policyalternatives.ca.

5 André Picard, "Wealth Begets Health: Why Universal Medical Care Only Goes So Far," *The Globe and Mail*, November 12, 2013.

6 Vincent Ferrao, "Paid Work," in Statistics Canada, *Women in Canada: A Gender-based Statistical Report* (89–503-X), 2013, www.statcan.gc.ca.

7 Pierre Fortin, Luc Godbout, and Suzie St-Cerny, "Impact of Quebec's Universal Low Fee Childcare Program on Female Labour Force Participation, Domestic Income, and Government Budgets," Université de Sherbrooke, Working Paper 2012/02, www.usherbrooke.ca.

Three: Increasing Inequality

1 Jelle Visser and Daniele Checchi, "Inequality and the Labor Market: Unions," in *The Oxford Handbook of Economic Inequality*, ed. Wiemer Salverda, Brian Nolan, and Tim Smeeding (Oxford: Oxford University Press, 2009), 230–56.

2 The Wagner Act is further discussed in chapter 4 of this book.

3 See Craig Riddell, "Unionization in Canada and the United States," in *Small Differences that Matter: Labor Markets and Income Maintenance in Canada and the United States* (Chicago: University of Chicago Press, 1993), 110; see also Bureau of Labor Statistics, "Union Members – 2012," news release, USDL-13–0105, January 23, 2013, www.bls.gov.

4 Organisation for Economic Co-operation and Development, "Divided We Stand: Why Inequality Keeps Rising" (Paris: OECD, 2011), www.oecd.org.

5 Mike Veall, "Top Income Shares in Canada: Recent Trends and Policy Implications," *Canadian Journal of Economics*, November 2012; Thomas Piketty and Emmanuel Saez, "Income and Wage Inequality in the United States, 1913–2002," in *The Oxford Handbook of Economic Inequality*.

6 Veall, "Top Income Shares in Canada: Recent Trends and Policy Implications." Surveys show that there has not in fact been much change in middle class household incomes in Canada over the last thirty years (see figure 3) – but because these surveys have very few respondents at the very top end, they cannot examine the top 1 per cent of income earners. The direct impact of unions of hourly wages (an issue that primarily affects the middle part of income distribution) has been much analyzed using survey data.

7 Lars Osberg, "Why Did Unemployment Disappear from Official Macro-Economic Policy Discourse in Canada?" in *New Directions for Intelligent Government in Canada: Papers in Honour of Ian Stewart*, ed. Fred Gorbet and Andrew Sharpe (Ottawa: Centre for the Study of Living Standards, 2011), 127–65.

8 CANSIM V1806037 and V1807573 confirm that average hourly real wages have continued to stagnate since then.

9 The distribution of annual incomes in a given year is a cross-sectional snapshot of individuals of different ages, many of whom will experience growth in earnings over their life cycle. For the downward shift in Canada of the age/earnings profiles of recently entering cohorts, see Paul Beaudry and David Green, "Cohort Patterns in Canadian Earnings: Assessing the Role of Skill Premia in Inequality Trends," *Canadian Journal of Economics* 33,4 (2000), 907–936.

10 Murphy, Roberts, and Wolfson make the same point with income tax data from 1982 to 2004 – very little change in real income for the bottom eight deciles. Alternative measurement choices (e.g., adjusting for household size or direct taxes) make little difference. Brian Murphy, Paul Roberts, and Michael Wolfson, "High-income Canadians," *Perspectives on Labour and Income*, Statistics Canada Cat No. 75–001-XIE (September 2007), 5–17.

11 Figures 1 and 4 can describe trends among the top 1 per cent (and fewer) because they are based on data drawn from income tax records, which all the top few of the income distribution have to fill out. Figure 3 and table 1 are based on data drawn from

surveys, which sample very few high-income households and face significant non-response among the very affluent. Incomes are also "top-coded" to prevent observation of the highest incomes, and hence cannot be depended on to track top income trends. Because the actual income gains of the top 20 per cent are, as figure 4 shows, mainly received by the top end of that top 20 per cent of households, and are poorly captured by survey methods, table 1 likely understates recent gains in top quintile income share.

12 Six-month moving averages reported. Source: Statistics Canada, CANSIM Table 282–0077 – Labour force survey estimates (LFS), employees by union coverage, North American Industry Classification System (NAICS), sex and age group, unadjusted for seasonality, monthly (persons).

13 See Bureau of Labor Statistics, "Union Members – 2012."

14 Riddell, "Unionization in Canada and the United States."

15 As well, Western argues that unions help set the norms of the "moral economy" and define ideas of fairness and minimum living standards, which are particularly important for low-income Canadians. Bruce Western and Jake Rosenfeld, "Unions, Norms, and the Rise in U.S. Wage Inequality," *American Sociological Review* 76 (2011), 513.

16 The capital-intensive nature of modern resource extraction limits greatly the number of unionized workers who could benefit.

17 See, for example, Benjamin I. Page, Larry M. Bartels, and Jason Seawright, "Democracy and the Policy Preferences of Wealthy Americans," *Perspectives on Politics* 11,1 (March 2013), 51–73.

Four: Labour Law and Labour Rights

1 Named after Senator Robert Wagner of New York, who sponsored the legislation in the U.S. Senate.

2 *National Labor Relations Act*, 29 U.S.C. 151–169, s.1: "The inequality of bargaining power between employees who do not possess full freedom of association or actual liberty of contract and employers who are organized in the corporate or other forms of business association . . . "

3 Ibid., "The inequality of bargaining power . . . tends to aggravate recurrent business depressions by depressing wage rates and the purchasing power of wage earners . . . "

4 *Ford Motor Co. and U.A.W.-C.I.O.* (1944–48), 18,001 Canadian Wartime Labour Relations Board Decisions 159 (Justice Ivan Rand), at 160: "In industry, capital must in the long run be looked upon as occupying a dominant position. It is in some respects at greater risk than labour; but as industry becomes established these risks change inversely. Certainly the predominance of capital against individual labour is unquestionable; and in mass relations, hunger is more imperious than passed dividends. . . . The power of organized labour, the necessary co-partner of capital, must be available to redress the balance of what is called social justice . . . "

5 Louis Brandeis, *The Curse of Bigness* (New York: Viking Press, 1934).

6 *National Labor Relations Act*, 29 U.S.C. 151–169, n1, s.1: "It is declared to be the policy of the United States to . . . [encourage] the practice and procedure of collective bargaining and by protecting the exercise by workers of full freedom of association . . . "; *Canada Labour Code*, R.S.C. 1985, c. L-2, preamble: "Whereas there is a long tradition in Canada of labour legislation and policy designed for the promotion of the common well-being through the encouragement of free collective bargaining and the constructive settlement of disputes."

7 Paul Krugman, *The Conscience of a Liberal* (New York: W.W. Norton, 2007), chap. 3–5.

8 Andrew Jackson, *Work and Labour in Canada,* 2nd ed. (Toronto: Canadian Scholars' Press Inc., 2009); Kim Moody, *US Labor in Trouble and Transition* (New York: Verso, 2007).

9 Over the past thirty-five years, the three Democratic presidential administrations all tried, and failed, to pass through Congress substantial labour reforms to the *National Labor Relations Act*: Jimmy Carter in 1978, Bill Clinton in 1994, and Barack Obama in 2009–10.

10 See, generally, Kris Warner, *Protecting Fundamental Labor Rights: Lessons from Canada for the United States* (Washington, D.C.: Center for Economic and Policy Research, 2012).

11 Joseph Stiglitz, *The Price of Inequality* (New York: W.W. Norton, 2012); Bruce Western & Jake Rosenfeld, "Unions, Norms and the Rise in US Wage Inequality," *American Sociological Review* 76 (2011), 513.

12 Organisation for Economic Co-operation and Development, *Divided We Stand: Why Inequality Keeps Rising* (Paris: OECD, 2011). Also see Nicole Fortin, et al., "Canadian Inequality: Recent Developments and Policy Options," *Canadian Public Policy* 38 (2012), 121.

13 See generally, Andrew Jackson, *Union Communities, Healthy Communities* (Ottawa: Broadbent Institute, 2013).

14 John Moylan, "Union Membership Has Halved Since 1980," BBC News, September 7, 2012, www.bbc.co.uk.

15 Peter Barnacle et al., *Employment Law in Canada,* 4th ed. (Toronto: LexisNexis, 2013), ch. 5.

16 Michael Lynk, "Disability and Work: The Transformation of the Legal Status of Employees with Disabilities in Canada," in *Law Society of Upper Canada Special Lectures 2007: Employment Law,* ed. Randall Echlin and Chris Paliare (Toronto: Irwin Law, 2008).

17 The lead ruling in the labour trilogy was *Reference Re Public Service Employee Relations Act,* [1987], 1 S.C.R. 313.

18 *Dunmore v. Ontario (Attorney General),* 2001 SCC 94.

19 *Health Services and Support – Facilities Subsector Bargaining Assn. v. British Columbia,* 2007 SCC 27.

20 *Ontario (Attorney General) v. Fraser,* 2011 SCC 20.

21 For example, see the following comment by Bastarache J. in *Dunmore v. Ontario,* n18 at para. 16: " . . . the law must recognize that certain union activities – making collective representations to an employer, adopting a majority political platform, federating with other unions – may be central to freedom of association even though they are inconceivable on the individual level."

22 *Health Services and Support v. B.C.,* n19 at para. 78.

23 For more detail on the labour legislation that has shrunk access to collective bargaining in recent years, see the listing compiled by the Canadian Foundation for Labour Rights: www.labourrights.ca/restrictive-labour-laws.

24 Judy Fudge and Eric Tucker, *Labour Before the Law: The Regulation of Workers' Collective Action in Canada, 1900–1948* (Toronto: Oxford University Press, 2001).

25 Ontario Progressive Conservative Caucus, *Paths to Prosperity: Flexible Labour Markets* (Toronto, 2012).

Five: Unions and Democratic Governance

1 For an analysis of various attempts to weaken unions by using an "impoverished" sense of democracy, see Michael Ford, "Citizenship and Democracy in Industrial Relations: The Agenda for the 1990s?" *Modern Law Review* 55 (1992), 241. Ford's analysis of the threats facing unions seems very relevant to the current Canadian discourse.

2 See the various accounts described at http://archive.uniondemocracy.org, Democracy for Unions, as well the tormented history of the U.S.-based International as Brotherhood of Teamsters.

3 Ford, "Citizenship and Democracy in Industrial Relations," 257.

4 (1984) 468 U.S. 609.

5 *Reference Re Public Service Employee Relations Act (Alta.)*, [1987] 1 S.C.R. 313; *PSAC* v. *Canada*, [1987] 1 S.C.R. 424; and RWDSU v. *Saskatchewan*, [1987] 1 S.C.R. 460.

6 Sopinka J. in *Professional Institute of the Public Service of Canada* v. *Northwest Territories (Commissioner)*, [1990] 2 S.C.R. 367.

7 *Health Services and Support – Facilities Subsector Bargaining Assn.* v. *British Columbia*, [2007] 2 S.C.R. 391.

8 *Ontario (Attorney General)* v. *Fraser*, 2011 SCC 20, [2011] 2 S.C.R. 3.

9 See Jacques Desmarais, "La liberté d'association, une liberté réduite," June 14, 2011, www.uqam.ca.

10 *Lavigne v. Ontario Public Service Employees Union*, [1991] 2 S.C.R. 211.

Six: Advancing Human Rights for All Canadians

1 The Rand formula, also known as compulsory dues check off, is a common feature of Canadian labour law (see discussion in chapter 1 of this book). It dates back to an arbitration decision by former Supreme Court of Canada Justice Ivan Rand in 1946 that was part of the settlement ending a United Auto Workers' strike at the Windsor, Ontario, Ford plant. At the heart of the decision was the recognition that union dues should be paid by all those who benefited from the union contract, not just the signed members of the union. The Rand formula ensures that employees in a unionized workplace cannot refuse to pay union dues while still benefiting from the union's collective bargaining activities, eliminating the "free-rider problem" that might otherwise exist.

2 Carmela Patrias and Ruth A. Frager, "'This Is Our Country, These Are Our Rights': Minorities and the Origins of Ontario's Human Rights Campaigns," *Canadian Historical Review* 82,1 (2001), 1.

3 Ibid., 10–11; and Ross Lambertson, "The Dresden Story: Racism, Human Rights, and the Jewish Labour Committee of Canada," *Labour/Travail* 47 (Spring 2001), 45–46.

4 One educational pamphlet from 1947 read: "Anti-semitism, anti-Negroism, anti-Catholicism, anti-French, anti-English as the case may be, and union-smashing are all parts of a single reactionary crusade of hatred and destruction." See Patrias and Frager, "'This Is Our Country, These Are Our Rights,'" 11.

5 Jack Williams, *The Story of Unions in Canada* (Toronto: J.M. Dent & Sons Ltd., 1975) 163–64 and 176–88.

6 Lambertson, "The Dresden Story," 50.

7 Ibid., 48.

8 Arnold Bruner, "The Genesis of Ontario's Human Rights Legislation: A Study in Law Reform," *University of Toronto Faculty of Law Review* 37,236 (1979), 238. Also see Patrias and Frager, "'This Is Our Country, These Are Our Rights,'" 11.

9 Lambertson, "The Dresden Story," 53. The Joint Committees in Toronto and Montreal were the most long-lasting, with short-lived ones in Hamilton, Calgary, and Halifax.

10 Patrias and Frager, "'This Is Our Country, These Are Our Rights,'" 11.

11 Lambertson, "The Dresden Story," 59–60.

12 Patrias and Frager, "'This Is Our Country, These Are Our Rights,'" 11–12.

13 Ibid, 12–13. Also see Lambertson, "The Dresden Story," 59–60.

14 Ibid., 11.

15 Bruner, "The Genesis of Ontario's Human Rights Legislation," 240, 251.

16 Patrias and Frager, "'This Is Our Country, These Are Our Rights,'" 18.

17 Lambertson, "The Dresden Story," 74. The committees were often represented in court by David Lewis, the future national NDP leader.

18 Ibid.

19 The Toronto Association for Civil Liberties presented a brief to Premier Frost in 1954 that referred to discrimination against blacks across Ontario, but noted that "the height of expression of Jim Crow in Canada is to be found in the town of Dresden, Ontario" (Lambertson, "The Dresden Story," 70). Two authors of the brief were Bora Laskin and David Lewis.

20 Kay's Cafe was originally acquitted in 1955, but the practices of owner Morley McKay didn't change. Union activists gathered more evidence and McKay was finally convicted in a second test case in 1956 (Lambertson, "The Dresden Story," 76–78). The conviction was maintained on appeal: *R. ex rel. Nutland* v. *McKay*, [1956] 5 DLR (2d) 403.

21 Lambertson, "The Dresden Story," 79.

22 Ross Lambertson, *Repression and Resistance: Canadian Human Rights Activists, 1930–1960* (Toronto: University of Toronto Press, 2005), 286.

23 Linda Briskin, "A Caucus of Caucuses: The Next Stage in Union Equity Organizing," *Just Labour* 8 (Spring 2006), 104.

24 *The Report of the Royal Commission on the Status of Women* (Ottawa, 1970), 54, para. 179.

25 Meg Luxton, "Feminism as a Class Act: Working Class Feminism and the Women's Movement in Canada," *Labour/Le Travail* 48,63 (Fall 2001), 68.

26 Luxton, "Feminism as a Class Act," 68, 70; Labour Canada, "Women in the Labour Force: Fact and Figures," (Statistics Canada: 1977).

27 Joan Sangster reviewed volumes 1 to 20 of *Labour Arbitration Cases* to reach this finding: see Joan Sangster, "Debating Maternity Benefits: Pacific Western Airlines and Flight Attendants' Struggle to 'Fly Pregnant' in the 1970s," in *Work on Trial: Canadian Labour Law Struggles*, ed. Judy Fudge and Eric Tucker (Toronto: Osgoode Society for Canadian Legal History, 2010), 308n18.

28 Ibid., 291.

29 Ibid., 292, 310n49. The author quoted the original case, a copy of which was obtained from the Canadian Labour Congress Papers at Library and Archives Canada.

30 Ibid., 292. According to Sangster, the age bar was conquered soon afterwards. By 1972, Air Canada estimated that 30 per cent of its stewardesses were married, and some had children.

31 Luxton, "Feminism as a Class Act," 69, 72.

32 The Royal Commission on the Status of Women reported in 1970 that collective agreements generally offered longer maternity leaves than were available in other workplaces. The Royal Commission produced a table of statutes from across the country that guaranteed the right to equal pay for women, although the commission did note that many employers tried to find ways to circumvent these legislative

protections. At the time, only B.C. and New Brunswick had legislation protecting the right to maternity leave. See *Report of the Royal Commission on the Status of Women*, 64, 72, 85, with table at 68–70.

33 Anne Porter, *Gendered States: Women, Unemployment Insurance and the Political Economy of the Welfare State in Canada, 1945–1997* (Toronto: University of Toronto Press, 2003), 77, 79; Luxton, "Feminism as a Class Act," 77.

34 Indeed, trade unions in the early 1900s were openly hostile as male unionists feared that women in the work force would lower wages: Maureen Baker and Mary-Anne Robertson, "Trade Union Reaction to Women Workers and Their Concerns," *Canadian Journal of Sociology* 6,19 (1981), 23.

35 Luxton, "Feminism as a Class Act," 77. Also see a more critical account in Baker and Robertson, "Trade Union Reaction to Women Workers and Their Concerns."

36 *Report of the Royal Commission on the Status of Women*, 64. In fairness, those same studies also showed that male unionists believed strongly that women as union members should have all the same rights and entitlements as men.

37 Quoted in Luxton, "Feminism as a Class Act," 77.

38 Luxton, "Feminism as a Class Act," 72.

39 *Robichaud* v. *Canada (Treasury Board)*, [1987] 2 S.C.R. 84.

40 In *Brooks* v. *Canada Safeway Ltd.*, [1989] 1 S.C.R. 1219, the Supreme Court of Canada overturned its earlier judgment in *Bliss* v. *Attorney General of Canada*, [1979] 1 S.C.R. 183 (quote at p. 190).

41 *British Columbia (Public Service Employee Relations Commission)* v. *BCGSEU*, [1999] 3 S.C.R. 3 (also known as *Meiorin*).

42 The Canadian Human Rights Tribunal upheld the PSAC's pay equity complaint in 1998 on behalf of approximately 200,000 people working in predominantly female occupations. The Federal Court affirmed the ruling in 1999 and the federal government subsequently reached a resolution worth $3.6 billion in payments. (See *Canada (Attorney General)* v. *Public Service Alliance of Canada* (1999), [2000] 1 F.C. 146.) The Indian Residential Schools' total individual settlements may end up being bigger, but that resolution was not made to satisfy a legal ruling.

43 Sangster, "Debating Maternity Benefits," 284.

44 Judy Fudge and Hester Lessard, "Challenging Norms and Creating Precedents: The Tale of a Woman Firefighter in the Forests of British Columbia," in *Work on Trial: Canadian Labour Law Struggles*, ed. Judy Fudge and Eric Tucker (Toronto: Osgoode Society for Canadian Legal History, 2010), 315–49.

45 See, e.g., *Canada (Attorney General)* v. *Johnstone*, 2013 F.C. 113. Of course, I am not suggesting that child care and parental obligations are only women's issues. However, studies still show that women overwhelmingly assume primary responsibility for child care in dual-income families. This is obviously a further equality issue in itself.

46 Bernard Adell, "The Rights of Disabled Workers at Arbitration and Under Human Rights Legislation," *Canadian Labour Law Journal* 1,46 (1992), 48, 53. Some collective agreements made special provision for "handicapped workers," providing rights to "transfer to more suitable job," and in some cases special seniority rights in layoff/recall situations.

47 M. Kaye Joachim, "Seniority Rights and the Duty to Accommodate," *Queen's Law Journal* 24,131 (1998), 134. The author cites a good review of the early case law in *Cameron* v. *Nel-Gor Castle Nursing Home* (1984), *Canadian Human Rights Reporter* 5, paras. 18392–409 (Ontario Board of Inquiry).

48 Michael Lynk, "Disability and Work: The Transformation of the Legal Status of Employees with Disabilities in Canada," in *Law Society of Upper Canada Special Lectures*

2007: *Employment Law*, ed. Randall Echlin and Chris Paliare (Toronto: Irwin Law, 2008), 190, 217.

49 Ibid., 190.

50 Fudge and Lessard described the union's support for the grievance as "crucial" to its success. They also noted that this was exceptional as the case was based on sex discrimination in a male-dominated job, with the risk of internal union conflict along gender lines. As it turned out, Ms. Meiorin had the full support of her male colleagues. See Fudge and Lessard, "Challenging Norms and Creating Precedents," 327.

51 Lynk, "Disability and Work," 224–25.

52 One of the earliest was the Members with Disabilities Ad Hoc Committee of the Public Service Alliance of Canada, formed in March 1990 PSAC, "Policy Statement and Background Paper on Disabilities Issues," January 1997, www.psac-afpc.org.

53 Briskin, "A Caucus of Caucuses," 105; and Canadian Labour Congress, *The MORE We Get Together: Disability Rights and Collective Bargaining Manual* (2004), www.canadianlabour.ca.

54 Lynk, "Disability and Work," 225.

55 In 1977, Quebec was the first province to include sexual orientation in its human rights legislation, with the next province, Ontario, following much later in 1986. Most other provinces started adding sexual orientation in the early 1990s: see Brian Etherington, "Promises, Promises: Notes on Diversity and Access to Justice," *Queen's Law Journal* 26,43 (2000), 44. The last holdout, Alberta, was forced to include it in 1998 as a result of the Supreme Court of Canada judgment in *Vriend* v. *Alberta* [1998] 1 S.C.R. 493.

56 Gerald Hunt, "Sexual Orientation and the Canadian Labour Movement," *Relations industrielles* 52,4 (1997), 791.

57 Hunt refers to research from 1983 indicating that "a few" collective agreements included sexual orientation in the "no discrimination" clauses: ibid., 789. In my own review of decisions reported in *Labour Arbitration Cases* (LACs), there were a few examples from the early 1980s referencing "no discrimination" clauses that included sexual orientation. These employers included Canada Post, the Toronto Public Library, and the University of British Columbia.

58 Efforts by the Public Service Alliance of Canada to include sexual orientation in collective agreements are described in *Moore* v. *Canada (Treasury Board)*, [1996] CHRD No. 8 (Canadian Human Rights Tribunal), at paras. 40–41.

59 See, e.g., *Carleton University and CUPE, Local 2424* (1988), 35 LAC (3d) 96; *Watson and Treasury Board*, [1990] CPSSRB No. 91; and *Hewens and Treasury Board*, [1992] CPSSRB No. 164.

60 See, e.g., *Lorenzen and Treasury Board*, [1993] CPPSRB No. 165; *CTEA and Bell Canada (Lee Grievance)*, (1994) 43 LAC (4th) 172 (MacDowell); *CBC* v. *Canadian Media Guild, Local 213 (Chabot Grievance)* (1995), 45 LAC (4th) 353 (D.R. Munroe); and *Moore*. In *Moore*, a Canadian Human Rights Tribunal case, the evidence shows at paras. 44–45 that PSAC referred thirty grievances on same-sex benefits to adjudication from 1987 to 1993. Sometimes, the federal government chose to settle sympathetic cases on a "without prejudice" basis, likely to avoid a negative precedent.

61 Hunt, "Sexual Orientation and the Canadian Labour Movement," 791 and 803.

62 See *Rosenberg* v. *Canada (Attorney General)* (1998), 38 OR (3d) 577 (ONCA). Hunt, "Sexual Orientation and the Canadian Labour Movement," mentions at p. 799 that CUPE funded an "unsuccessful" challenge, but his paper was published before CUPE won on appeal.

63 The evidence in *Moore* at para. 53 shows that the Professional Institute of the Public Service donated money to EGALE to intervene in the Supreme Court of Canada case

(*Egan* v. *Canada* [1995] 2 S.C.R. 513) that established sexual orientation as an analogous ground protected by s. 15 of the *Charter*.

64 Hunt, "Sexual Orientation and the Canadian Labour Movement," 798–800.

65 *Lavigne* v. *OPSEU*, [1991] 2 S.C.R. 211 at 335.

66 Lambertson, *Repression and Resistance*, 286; Sangster, "Debating Maternity Benefits," 284; and Lynk, "Disability and Work," 225.

67 Christopher Schenk and Elaine Bernard, "Social Unionism: Labor as a Political Force," *Social Policy* (Summer 1992), 44.

Seven: A Changing Union Tide Hurts Vulnerable Workers

1 Richard Wilkinson and Kate Pickett, *The Spirit Level: Why Equality Is Better for Everyone* (London: Penguin, 2010).

2 See, for example, Eric Liu, "Viewpoint: The Decline of Unions Is Your Problem Too," *Time Magazine*, January 29, 2013, http://ideas.time.com; Jeannette Wicks-Lim, "Creating Decent Jobs in the United States: The Role of Labor Unions and Collective Bargaining" (Amherst: Political Economy Research Institute, 2009); Wilkinson and Pickett, *The Spirit Level*.

3 Patti Domm, "Dow Hits Fresh High Above 15,000; S&P Pushes to New Record," May 7, 2013, CNBC, www.cnbc.com.

4 In Canada, some refer to workers who come to Canada under the federal government's Temporary Foreign Worker Program as "temporary foreign workers." The preferred and less exclusionary terminology describing such individuals as "migrant workers" is used in this paper; this terminology is used in a number of countries and by the United Nations.

5 Citizenship and Immigration Canada, "Canada – Temporary foreign workers present on December 1st by province or territory and urban area, 2007–2011, RDM, Preliminary 2011 Data," www.cic.gc.ca.

6 Citizenship and Immigration Canada, "Canada: Facts and Figures 2011 – Immigration Overview: Permanent and Temporary Residents," www.cic.gc.ca.

7 Ibid. The exact number was 248,748 people becoming permanent residents in 2011.

8 For a more comprehensive analysis of the situation facing many so-called low-skilled migrant workers in Canada, see Naveen Mehta, *Report on the Status of Migrant Workers in Canada* (Toronto: UFCW Canada, 2012).

9 *Dunmore* v. *Ontario (Attorney General)*, [2001] 3 S.C.R. 1016, 2001 SCC 94.

10 The Supreme Court of Canada held that there was "substantial interference" with farm workers' *Charter* rights to freedom of association due to the lack of a positive framework to protect farm workers from employer reprisals when exercising their associational rights.

11 2011 SCC 20, [2011] 2 S.C.R. 3.

12 With regard to the nature of the court challenge, UFCW Canada alleged that section 21 amounted to a violation of section 2(d) of the *Charter* because it denies agricultural workers employed on farms that have three or fewer employees the right to join a union and bargain collectively. UFCW Canada launched a *Charter* challenge before the Quebec Labour Commission, where it sought certification of a bargaining unit constituted exclusively of migrant workers from Mexico. Relying on *B.C. Health* (and before *Fraser*), the Board found in April 2010 the provision was unconstitutional as it denied agricultural workers the guarantee of freedom of association. The Quebec Attorney General and the farm lobby group FERME appealed that decision to the Quebec Superi-

or Court. On March 11, 2013, the Quebec Superior Court ruled that "in relationship to agricultural workers who work on farms which ordinarily and continuously employ less than three workers, section 21 of the *Code* is discriminatory as being a significant hindrance on their ability to exercise their fundamental right of freedom of association." Section 21 was struck down by the courts and the government of Quebec will not appeal the decision. Therefore, agriculture workers are able to organize with no hindrance to their collective bargaining or freedom of association rights in Quebec.

13 For example, the hundreds of thousands of immigrant workers who come to Canada every year, the millions of racialized workers, disabled workers, and LGBTQ workers, and of course, women. These equity-seeking groups are still working towards a balanced playing field in society and the workplace.

Eight: Who Owns *Charter* Values?

1 *Cooper v. Canada (Human Rights Commission)*, [1996] 3 S.C.R. 854, per McLachlin J. (as she then was) at para. 70.

2 *R. v. Oakes*, [1986] 1 S.C.R. 103 at para. 64.

3 *Health Services and Support – Facilities Subsector Bargaining Assn. v. British Columbia*, 2007 SCC 27, [2007] 2 S.C.R. 391.

4 The English Jacobins were a loose group of radical reformers primarily concerned with extending democratic rights to the bulk of the English people who were disenfranchised and protecting civil liberties. Because they were sympathetic to the French Revolution, at least in its early stages, they were labelled as Jacobins and viewed as a threat to the established order. See Carl B. Cone, *The English Jacobins* (New York: Scribner, 1968).

5 James Vernon, *Politics and the People: A Study of English Political Culture, c. 1815–1867* (Cambridge: Cambridge University Press, 1993), 298.

6 James A. Epstein, *Radical Expression: Political Language, Ritual, and Symbol in England, 1790–1850* (New York: Oxford University Press, 1994), 20.

7 Dror Wahrman, "Public Opinion, Violence and the Limits of Constitutional Politics" in James Vernon, ed., *Re-reading the Constitution* (Cambridge: Cambridge University Press, 1996), 83.

8 James Gray Pope, "Labor's Constitution of Freedom," *Yale Law Journal* 106 (1997), 941, 943–44.

9 Ibid., 958–59.

10 Section 1 of the *Charter* states: "The *Canadian Charter of Rights and Freedoms* guarantees the rights and freedoms set out in it subject only to such reasonable limits prescribed by law as can be demonstrably justified in a free and democratic society."

11 *R. v. Oakes*, above note 2, at para. 64.

12 Ibid.

13 *R. v. Edwards Books and Art*, [1986] 2 S.C.R. 713 at 779.

14 Kettling is the highly controversial police tactic of completely surrounding a group of people, refusing them an opportunity to leave the area, and subsequently arresting everyone, whether they are involved in a demonstration or simply bystanders caught up in the police sweep.

15 Canadian Civil Liberties Association and NUPGE, *Breach of the Peace: G20 Summit: Accountability in Policing and Governance* (Ottawa: NUPGE and CCLA, February 2011).

16 See, for example, "Share Our Future – The CLASSE Manifesto," July 2012, www.stopthehike.ca.

Nine: Freedom of Association

1 For a more in-depth discussion of this subject matter, see our book chapter, "Freedom of Association: How Fundamental Is the Freedom? – Section 2(d)," in *The Charter at Thirty*, ed. R. Gilliland (Toronto: Canada Law Book, 2012).

2 See, for example, *Lavigne v. Ontario Public Service Employees Union*, [1991] 2 S.C.R. 211.

3 *Health Services and Support – Facilities Subsector Bargaining Assn. v. British Columbia*, 2007 SCC 27 ("*B.C. Health Services*").

4 *Ontario (Attorney General) v. Fraser*, 2011 SCC 20.

5 *Reference Re Public Service Employee Relations Act (Alta.)*, [1987] 1 S.C.R. 313; *PSAC v. Canada*, [1987] 1 S.C.R. 424; and *RWDSU v. Saskatchewan*, [1987] 1 S.C.R. 460.

6 *Reference Re Public Service Employee Relations Act (Alta.)*, at para. 22, per Dickson CJ. See paras. 156 and 173 of McIntyre J.'s reasons.

7 Ibid., para. 153.

8 As stated by Chief Justice Dickson, " . . . freedom of association is not explicitly protected in the United States Constitution, as it is in the *Charter*. Instead, it has been implied by the judiciary as a necessary derivative of the First Amendment's protection of freedom of speech, 'the right of the people to peaceably assemble,' and freedom to petition." Ibid. at para. 48. See also paras. 83–84.

9 Ibid., para. 81.

10 Ibid., para. 82.

11 Ibid., para. 27.

12 *Dunmore v. Ontario (Attorney General)*, 2001 SCC 94.

13 *B.C. Health Services* at para. 22.

14 Ibid., para. 66.

15 The Wagner Act, also known as the *National Labor Relations Act*, was an important piece of Depression-era American legislation that sought to prevent an employer's interference with workers organizing into unions (see chapter 4 of this book). Notably, it did not cover agricultural workers or domestic labourers.

16 *Mounted Police Association of Ontario et al. v. Attorney General (Canada)*, 2012 ONCA 363. The Supreme Court of Canada has granted leave to appeal from the Ontario Court of Appeal's decision in the case. It is expected to be heard by the Court in 2014.

17 *Mounted Police Association of Ontario v. Canada*, 2012 ONCA 363.

18 *Association of Justice Counsel v. Canada (Attorney General)*, 2012 ONCA 530. The Supreme Court of Canada denied leave to appeal to the Association of Justice Counsel.

19 Ibid., para. 41.

20 Ibid., para. 32.

Ten: Constitutional Protection for the Right to Strike

1 *B.C. Health Services and Support – Facilities Subsector Bargaining Assn. v. British Columbia*, 2007 SCC 27, [2007] 2 S.C.R. 391 [*B.C. Health Services*] para. 89 ("The constitutional right to collective bargaining concerns the protection of the ability of workers to engage in associational activities, and their capacity to act in common to reach shared goals related to workplace issues and terms of employment.")

2 See, e.g., ibid., paras. 11, 92, 111, and 113.

3 As established in the so-called labour trilogy: *Reference Re Public Service Employee Relations Act (Alta)*, [1987] 1 S.C.R. 313 [*Alberta Reference*]; *PSAC v. Canada*, [1987] 1 S.C.R. 424 [*PSAC*]; *RWDSU v. Saskatchewan*, [1987] 1 S.C.R. 460 [*Dairy Workers*].

4 *B.C. Health Services*, para. 27.

5 *Ontario (Attorney General) v. Fraser*, 2011 SCC 20, [2011] 2 S.C.R. 3 [*Fraser*].

6 See generally the various analyses of *Fraser* in Alan Bogg and Keith Ewing, "A (Muted) Voice at Work? Collective Bargaining in the Supreme Court of Canada," *Comparative Labor Law and Policy Journal* 379, 33 (2011–2012), 384–87; Steven Barrett, "The Supreme Court of Canada's Decision in *Fraser*: Stepping Forward, Backward or Sideways?" *Canadian Labour and Employment Law Journal* 331,16 (2012), 338–40; Peter W. Hogg, *Constitutional Law of Canada*, 5th ed., looseleaf (Toronto: Carswell, 2012), 44.3(c); Eric Tucker, "Labour's Many Constitutions," *Comparative Labor Law and Policy Journal* 101 (2012), 107; Alison Braley, "I Will Not Give You a Penny More Than You Deserve: *Ontario v. Fraser* and the (Uncertain) Right to Collectively Bargain in Canada," *McGill Law Journal* 351 (2011–2012), 57; Judy Fudge, "Constitutional Rights, Collective Bargaining and the Supreme Court of Canada: Retreat and Reversal in the *Fraser* Case," *Industrial Law Journal* 1 (2012), 41; Steven Barrett and Ethan Poskanzer, "What *Fraser* Means for Labour Rights in Canada," in Fay Faraday, Judy Fudge, and Eric Tucker, *Constitutional Labour Rights in Canada: Farm Workers and the Fraser Case* (Toronto: Irwin Law, 2012), 232; Benjamin Oliphant, "Exiting the Fraser Labyrinth: Resurrecting the Parallel Liberty Standard under s. 2(d), and Saving the Freedom to Strike," *University of Toronto Faculty of Law Review* 71 (2013).

7 *Fraser*, para. 50, citing *B.C. Health Services*, para. 114.

8 *Ontario (Attorney General) v. Fraser*, 2011 SCC 20, [2011] 2 S.C.R. 3, paras. 40, 46, 54, 66, and 99.

9 Indeed, this was the very reading of the Ontario Court of Appeal in the *Fraser* case, which had found, applying its understanding of the Court's protection of meaningful collective bargaining in *B.C. Health Services*, that the failure to enact essential protections of the U.S. Wagner Act model (particularly majoritarian exclusivity, certification, a duty to bargain in good faith, and a dispute resolution mechanism to resolve collective bargaining impasses) interfered with the ability of agricultural employees to engage in "meaningful collective bargaining," and therefore infringed section 2(d): see *Fraser v. Ontario (Attorney General)*, 2008 ONCA 760, paras. 11, 51, 52, 57, and 79–96.

10 See *Fraser*, para. 47.

11 While the Court refers to good faith bargaining in several passages (see, for example, paras. 37, 40, and 73), stating at one point that "individuals have a right against the state to a process of collective bargaining in good faith, and that this right requires the state to impose statutory obligations on employers" (para. 73), it also stated that this merely requires the employer to engage "in a process of meaningful discussion" (para. 54) and merely afforded a right "to make collective representations and to have their collective representations considered in good faith" (para. 51). Similar references to good faith consideration, negotiations, or exchanges are found in paras. 43, 51, 90, 99, and 101–108. These latter articulations of the content of the "right" may be less than a formal "duty to bargain in good faith" as the term is used in the labour relations context and understood by anyone familiar with Canadian labour relations. See, e.g., Bogg and Ewing, *"A (Muted) Voice at Work?,"* 384–87.

12 Patrick Monaghan and Chanakya Sethi, "Constitutional Cases 2011: An Overview" (2012) 58 SCLR 1 at 17. We prefer Abella J.'s more conventional method of statutory interpretation, which we think displays greater fidelity to the words as written and intended. *Fraser*, paras. 328–334. See further Hogg, *Constitutional Law of Canada*, 44.3(c).

13 *Fraser*, para. 54.

14 On the relevance of the distinction between "rights" and "freedoms" in this context, see Brian Langille, "Why the Right-Freedom Distinction Matters to Labour Lawyers – And to All Canadians," *Dalhousie Law Journal* 34 (2011), 143; Judy Fudge and Eric Tucker, "The Freedom to Strike in Canada: A Brief Legal History," *Canadian Labour Law and Employment Journal* 15 (2009–2010), 333 and 336–37; Barrett, "The Supreme Court of Canada's Decision in *Fraser*," 366–67.

15 We follow here the terminology used by Brian Langille and others. See, e.g., Langille, "Why the Right-Freedom Distinction Matters to Labour Lawyers," 157–63.

16 *Big M Drug Mart Ltd*, [1985] 1 S.C.R. 295 at 344.

17 *Alberta Reference*, para. 86.

18 Ibid., para. 91 ("the conditions in which a person works are highly significant in shaping the whole compendium of psychological, emotional and physical elements of a person's dignity and self-respect"). Dickson CJ sounded similar notes in *Slaight Communications Inc v. Davidson*, [1989] 1 S.C.R. 1038 at 1054–1055.

19 *Alberta Reference*, para. 97.

20 Ibid., paras. 79–82. For a more thorough razing of the notion that freedom of association protects only the freedom to join a union, see the judgments of Bayda CJ and Cameron J in the Court of Appeal decision in *Dairy Workers: Retail, Wholesale and Department Store Union, Local 544 v. Saskatchewan*, 1985 CanLII 184 (SK CA).

21 See, e.g., Jamie Cameron, "The Labour Trilogy's Last Rites: *B.C. Health* and a Constitutional Right to Strike," *Canadian Labour Law and Employment Journal* 15,297 (2009), 307; and Dianne Pothier, "Twenty Years of Labour Law and the *Charter*," *Osgoode Hall Law Journal* 40,369 (2002), 397. We do not mean to suggest that the Chief Justice did not identify factors that may be relevant to determining the scope of protection under section 2(d). See Steven Barrett, "*Dunmore* v. *Ontario (Attorney General)*: Freedom of Association at the Crossroads," *Canadian Labour Law and Employment Journal* 10,83 (2002), 93.

22 *Alberta Reference*, para. 87.

23 A similar reasoning process was employed by the Chief Justice in *Big M Drug Mart*, 346–47 ("For the present case it is sufficient in my opinion to say that *whatever else freedom of conscience and religion may mean, it must at the very least mean this*: government may not coerce individuals to affirm a specific religious belief or to manifest a specific religious practice for a sectarian purpose.")

24 *Alberta Reference*, para. 57–59.

25 That is, if a wide range of authorities consider protection for collective action an indispensable element of freedom of association, that would seem to be strong evidence – even amounting to a "presumption" – that it is a necessary incident of the concept itself. See, e.g., *Alberta Reference* para. 59.

26 *International Covenant on Economic, Social and Cultural Rights*, 16 December 1966, 993 UNTS 3 [ICESCR], art. 8(d) ("The States Parties to the present Covenant undertake to ensure . . . (d)The right to strike, provided that it is exercised in conformity with the laws of the particular country").

27 *International Covenant on Civil and Political Rights*, December 16, 1966, 999 UNTS 171, arts. 7, 24 [ICCPR], art. 22 ("Everyone shall have the right to freedom of association with others, including the right to form and join trade unions for the protection of his interests.") While historically this has not been interpreted to include a right to strike – given its explicit protection in the *ICESCR* – more recent articulations appear to suggest such protection. See generally Urfan Khaliq and Robin Churchill, "The Protection of Economic and Social Rights: A Particular Challenge?" in *UN Human Rights Treaty Bodies: Law and Legitimacy*, ed. Helen Keller and Geir Ulfstein (Cambridge: Cam-

bridge University Press, 2012), 250–52. See also Patrick Macklem, "The Right to Bargain Collectively in International Law: Workers' Right, Human Right, International Law?" in *Labour Rights as Human Rights*, ed. Philip Alston (New York: Oxford University Press, 2005).

28 *Alberta Reference*, para. 68 ("The general principle to emerge from interpretations of Convention No. 87 by these decision-making bodies is that freedom to form and organize unions, even in the public sector, must include freedom to pursue the essential activities of unions, such as collective bargaining and strikes, subject to reasonable limits").

29 *Convention (No. 87) Concerning Freedom of Association and Protection of the Right to Organize*, 68 UNTS 17 [Convention No 87]. See also Committee on Freedom of Association, *Digest of Decisions and Principles of the Freedom of Association Committee of the Governing Body of the ILO*, 5th ed. (Geneva: International Labour Organization, 2006), para. 522.

30 See Committee on Freedom of Association, *Digest of Decisions and Principles of the Freedom of Association Committee*, para. 522–25. See further Roy Adams, "*Fraser v. Ontario* and International Human Rights: A Comment," *Canadian Labour Law and Employment Journal* 14 (2008), 377.

31 *Alberta Reference*, para. 72.

32 Put differently, the fact that other bodies, jurisdictions, and interpreters have recognized it as such demonstrates that the right to strike simply is central to what freedom of association means, as applied to the workplace. On this conception, "protection of freedom of association is effectively understood by the international community as a code for protection of workers' collective action in general, and collective bargaining and the right to strike in particular." Steven Barrett and Ethan Poskanzer, "What *Fraser* Means for Labour Rights in Canada," in *Constitutional Labour Rights in Canada: Farm Workers and the Fraser Case*, ed. Fay Faraday, Judy Fudge, and Eric Tucker (Toronto: Irwin Law, 2012), 232.

33 While the European Court of Human Rights had, at the time Dickson CJ was writing, rejected the notion that a stand-alone right to strike was protected (see, e.g., *Schmidt and Dahlstrom v. Sweden* (1976) 1 EHRR 632), a string of recent cases has found that protection for collective action is indeed afforded by article 11 of the European Convention, guaranteeing freedom of association "including the right to form and to join trade unions for the protection of his interests." See, e.g., *Enerji Yapi-Yol Sen v. Turkey*, Application 68959/01, April 21, 2009; *Saime Özcan v. Turkey*, Application No 22943/04, September 15 2009; *Kaya and Seyhan v. Turkey*, Application 30946/04, September 15, 2009; *Karaçay v. Turkey*, Application No 6615/03, June 27, 2007; *Danilenkov v. Russia*, Application No 67336/01, July 30, 2009. See further K.D. Ewing and John Hendy, "The Dramatic Implications of *Demir and Baykara*," *Canadian Labour Law and Employment Journal* 15 (2009–2010), 165. With respect to the right to strike under the European Social Charter, see generally Erika Kovács, "The Right to Strike in the European Social Charter," *Comparative Labor Law & Policy Journal* 26 (2005), 445. See generally T. Novitz, *International and European Protection of the Right to Strike* (Oxford: Oxford University Press, 2003).

34 E.g., Judy Fudge, "Brave New Words: Labour, The Courts and the Canadian Charter of Rights and Freedoms," Windsor *Yearbook of Access to Justice* 28,23 (2010), 34–35. See also Judy Fudge, "The New Discourse of Labour Rights: From Social to Fundamental Rights?" *Comparative Labor Law & Policy Journal* 29 (2007); Roy J. Adams, "From Statutory Right to Human Rights: The Evolution and Current Status of Collective Bargaining," *Just Labour* 12 (2008), 48; Ken Norman, "ILO Freedom of Association Principles

as Basic Canadian Human Rights: Promises to Keep," *Saskatchewan Law Review* 67 (2004), 591. See also James A. Gross, "A Human Rights Perspective on United States Labor Relations Law: A Violation of the Right of Freedom of Association," *Employment Rights & Employment Policy Journal* 3 (1999), 65; David Gregory, "Right to Unionize as a Fundamental Human and Civil Right," *Mississippi College Law Review* 9 (1988), 135; Lee Swepston, "Human Rights Law and Freedom of Association, Development through ILO Supervision," *International Labour Review* 137 (1998), 169.

35 The method of using international law and norms in defining the proper scope of section 2(d) has been endorsed by the Supreme Court in each of its most recent freedom of association decisions following the labour trilogy. See *Dunmore v. Ontario (Attorney General)*, 2001 SCC 94, [2001] 3 S.C.R. 1016 paras. 13–18; *B.C. Health Services*, para. 78; *Fraser*, paras. 91–95. This approach has its adherents, while others have sounded a more cautionary tone. See, e.g., Roy J. Adams, "From Statutory Right to Human Right: The Evolution and Current Status of Collective Bargaining," *Just Labour* 12 (2008), 48; Brian Langille and Benjamin Oliphant, "From the Frying Pan into the Fire: *Fraser* and the Shift from International Law to International 'Thought' in Charter Cases," *Canadian Labour Law and Employment Journal* 16 (2012), 181.

36 See *Dunmore v. Ontario (Attorney General)*, 2001 SCC 94, [2001] 3 S.C.R. 1016 paras. 13–18 (courts must adopt a purposive approach "which aims to protect the full range of associational activity contemplated by the *Charter* and to honour Canada's obligations under international human rights law").

37 See, e.g., *B.C. Health Services*, paras. 69–79, 89; *Fraser*, paras. 38, 91–95.

38 *SEIU, Local 204 v. Broadway Manor Nursing Home* (1983), 44 OR (2d) 392 (Div. Ct), 4 DLR (4th) 231 at 302, Smith J [*Broadway Manor Nursing Home*].

39 Geoffrey England, "Some Thoughts on a Constitutional Right to Strike," *Queen's Law Journal* 13,168 (1998), 177.

40 See *Alberta Reference*, paras. 94–97. Dickson CJ quoted the Woods Task Force for the proposition that "strikes and lockouts are an indispensable part of the Canadian industrial relations system and are likely to remain so in our present socio-economic-political society."

41 England, "Some Thoughts on a Constitutional Right to Strike," 177.

42 According to pre-eminent international labour law scholar Otto Kahn-Freund: "The power to withdraw their labour is for the workers what for management is its power to shut down production, to switch it to different purposes to transfer it to different places. A legal system which suppresses that freedom to strike puts the workers at the mercy of their employers. This – in all its simplicity – is the essence of the matter." Cited in Bob Hepple, "The Right to Strike in an International Context," *Canadian Labour Law and Employment Journal* 15,133 (2009–2010), 140.

43 The freedom to withdraw one's labour has long been described as essential in the collective bargaining context. Seventy years ago, the House of Lords observed: "Where the rights of labour are concerned, the rights of the employer are conditioned by the rights of the men to give or withhold their services. The right of workmen to strike is an essential element in the principle of collective bargaining." (*Crofter Hand Woven Harris Tweed Co v. Veitch*, [1942] 1 All ER 142 (HL) at 158–59, Wright LJ.)

44 *Broadway Manor Nursing Home*, 249–50, Galligan J. As Justice O'Leary stated in a concurring opinion: "The right to organize and bargain collectively is only an illusion if the right to strike does not go with it. . . . To take away an employee's ability to strike so seriously detracts from the benefits of the right to organize and bargain collectively as to make those rights virtually meaningless." (Ibid., 284).

45 See, e.g., Committee on Freedom of Association, *Digest of Decisions and Principles of the*

Freedom of Association Committee, para. 522 ("The right to strike is one of the essential means through which workers and their organizations may promote and defend their economic and social interests"); and Roy Adams, "The Revolutionary Potential of *Dunmore*," *Canadian Labour Law and Employment Journal* 10, 117 (2002), 131 ("International labour theory suggests that, to be substantively meaningful, representations made by employee spokespersons to employers need to be backed by the availability of sanctions against a recalcitrant listener."). For an example of this reasoning at the European Court of Human Rights (ECtHR), see *Wilson and Palmer* v. *United Kingdom* [2002] ECHR 552 para. 46 (" . . . it is of the essence of the right to join a trade union for the protection of their interests that employees should be free to instruct or permit the union to make representations to their employer or to take action in support of their interests on their behalf. If workers are prevented from so doing, their freedom to belong to a trade union, for the protection of their interests, becomes illusory." According to Ewing and Hendy, the ECtHR thereby recognized that "freedom to strike was a necessary alternative to a right to compel an employer to bargain collectively" ("The Dramatic Implications of *Demir and Baykara*," 179).

46 See, e.g., Judy Fudge, "The Supreme Court of Canada and the Right to Bargain Collectively: The Implications of the Health Service and Support Case in Canada and Beyond," *Industrial Law Journal* 37,25(2008), 42; Jamie Cameron, "The Labour Trilogy's Last Rites: *B.C. Health* and a Constitutional Right to Strike," *Canadian Labour Law and Employment Journal* 15,297 (2009), 302–303; Barrett, "*Dunmore* v. *Ontario (Attorney General)*: Freedom of Association at the Crossroads"; Roy Adams, "The Revolutionary Potential of *Dunmore*," *Canadian Labour Law and Employment Journal* 10 (2002), 117.

47 Paul Weiler, *Reconcilable Differences: New Directions in Canadian Labour Law* (Toronto: Carswell, 1980) at 240.

48 *Saskatchewan* v. *Saskatchewan Federation of Labour*, 2012 SKQB 62 (*SFL*, SKQB). Justice Ball of the Saskatchewan Court of Queen's Bench ruled that the Saskatchewan government's *Public Services Essential Services Act* (Bill 5) infringed section 2(d), because it deprived employees of what he found to be the constitutionally protected right to strike.

49 *SFL*, SKQB, para. 92.

50 Ibid., para. 61. Justice Ball accepted that it is typically the threat of economic pressure that places incentives on parties to resolve collective agreements, and makes the entire system workable. Ball J. cites Arbitrator Rayner for the proposition that "the ultimate truth of free collective bargaining is that it can only operate effectively, in market terms, if it is backed up by the threat of economic sanction." Ibid., para. 62, citing W. B. Rayner, *Canadian Collective Bargaining Law*, 2nd ed. (Markham, ON: LexisNexis, 2007), 541.

51 And Ball J was convinced they were. See *SFL*, SKQB, para. 91.

52 As noted under Recent Developments, this decision was recently overturned by the Saskatchewan Court of Appeal: *Saskatchewan* v. *Saskatchewan Federation of Labour*, 2013 SKCA 43 [*SFL*, SKCA]. In effect, the Court of Appeal ducked the issue, ruling that until the Supreme Court of Canada holds otherwise, the original ruling in the 1987 labour trilogy that the right to strike is not constitutionally protected must stand.

53 *Fraser*, para. 125 ("In my view, s. 2(d) protects the liberty of individuals to associate and engage in associational activities. Therefore, s. 2(d) protects the freedom of workers to form self-directed employee associations in an attempt to improve wages and working conditions.") and para. 270 ("I am, however, of the view that s. 2(d) does protect a voluntary association of workers who wish to use their associational

freedoms to come together and attempt to improve their wages and working conditions.")

54 This "parallel liberty" approach was the central pillar of section 2(d) protection prior to *Dunmore*. It was later consolidated with other principles from the labour trilogy by Justice Sopinka in *Professional Institute of the Public Service of Canada* v. *Northwest Territories (Commissioner)*, [1990] 2 S.C.R. 367 at 401–402, which was eventually endorsed by a majority of the Court in *Delisle* v. *Canada (Deputy Attorney General)*, [1999] 2 S.C.R. 989 [*Delisle*] and *Canadian Egg Marketing Agency* v. *Richardson*, [1998] 3 S.C.R. 157 [*CEMA*]. While *Dunmore* found that the section 2(d) analysis should start with the parallel liberty approach, it was no longer the exclusive avenue for establishing a violation of section 2(d) (*Dunmore*, para. 18).

55 *Fraser*, para. 275 ("Section 2(d) protects the ability of individuals to form associations and to do in association what they can lawfully do alone. Because individuals are generally free to bargain with their employer individually, it follows that s. 2(d) must protect the decision of individuals to come together, to form a bargaining position and to present a common and united front to their employers. However, just as an employer is not obliged to bargain with an individual employee, s. 2(d) does not oblige an employer to bargain with a group of employees.")

56 This point has been addressed elsewhere and will not be belaboured here in great detail. See Brian Langille, "The Freedom of Association Mess: How We Got into It and How We Can Get out of It," *McGill Law Journal* 54, 177 (2009), 199–201; Langille, "Why the Right-Freedom Distinction Matters to Labour Lawyers"; David Beatty and Steve Kennett, "Striking Back: Fighting Words, Social Protest and Political Participation in Free and Democratic Societies," *Queen's Law Journal* 13 (1998), 214; Pothier, "Twenty Years of Labour Law and the Charter," 376–77; Barrett & Poskanzer, "What *Fraser* Means for Labour Rights in Canada," 225–26; Oliphant, "Exiting the Fraser Labyrinth."

57 *Alberta Reference*, para. 89 ("I believe that Bayda C.J.S. was right in holding that s. 2(d) normally embraces the liberty to do collectively that which one is permitted to do as an individual . . . However, it is not in my view correct to regard this proposition as the exclusive touchstone for determining the presence or absence of a violation of s. 2(d).")

58 *Alberta Reference*, paras. 177–78.

59 See Beatty and Kennett, "Striking Back," 229–36; Pothier, "Twenty Years of Labour Law and the Charter," 376–77; Patrick Macklem, "Developments in Employment Law: The 1990–91 Term," Supreme Court Law Review 3,277 (1992), 230–31; Langille, "The Freedom of Association Mess," 183–84.

60 Beatty and Kennett, "Striking Back," 236.

61 Pothier, "Twenty Years of Labour Law and the Charter," 376, 378.

62 *Fraser*, para. 185 ("In my view, the question is not whether the activity is susceptible of being performed, *in exactly the same manner*, by an individual acting alone. A choir singing harmony may produce sound that is qualitatively distinct from an individual voice, but it is nonetheless produced by a group of individuals voluntarily singing together.") See also para. 272 ("While greater economic clout or political power may flow from the very act of association in a way that makes the associational activity 'qualitatively' different from the individual activity, the legal rights and freedoms granted to individuals acting in association under s. 2(d) are nonetheless limited to the same rights and freedoms afforded to individuals acting alone.") Both passages recognize that the mere fact that collective activity may produce a qualitatively different outcome is no reason to deny constitutional protection under the parallel liberty approach.

63 *Fraser*, para. 179.

64 There is nothing necessarily exclusive in any of these approaches, and their separa-
tion from a doctrinal perspective is to a certain extent artificial. The acceptance of one
of these methods of finding constitutional protection for strike action neither requires
nor necessarily precludes adopting another. The Court in *B.C. Health Services*, for
instance, clearly followed much of Dickson CJ's reasoning; Dickson CJ himself incor-
porated the parallel liberty approach into his conception of section 2(d); and Rothstein J. adopted the parallel liberty approach while seeming to accept *Dunmore's* call
for the protection of certain inherently collective activities. Indeed, the authors of this
piece disagree on the wisdom of the various approaches in the context of section 2(d)
(see Barrett, "The Supreme Court of Canada's Decision in *Fraser*," and Oliphant, "Exiting the Fraser Labyrinth"). The important point for our purposes here is that on any
of the approaches adopted by the Court to date, the freedom to strike is protected.

65 Harry Arthurs, "'The Right to Golf': Reflections on the Future of Workers, Unions and
the Rest of Us Under the *Charter*," *Queen's Law Journal* 13,17 (1988), 18.

66 See, for example, *B.C. Health Services*, paras. 80–85.

67 *SFL*, SKCA.

68 Ibid., para. 51.

69 Ibid., para. 46.

70 Ibid., para. 52.

71 *Professional Institute of the Public Service of Canada* v. *Northwest Territories (Commissioner)*, [1990] 2 S.C.R. 367.

72 *Dunmore*, para. 16.

73 *B.C. Health Services*, para. 20.

74 This seemed to be an argument that Richards J. rejected. See, e.g., *SFL*, SKCA, para.
67. ("In other words, the Court's recent decisions have not undermined the *Labour
Trilogy* to the point where, even if they were entitled to anticipate the reversal of a
binding precedent, either this Court or the Court of Queen's Bench should disregard
what has been decided about the relationship between the right to strike and s. 2(d)
of the *Charter*.")

75 *SFL*, SKCA, para. 52.

76 Ibid., paras. 53 and 61.

77 Ibid., para. 54. ("But, at least to this point, the Supreme Court has not mapped the
freedom to bargain collectively in these broad terms. Rather, it has said that collective
bargaining involves only: the right of employees to organize, to make collective representations to their employers and to have those representations considered in good
faith. This is clearly illustrated by *Fraser*.")

78 These two inquiries must be treated differently as a matter of law. See Oliphant, "Exiting the Fraser Labyrinth"; and Langille, "Why the Right-Freedom Distinction Matters
to Labour Lawyers."

79 According to the Court of Appeal, the "right to strike" is a "function of a specific
statutory system." *SFL*, SKCA, paras. 61–64.

80 Ibid., para. 64.

81 As the Court held in *B.C. Health Services*, para. 25: "The first suggested reason was that
the rights to strike and to bargain collectively are 'modern rights' created by legislation, not 'fundamental freedoms' (*Alberta Reference, per* Le Dain J., writing on behalf of
himself, Beetz and La Forest JJ., at p. 391). The difficulty with this argument is that it
fails to recognize the history of labour relations in Canada. As developed more thor-
oughly in the next section of these reasons, the fundamental importance of collective
bargaining to labour relations was the very reason for its incorporation into statute.
Legislatures throughout Canada have historically viewed collective bargaining rights

as sufficiently important to immunize them from potential interference. The statutes they passed did not create the right to bargain collectively. Rather, they afforded it protection. There is nothing in the statutory entrenchment of collective bargaining that detracts from its fundamental nature." While the Saskatchewan Court of Appeal specifically acknowledged this passage (para. 64 of its reasons), it was seemingly unprepared to accept that its reach and logic extends to the right to strike.

Eleven: Working towards Equality

1 *Vriend* v. *Alberta*, [1998] 1 S.C.R. 493 at para. 67–68; *Law* v. *Canada*, [1999] 1 S.C.R. 497 at para. 2.
2 Fay Faraday, Margaret Denike and M. Kate Stephenson, "In Pursuit of Substantive Equality," in *Making Equality Rights Real: Security Substantive Equality Under the Charter*, ed. Faraday, Denike, and Stephenson (Toronto: Irwin Law, 2006), 9.
3 Sheila McIntrye, "Answering the Siren Call of Abstract Formalism with the Subjects and Verbs of Domination," in *Making Equality Rights Real*, above note 2 at 108.
4 *Andrews* v. *Law Society of British Columbia*, [1989] 1 S.C.R. 143 at p. 185.
5 In 1995, the Court released a trilogy of section 15 cases in which the nine judges divided into four camps, setting out three wholly distinct legal tests with a fourth variation on one of them. None of the positions had majority support: *Egan* v. *Canada*, [1995] 2 S.C.R. 513; *Miron* v. *Trudel*, [1995] 2 S.C.R. 418; *Thibaudeau* v. *Canada*, [1995] 2 S.C.R. 627. This confusion continued until a unanimous decision was released in 1999 confirming and building on the *Andrews* framework: *Law* v. *Canada*, above note 1.
6 The legal test that focused on a violation of "human dignity," adopted in 1999 in *Law* v. *Canada*, above note 1, was explicitly rejected as a legal test in 2008 in *R* v. *Kapp*, [2008] 2 S.C.R. 483. A requirement, adopted in 2004 in *Hodge* v. *Canada*, [2004] 3 S.C.R. 357, that discrimination be assessed using "mirror comparators" – comparing a claimant to a group that "mirrored" them in all respects except for the ground at issue – was explicitly rejected in 2011 in *Withler* v. *Canada*, [2011] 1 S.C.R. 396. Finally, a narrow focus on proving discrimination with reference to "stereotype and prejudice," adopted in 2008 in *R.* v. *Kapp*, was explicitly rejected in 2013 in *Quebec* v. *A*, 2013 SCC 5 in favour of a test that recognizes that stereotypes and prejudice are only two out of many different ways in which discrimination may arise.
7 In *Lovelace* v. *Ontario*, [2000] 1 S.C.R. 950, section 15(2) was characterized as an interpretive aid to section 15(1) to provide conceptual depth to the meaning of substantive equality. Beginning in 2008, a line of jurisprudence is emerging with *R.* v. *Kapp*, above note 6, and *Alberta* v. *Cunningham*, [2011] 2 S.C.R. 670 that applies section 15(2) independently of section 15(1) to protect ameliorative programs against charges of discrimination.
8 *Withler* v. *Canada*, above note 6 at para. 2 and 39.
9 *Law* v. *Canada*, above note 1, at para. 93.
10 Fay Faraday, "Envisioning Equality: Analogous Grounds and Farm Workers' Experience of Discrimination," in *Constitutional Labour Rights in Canada: Farm Workers and the Fraser Case*, ed. Fay Faraday, Judy Fudge, and Eric Tucker (Toronto: Irwin Law, 2012), 114.
11 See further discussion of migrant workers in chapter 7 of this book.
12 See Fay Faraday, *Made in Canada: How the Law Constructs Migrant Workers' Insecurity* (Toronto: Metcalf Foundation, 2012), www.metcalffoundation.com.

13 Section 15 of the *Charter* took effect in 1985, three years after the other provisions in the *Charter*.

14 Bruce Porter, "Expectations of Equality," in *Diminishing Returns: Inequality and the Canadian Charter of Rights and Freedoms*, ed. Sheila McIntyre and Sanda Rodgers (Markham, ON: LexisNexis Butterworths, 2006), 23–44.

15 Ibid., 34–35.

16 Ibid., 24.

Twelve: The Power of Collective Bargaining

1 Britain has the second-worst economic performance in the G7. Its credit rating – maintenance of which the Chancellor of the Exchequer called the acid test of the ConDem government's economic policy – was reduced in February 2013 from AAA. Investment in production has fallen by at least 15 per cent below 2007 levels, and corporations are sitting on some £777 billion of funds that could be put to productive use. The impact on living standards has been dramatic, with the real value of wages plummeting as the levels of top income have continued their skyward ascent.

2 David Harvey, *A Brief History of Neoliberalism* (Oxford: Oxford University Press, 2007); Kean Birch and Vlad Mykhnenko, eds., *The Rise and Fall of Neo-liberalism* (London: Zed Books, 2010).

3 On the role of financialization and globalization in the decline of wages in the share of income, see Engelbert Stockhammer, *Why Have Wage Shares Fallen?* (Geneva: International Labour Office, 2012).

4 Richard Wilkinson, *Unhealthy Societies: The Afflictions of Inequality* (London: Routledge, 1996); Richard Wilkinson, *The Impact of Inequality: How to Make Sick Societies Healthier* (London: Routledge, 2005); Richard Wilkinson and Kate Pickett, *The Spirit Level: Why Greater Equality Makes Societies Stronger* (London: Penguin, 2010); Stewart Lansley, *Rising Inequality and Financial Crises: Why Greater Equality Is Essential for Recovery* (London: Centre for Labour and Social Studies, 2012).

5 See chapter 18 in Friedrich A. Hayek, *The Constitution of Liberty* (Chicago: University of Chicago Press, 1959). His chief complaint against trade unions seems not so much their function of using industrial power for wage bargaining but their "coercion" of workers to achieve "complete unionisation." Now that coercion and complete unionization are rarely a feature of modern trade unionism, Hayek's disciples focus on trade union wage bargaining as the distorting feature of the labour market that must be eradicated.

6 See *International Transport Workers' Federation and Another* v. *Viking Line ABP* (Case C-438/05) [2008] I.C.R. 741 and the parallel *Laval un Partneri Ltd* v. *Svenska Byggnadsarbetareförbundet* (Case C-341/05 [2007] ECR I-11767) in the Court of Justice of the European Union (CJEU); *Metrobus* v. *UNITE* [2008] [2010] ICR 173) in the U.K.; and, in Canada, *Ontario (AG)* v. *Fraser* (2011 SCC 20), and *Saskatchewan* v. *Saskatchewan Federation of Labour*, 2013 SKCA 43.

7 See the description by the ILO Committee of Experts on the Application of Conventions and Recommendations, *General Survey on the Fundamental Conventions concerning Rights at Work in Light of the ILO Declaration on Social Justice for a Fair Globalisation*, 2008 (ILO, 2012), 46–50.

8 Article 53(3) of the Charter of Fundamental Rights of the EU provides that the meaning and scope of the fundamental rights there enshrined shall be the same as those laid down in the European Convention.

9 *OFS* v. *Norway* (*Federation of Offshore Workers Trade Unions* v. *Norway*, Application No. 381/97, (2002) ECHR 2002-VI, 301); *UNISON* v. *UK* ([2002] IRLR 497); *Wilson, Palmer* v. *UK* ([2002] IRLR 568); *Dilek et al* v. *Turkey* (On July 17, 2007, the judgment was under the name of *Satlimiş* v. *Turkey* and the final version was dated January 30, 2008. This was rectified on April 28, 2008, when the name was corrected to *Dilek* v. *Turkey*, Application Nos 74611/02, 26876/02, and 27628/02). *Enerji Yapi-Yol Sen* v. *Turkey* (Application No 68959/01, judgment dated April 21, 2009); *Danilenkov. & Others* v. *Russia* (Application No 67336/01, July 30, 2009, definitive version December 10, 2009); *Urcan* v. *Turkey* (Application No 23018/04 etc., July 17, 2008, definitive judgment October 17, 2008, only in French); *Saime Özcan* v. *Turkey* (Application No 22943/04, September 15, 2009, judgment in French only); *Kaya and Seyhan* v. *Turkey* (Application No 30946/04, September 15, 2009); *Karaçay* v. *Turkey* (Application No 6615/03, March 27, 2007, definitive version of the judgment on June 27, 2007, only in French); *Çerikçi* v. *Turkey* (Application 33322/07, October 13, 2010).

10 (2009) 48 EHRR 54, [2009] IRLR 766, Appn No 34503/97, November 12, 2008. (This case was a close parallel of *Health Services and Support – Facilities Subsector Bargaining Assn.* v. *British Columbia* 2007 SCC 27, [2207] 2 S.C.R. 391.) The Grand Chamber unanimously upheld the unanimous judgment of the Second Chamber (see paras. 98–101, 147–151). Since there was only one judge in common, it can be said that, in Demir, 23 judges of the ECtHR came to similar conclusions. The significance of this case is discussed in K.D. Ewing and John Hendy, "The Dramatic Implications of Demir and Baykara," *Industrial Law Journal* 39,2 (2010).

11 Ewing John Hendy, "The Dramatic Implications of Demir and Baykara," para. 154.

12 See the discussion of the *Fraser* case elsewhere in this book, especially chapters 9 and 10.

13 See, e.g., *Texas and New Orleans Railway Company* v. *Brotherhood of Railway and Steamship Clerks* (1930) upholding the Act's prohibition of interference in the selection of collective bargaining delegates.

14 See chapter 4 of this book for more on the Wagner model in Canada.

15 Ministry of Reconstruction, Committee on Relations between Employers and Employed, Final Report, Cmd 9153, 1918, para. 1.

16 Cmd. 8606, 1917, para. 6.

17 Ministry of Reconstruction, Committee on Relations between Employers and Employed, Final Report, Cmd 9153, 1918, para.1.

18 Passed by the House of Commons, 1891, 1909, and 1946.

19 Ministry of Labour, Annual Report, 1934, 74.

20 Wanrooy et al., WERS 2011, First Findings, Dept. BIS, 2012, 22. It was 72 per cent by 1984, dropping to 47 per cent by 1995. By 2004 the rate was 29 per cent. Thus the level has been falling at a rate of 1–2 per cent per annum.

21 In France collective bargaining coverage is over 90 per cent, whereas trade union membership is below 10 per cent, although French unions can call on massive support for demonstrations.

22 See, e.g., Guy Vernon and Mark Rogers, "Where Do Unions Add Value? Predominant Organizing Principle, Union Strength and Manufacturing Productivity Growth in the OECD," *British Journal of Industrial Relations* 51,1 (2013).

23 E.g., David Coats, *Just Deserts? Poverty and Income Inequality: Can Workplace Democracy Make a Difference?* (The Smith Institute, Webb Memorial Trust, 2013).

24 Stockhammer, *Why Have Wage Shares Fallen?*, 43.

Contributors

Steven Barrett is a managing partner of Sack Goldblatt Mitchell LLP. He practises in the areas of labour law, constitutional litigation, and public interest litigation. Steve has represented trade union clients in numerous appeals before the Supreme Court of Canada and has argued many judicial review applications and appeals before Ontario courts. He is a member of the Canadian Association of Labour Lawyers, the Canadian Bar Association, and the Canadian Foundation for Labour Rights.

Paul J.J. Cavalluzzo is the senior partner of Cavalluzzo Shilton McIntyre & Cornish LLP. He is a leading constitutional labour law lawyer and has argued significant cases before the Supreme Court of Canada. Most recently, he represented UFCW Canada in the *Fraser* case all the way to the Supreme Court of Canada. He is a board member of the Canadian Foundation for Labour Rights. In 2005, Paul was awarded the Law Society Medal of Upper Canada, in 2012, he received the Order of Ontario, and in 2013, he received the Order of Canada.

Paul Champ is a labour and human rights lawyer with Champ & Associates in Ottawa. He has acted as counsel in several important constitutional law cases dealing with fundamental human rights and civil liberties, and has been a lecturer at the University of Ottawa on social justice and the law. In 2010, Paul was the recipient of the Reg Robson Civil Liberties Award. Paul is a board member of the Canadian Foundation for Labour Rights.

James Clancy has been the National President of the 340,000-member National Union of Public and General Employees (NUPGE) since 1990. Prior to that, he was President of NUPGE's largest component, the Ontario Public Service Employees Union. James is also a General Vice-President of the Canadian Labour Congress and a board member of the Canadian Foundation for Labour Rights. Under his leadership, NUPGE has gained a strong reputation for its aggressive defence of labour rights as human rights in Canada and internationally.

Nathalie Des Rosiers has been the Dean of Law at the University of Ottawa since July 2013. Prior to that, she was General Counsel of the Canadian Civil Liberties Association for four years. Nathalie serves on the board of the Canadian Foundation for Labour Rights. She was named one of Canada's 25 most influential lawyers in 2011 and 2012 by *Canadian Lawyer* magazine, and one of Canada's 10 nation builders in 2010 by *The Globe and Mail.*

Fay Faraday is a human rights lawyer and a Visiting Professor at Osgoode Hall Law School, where she teaches courses in ethical lawyering, the *Charter,* and human rights law. She is the co-author/co-editor of three books, including *Constitutional Labour Rights in Canada: Farm Workers and the* Fraser *Case* (2012). Fay holds an Innovation Fellowship with the Metcalf Foundation, where she is engaged in research addressing the rights of migrant workers.

Derek Fudge is the National Director of Policy Development for the 340,000-member National Union of Public and General Employees (NUPGE) and a former Vice-President (Disability Rights) of the Canadian Labour Congress. He has published numerous articles in labour relations and human rights journals and is the author of *Collective Bargaining in Canada: Human Right or Canadian Illusion* (2006). Derek serves as the secretariat to the Canadian Foundation for Labour Rights.

John Hendy, QC, is a senior partner with Old Square Chambers, a widely respected labour law firm in Britain. John has a particular interest in international labour law, having acted in three of the most significant cases in the European Court of Human Rights concerning Article 11 (Freedom of Assembly and Association) of the European Convention on Human Rights. He is President of the International Centre for Trade Union Rights and Chair of the Institute of Employment Rights. In 2011, he was given the Liberty Lifetime Achievement Award in recognition of a career dedicated to defending and upholding the rights of workers and trade unionists in the United Kingdom.

Michael Lynk is associate professor at the Faculty of Law, University of Western Ontario, where he teaches labour, human rights, constitutional, and administrative law. Michael is the co-author of *Trade Union Law in Canada* (Canada Law Book), and the co-editor, with John Craig, of *Globalization and the Future of Labour Law* (2006). He is a senior co-editor of the *Labour Law Casebook* (7th and 8th eds.).

Naveen Mehta is the General Counsel and Director of Human Rights, Equity and Diversity for United Food and Commercial Workers (UFCW) Canada. He has been active in a variety of legal, labour, and human rights based organizations including the International Bar

Association (Industrial Relations, Human Rights, Immigration Law Committees). He was an adviser to the Law Commission of Ontario on Precarious Work.

Benjamin Oliphant graduated with honours from the University of Toronto Faculty of Law in 2012, and articled at Sack Goldblatt Mitchell LLP. During law school, he worked with the Canadian Civil Liberties Association and the David Asper Centre for Constitutional Rights, and his academic writing on discrimination, labour, and constitutional law has appeared in a range of publications. He is currently clerking for the 2013–2014 term.

Lars Osberg is a professor and Chair of the Department of Economics at Dalhousie University. He is well known internationally for his research and published contributions on the extent and causes of poverty and economic inequality. Lars has published numerous articles in academic journals and has authored eight books, including *Economic Inequality in Canada* and his most recent, *The Economic Implications of Social Cohesion*.

Garry Sran is a PhD candidate in Economics at York University. He received an honours degree in Economics from the University of Manitoba. He regularly speaks at various social justice events and helps organize events and workshops to engage the broader community in building a more democratic, equitable society.

Adrienne Telford is an associate with Cavalluzzo Shilton McIntyre & Cornish LLP. She practises in the areas of constitutional, labour, and administrative law. Adrienne has worked on a number of *Charter* cases and is currently co-counsel to the Canadian Union of Postal Workers and the International Association of Machinists and Aerospace Workers in constitutional challenges to back-to-work legislation. She has published numerous articles in the area of equality and freedom of association.

Eric Tucker is a professor at Osgoode Hall Law School, York University. He has published extensively on the history and current state of labour and employment law and occupational health and safety regulation. He is the author of *Administering Danger in the Workplace* (1990), co-author of *Labour before the Law* (2001) and *Self-Employed Workers Organize* (2005), and co-editor of *Work on Trial: Canadian Labour Law Struggles* (2010) and *Constitutional Labour Rights in Canada: Farm Workers and the* Fraser *Case* (2012).

Armine Yalnizyan is a senior economist with the Canadian Centre for Policy Alternatives. She is one of Canada's leading progressive economists. Armine writes for *The Globe and Mail*'s online business feature, Economy Lab, and provides business commentary twice a week for Toronto's most popular morning radio show, CBC's *Metro Morning*. She punches above her weight every week on the Big Picture Panel, featured Thursdays on Canada's premier business show, CBC's *Lang & O'Leary Exchange*.